INTERNATIONAL BANKING

Nicholas L. Deak

JoAnne Celusak

New York Institute of Finance
Prentice-Hall, Inc.

Library of Congress Cataloging in Publication Data
Deak, Nicholas L.
  International banking.

  Bibliography:
  Includes index.
   1. Banks and banking, International—Law and legis-
lation.   2. Banks and banking, International.   I. Celusak,
JoAnne. II. Title.
K1066.D4   1984   346'.08215   84-3397
ISBN 0-13-471061-4   342.68215

New York Institute of Finance
(NYIF Corp.)
70 Pine Street
New York, New York 10270

Contents

Foreword v

Introduction vii

1
Balance of Payments 1

2
International Banking Entities 13

3
Letters of Credit 35

4
Bankers' Acceptances 74

5
Collections 85

6
Checks 95

7
Foreign Exchange 110

8
Eurodollar Lending 165

9
Bank Examination and Supervision 192

10
Bank Holding Companies 210

11
Swiss Banking 223

12
European Monetary Systems 239

13
International Lending Agencies 253

14
Glossary 272

Index 284

Foreword

A proverb, wrote Cervantes, is a short sentence based on long experience. The complexities of international finance are not so easily reduced
to succinct dictums. So Nicholas Deak and JoAnne Celusak have given
us a volume, but one with cogency and based on a life lived on both the
back paths and carriageways of multinational commerce.

I welcome this book, as should all who wish to sharpen their
understanding of international banking and finance. It is a useful text for
the motivated novitiate and the seasoned practitioner alike. Given the
ever-shifting mosaic we know as international finance, Mr. Deak and Ms.
Celusak have captured a portrait that will endure. An intricate terrain
has been charted with wisdom and care.

JOHN F. MCGILLICUDDY
Chairman of the Board
Manufacturers Hanover Corporation

Introduction

With the expansion of American banks abroad and of foreign banks in the United States, and with the related international activities, there is a crying need for a textbook on international banking, which can be used in universities and colleges.

More and more students, on undergraduate and graduate levels, are seeking expertise in the international financial field. A growing number of law schools are providing their students with facilities to expand their legal knowledge and the basis for their future professional activities in this area.

During my classes in international banking at the New York Law School, students called to my attention the need for more up-to-date textbook material to facilitate their studies. The former Dean of the New York Law School, E. Donald Shapiro, and the Associate Dean, Margaret S. Bearn, gave me encouragement to attend to this task.

The greatest incentive, however, to tackle the job of writing this textbook, came from one of my students, JoAnne Celusak, who volunteered to assemble a group of students to cooperate with me in doing research, preparing the material, and making corrections wherever necessary. All the students were in the graduating class of the New York Law School. Their contribution under the leadership of JoAnne Celusak was especially commendable since, in the meantime, they graduated and became engaged in various aspects of the legal profession.

Without JoAnne Celusak and her team, this book could not have been accomplished.

We do not claim completeness; we do not claim perfection. We do believe, however, that this book contains superior material for the mature students interested in international banking, international finance, and advanced economics. We feel that professionals, bankers, economists, will find this book valuable and useful to them.

As time goes by, and as new editions might become necessary, we intend to upgrade the book with additional information as it becomes available.

We wish to thank the following individuals for their cooperation and assistance in the preparation of this text: in particular, David Roulston, for his skillful editorial work and helpful contributions, along with Joyce Moffatt, Richard O'Connor, Karin Burke, Brian Platton, Celeste Miller, Simon Kogan, and other New York Law School graduates for their assistance in preparation of the drafts. A special thank you goes to Inez Bruelhmann as well as to Frances Lauder for their extraordinary secretarial skills in producing the final manuscript.

Dr. Nicholas L. Deak
Adjunct Professor of Law
New York Law School

1

Balance of Payments

The concept of balance of payments is important to understanding the economic forces behind events affecting international banking. Numerous studies have analyzed the intricacies and theories of balance of payments. However, this discussion approaches balance of payments with the purpose of explaining components that have immediate as well as long-term effects upon a nation's currency and banking transactions. Therefore, let us first define the often used term, "balance of payments."

The *balance of payments* of a nation refers to a whole complex of international business and financial transactions involving payments made and received by the residents of one nation to and from the residents of other nations. The measurement of payments is not necessarily restricted to payments made in monetary form. Currently, the United States balance of payment data is officially called "United States International Transactions."

Thus, the balance of payments records economic transactions made during a specific period between residents and nonresidents. It is a complex structure consisting of many tangible and intangible movements of funds. A nation's balance of payments must be carefully monitored and studied since it indicates not only the internal but also the external economic strength of a country. In fact, it would be inaccurate to think of the balance of payments as a disconnected phenomenon that is unrelated to the domestic economy.

It is clear that international economic relationships will affect the balance of payments between the United States and the rest of the world. Moreover, the balance of payments will influence the well-being of a nation. In addition, it has a significant effect upon everyday political, economic, and monetary decisions. For example, since the United States dollar is so widely used to settle many business transactions here and abroad, the condition of the balance of payments in the United States is of importance to many nations. Similarly, investors turn to balance of payment figures as the key starting point for the study of a nation's economic condition.

In general, a balance of payments surplus indicates a healthy economy that holds enough foreign currency reserves to finance outstanding foreign debt. On the other hand, a balance of payments deficit implies a drain on the economic resources of a nation, which will produce harmful consequences. Causes and effects of these conditions will be examined later in this chapter.

Overall, however, we will see that every act involving some form of payment between a resident and a nonresident will affect the balance of payments. For example, if an individual travels outside the United States, purchases goods manufactured abroad, or sends money to help a friend or relative residing abroad, these acts affect the balance of payments. Other examples include: making a loan to a foreign enterprise, opening a foreign bank account, or purchasing insurance through a foreign company. The list of possibilities is endless since virtually every form of international economic transaction is added to the balance of payments picture.

However, for analytical purposes, a distinction should be made between the various types of transactions that comprise the balance of payments. Therefore, the balance of payments can be subdivided into five major components including:

- Balance of Trade
- Balance of Services
- Balance of Short-Term Capital Movements
- Balance of Long-Term Capital Movements
- Errors and Omissions

By looking at these components individually or in combinations, analysts can determine the areas of economic strength and weakness of a national economy, thereby locating growth and decline in specific domestic and international sectors. Although balance of payments data is a reflection of the past, economic trends may be projected when supplemental information is also considered. It is important to note, however, that the "errors and omissions" component, now officially called "statistical discrepancy," should be seriously taken into consideration by analysts since this category can be substantial and lessen the degree of reliability of the data. In addition to the possibility of a large number of transactions being incorrectly reported or altogether omitted, about 30% of the United States economy might be underground. This further adds to the unreliability of official balance of payments data. Nevertheless, for reasons to be explained, the true barometer of a nation's balance of payments condition is its currency. That is, we can determine the positiveness or negativeness of the balance of payments through the relative strength or weakness of its currency. If the currency strengthens, we know that the balance of payments is positive. Conversely, if the rate of exchange of a nation's currency weakens versus other countries, we know that the balance of payments of that country is negative at that point in time.

Before examining the various components of the balance of payments in depth, it is useful to understand the basic differences between each of the components and see the manner in which the data is compiled and published by the authorities.

The first subdivision mentioned was the *balance of trade.* This component measures the balance or net between all the merchandise exported and all the merchandise imported into a country during the measuring period. It measures the competitive position of U.S. products. The Customs Service is the agency that processes figures for imports and exports using documents accompanying the goods.

The second subdivision covers *balance of services.* This component includes all expenditures and receipts that are neither connected with the trade of merchandise nor included in the categories of capital movements. Services are often provided between residents of separate nations, such as when tourists travel to see the scenery. Services include payments for franchises and interest on the use of money in a loan transaction. Thus, interest paid or received on the use of funds is considered payment for a service provided and is classified under balance of services. In order to compile these figures, an average expenditure is calculated using a group of questionnaire survey responses, sometimes obtained from tourists returning to the United States. In addition, total receipts and expenditures for various measurable services are also included in the balance of services. However, unlike the balance of trade, figures for the balance of services are not as easily obtainable.

The third subdivision mentioned was *short-term capital movements.* These include financial transactions, namely capital investments with a maturity of generally less than one year. Overall changes in assets and liabilities held are measured. Short-term capital movements can be defined either as a transfer of funds that can be withdrawn at any time in the discretion of the originator or as a transfer of funds for a specific length of time, mostly one year or less. It should be mentioned, however, that a few economists consider three years to be the distinguishing time factor between short- and long-term capital movements. Regarding the computation of capital movement figures, the reporting requirements imposed on certain transactions facilitate the collection of data to measure both short- and long-term movements of capital. However, great statistical difficulty is involved in calculating this most important subdivision of balance of payments.

The fourth subdivision, *long-term capital movements*, refers to investments of a more permanent nature, which are not callable or returnable on short notice. Therefore, transactions in assets or liabilities with original maturities of more than twelve months are generally classified as long-term capital movements.

As was mentioned for the short-term capital movement figures, the source of data for long-term transactions is obtained mainly from Department of the Treasury reports that various organizations are required to file. For example, banks, large corporations, and some securities firms must file reports indicating changes in capital movements based on either a transaction or net position. Securities firms make reports on a transaction basis, whereas figures for banks are sometimes estimated using the balances outstanding at the end of the reporting period. Thus, whereas the shift of funds between banking centers may be large in volume, the overall change in capital movements is taken from the net position at the end of the reporting period. It should be mentioned that, in countries having exchange controls, data regarding transfers of funds between residents and nonresidents through the domestic banking system will probably be one of the main sources of balance of payments data.

The fifth and final subdivision in balance of payments is called *errors and omissions*. A statistical discrepancy occurs despite attempts to collect relevant data by means of mandatory reports and other methods. All the movements of funds and payments that statisticians did not measure are entered into the category of errors and omissions. Furthermore, the reliability of balance of payment data is not assured once errors and omissions are tallied. This is due to the fact that it is not known into which category or categories the discrepancy should be placed.

In order to eliminate this inaccuracy, which became very large in 1980–81, a committee was set up to study causes and suggest solutions to the reporting problem. Although adjustments were made in reporting requirements, the problem of a large statistical discrepancy still exists.

Nevertheless, by adding up the positive and negative side of the first four subdivisions of the balance of payments, we would have a good indication of the nation's economic position. This is possible because of the method of recording the balance of payment transactions, known as the *double entry system*. Similar to business accounting, a debit entry shows an increase in assets (or a decrease in liabilities), whereas a credit entry shows an increase in liabilities (or a decrease in assets). Each transaction within the balance of payments system is shown with two entries, one positive and one negative in real terms.

To illustrate this double entry system, assume that goods (such as trucks) are being exported from country A to country B. Two entries are made to represent the exportation of goods and payment therefore. Namely, since country A now has less goods, a credit (or minus) entry is made in that category. However, a debit (plus) entry must also be made under payments since funds are due for payment of the goods. The opposite entries will be made for country B's balance of payments, since goods are being gained (debit or plus entry) while funds are being reduced (credit or minus entry).

Theoretically, these transactions balance. Thus, the components of the balance of payments of a nation must always balance due to its nature as a double entry system. The ideal balance is known as *balance of payments equilibrium.*

It is important to examine the reality of the total balance of payments system, however. It is likely that the amount of goods exported will not equal the amount of goods imported to a nation. Therefore, the possibility of balance of payment disequilibrium between two or more nations exists. In other words, one country may be exporting more goods to other nations and receiving more funds in payment than others. In this situation, assuming a surplus is created, the balance of trade of the exporting nation will be positive.

Conversely, if foreign claims on a country's currency to pay for imports increase to the point of creating a deficit, the balance of trade will be negative. Although surplus and deficit concepts are more suspect due to the shift from fixed to floating exchange rates, the strength or the weakness of a currency will indicate a balance of payments position. Thereafter, an adjustment mechanism might operate when the demand or supply of a nation's currency is substantially increased so as to alter the exchange rate of a currency. That is, an exchange rate adjustment may occur at some point in time to equalize the purchasing power of the currencies and reduce the balance of payment disequilibrium between the nations. However, as will be examined in the chapter on foreign exchange, a variety of forces continually operate on the value of a currency. Nevertheless, it is important to realize that there is a correlation between the balance of payments and the currency value of a nation.

For example, the value of the dollar outside the United States depends mainly upon our balance of payments. Outside the United States, our currency is a commodity, since it is not legal tender abroad. An excess of any commodity forces prices down. As shown, if the United States balance of payments is negative, it means that more dollars have been spent abroad than were taken in from nonresidents. Therefore, if the supply of U.S. dollars abroad is greater than the demand, the value of the dollar will decrease.

Until about 1968, the balance of trade of the United States was positive due to the fact that more goods were exported than imported. However, with the exception of one year, the United States balance of trade has remained negative. In addition, the United States balance of payments turned negative in 1982, resulting, years later, in a vast depreciation of the value of the dollar abroad. The reality of the situation is that U.S. residents have to pay higher prices (in terms of U.S. dollars) for foreign goods and services. At the present time there is no indication that our balance of trade will become positive.

It is evident why the individual and combined components of the balance of payments accounts are of such interest to analysts and governmental officials. Let us now look more closely at the various subdivisions of a nation's balance of payments.

The balance of trade can be positive or negative, as it measures the difference between all the merchandise exported and imported into a country. It is a sizable part of the balance of payments, and, in foreign countries especially, balance of trade figures have great importance. However, it should be understood that in the United States the importance of balance of trade is not as great as it is in some other countries. As a general matter, the importance of balance of trade figures can be judged based upon the percentage that exports contribute to GNP amounts. The greater the proportion of exports to GNP totals, the more significant the balance of trade figures will be in ascertaining a particular nation's economic position.

For example, the United States exports less than 10% of its gross national product. This is much less than the proportionate export of some other countries. Some countries export over 30% of their GNP. As a result, the balance of trade of those countries is more crucial and has a greater effect on the balance of payments than in the United States. Nevertheless, the majority of people either mistake balance of trade for the balance of payments or lend greater significance to balance of trade figures than is required. Therefore, news of negative United States balance of trade figures produces more of a reaction than is warranted under the circumstances.

It is also important to look behind the balance of trade figures for additional useful information. For example, an unfavorable deficit in the balance of trade may in the long run be productive if so-called capital goods are being acquired to be utilized to increase future exports or to lessen future dependency on imports. Similarly, one should be aware that, since balances are derived by computing the next excess of debits or credits in merchandise accounts, the possibility of a valuation error is present. All entries are supposed to be recorded on a uniform valuation basis, which should achieve uniformity in the freight and insurance entries. However, establishing the value of goods shipped and received is not simple. For example, should cost of goods to importers and exporters be the valuation, or should additional costs—such as commissions, insurance premiums, freight and handling charges, and the like—also be included? Detailed sets of rules of the U.S. Customs Service provide valuation guidelines for U.S. trade statistics. Valuation basis is normally FOB (free on board) at the customs frontier of the exporting country for both exports and imports. However, if a country is unable to report imports on this basis, the alternative valuation of CIF (cost, insurance, freight) at the customs frontier of the importing country is also used. For example, the United States, Canada, and Australia value imported goods FOB foreign port of origin. The thorough collection of statistical data through the U.S. Customs Service provides figures reflecting monthly, quarterly, and yearly balances of trade. Nevertheless, the valuation of merchandise is a crucial factor in the accuracy of these statistics. Furthermore, since different nations compile data using different systems of valuation, comparison of those figures is often inconclusive. Finally, it should be mentioned that a special classification is made for military merchandise, which leaves the country but for which no payment is made. Assuming that no payments were made and the shipments are going to be used by our own military abroad, it is not considered a true "export," and it might be added to the errors and omissions category.

Another category that contains a variety of classifications is the balance of services. As was mentioned earlier, expenditures and receipts that are not connected with trade or merchandise and that are not in the category of capital movements are entered in balance of services. Principal areas include shipping services, other transportation, travel, investment income such as interest and dividends, official services and private services such as insurance premiums unrelated to merchandise. In some countries, the balance of services may be a significant category in the balance of payments measurement inasmuch as large amounts of foreign currency earnings are generated by the nation's sale of various services. For example, a country largely dependent on tourist trade will attribute a greater significance to balance of service figures. Additional examples of expenditures that would fall within the balance of services include: expenditures of embassies abroad; payments received for use of patents, royalties, and fees; medical and student expenses; film right payments; supplying know-how and labor; foundation payments supporting universities, educational institutions, hospitals, and churches; expenditures of various American missions; legal fee expenditures; plus many more. An interesting illustration of a balance of service entry is the payment made to the Canadian government for permitting the use of their territory for the transit of oil by pipeline from Alaska. Since the oil originates in U.S. territory, the royalty paid for the right to transport the oil across Canada is not for import but rather for services. The sum total of these service expenditures will yield the balance of services. Again, this total may be either positive or negative and is another element in the final balance of payments calculation.

This brings us to a discussion of short-term capital movements, which is a most significant factor in a nation's balance of payments. While the officially prepared United States International Transactions groups capital flows into private and governmental capital flows, with remittances and transfers under a separate heading, a clear understanding of the causes and effects of short-term capital flows is still essential. Short-term investments of one year or less create a vast amount of readily movable funds that respond to identifiable catalysts. In particular, the interest rate differentials existing in worldwide money markets are responsible for attracting short-term capital flows. Naturally, costs incurred, such as those involved in conversion of one currency to another and in hedging exchange risks, must be considered when calculating the most favorable investment yield. In addition, market factors, such as perceived risk and stability existing in the country of investment, also play important roles in the choice of location of short-term investments. For example, when the United States devalued its dollar repeatedly and closed the gold window in 1971, many individuals in the United States and abroad lost faith in the monetary policy of the United States government. A huge outflow of short-term capital from the United States to foreign banks occurred in response to the concern that the U.S. dollar would be further depreciated. Thus, we see that a lack of confidence creates a flow of short-term capital, which may assume abnormal proportions.

The most commonly known forms of short-term capital movements include: opening accounts abroad, purchase of foreign securities, or the purchase of certificates of deposit by nonresidents if the maturity is one year or less. Thus, since most certificates of deposit or commercial paper are for three-, six-, or nine-month periods, funds moving out of a country into foreign certificates would be considered short-term. If the certificates of deposit were to be renewed or rolled over so as to extend the total time, the funds would still not be considered long-term. There would be two short-term movements—one for the original duration and one for the renewal period. It should be remembered, however, that the interest resulting from these short-term deposits would be categorized under balance of services.

The free, unrestricted flow of short-term funds into as well as out of the nation has advantages. For example, international trade will be facilitated through the availability of funds for payment. Foreign ex-

change markets will operate more smoothly by having arbitrage channels available for purchase and sale of currency. Finally, the possibility
of turning short-term capital movements into long-term investments is
better when the international financial market is active.

Difficulties arise, however, when conditions in a nation do not
permit the establishment of a free market interest rate. Confidence in the
safety of investments and faith in continued free market conditions are
vital if a market is to continue to attract short-term funds. Therefore, if
foreign governments and foreign enterprises have faith in the U.S. dollar, they will purchase U.S. dollars for deposit in the United States. This
flow of funds into the country will improve the U.S. balance of payments. Conversely, if confidence in the monetary system of a nation
falters, the resulting withdrawal of short-term funds will weaken the
balance of payments. When this outward movement of funds is
prompted by loss of market confidence beyond a shift of short-term
interest rate levels, the international flow of funds will rapidly become
substantial. This phenomenon is known as *flight of capital*. The movement of funds out of a nation due to an international weakening of faith
in the currency of that country accounts for a large percentage of short-
term capital movement. Therefore, it is a most important factor in a
nation's balance of payments.

Many events may prompt the flight of capital. A loss of faith in the
economy or the stability of the government may be the cause. Threats of
outside aggression or domestic upheavals will invariably prompt residents to seek out more stable conditions and move funds to safer countries, rather than hold a currency exposed to unfavorable pressures. For
example, in countries such as Argentina, Brazil, Uruguay, and Israel,
those earning money in excess of their daily needs exchange their local
money into other currencies in order to preserve their wealth. The added
pressure created by flight capital prevents these countries from maintaining a positive balance of payments.

Naturally, in the attempt to alleviate this added pressure on currency, governments seek to prevent flight of capital. Controls on capital
movements are frequently enacted in the forms of exchange restrictions
discussed in more detail in the chapter on foreign exchange. However,
the effectiveness of such controls has not been proven. It is more likely
that removal of the cause triggering the flight of capital would stem the
outflow of funds more effectively than exchange restrictions.

An example of efforts made to control foreign investment outflows
is seen in the United States capital controls introduced in the 1960s. The
increasing weakening of the U.S. dollar and continuing deficit in the
balance of payments caused by corporate expansion overseas, war expenditures, and capital outflow prompted measures such as the Interest
Equalization Tax and the Voluntary Credit Restraint Program. These

programs were designed to limit the flow of investments abroad. Although banking and business sectors complied to some degree, these controls did not limit the amount of private capital leaving the United States. It should be mentioned that, unlike many nations, these capital controls were not combined with exchange controls. Nevertheless, if the motivation prompting flight capital is strong enough, experience shows that controls will not alleviate the situation. Especially in nations ruled by dictatorships or those prone to revolution, residents transfer their excess funds to foreign banks. The exchange and transfer restrictions designed to prevent the transfer of funds abroad are therefore inadequate solutions. As mentioned earlier, unreported items in a country's balance of payments may form a substantial errors and omissions category.

There is another potential problem for countries, such as the United States, that offer interest rates high enough to attract substantial amounts of short-term capital. The high rate of interest in a country reflects inflationary pressure that is due to budgetary deficits on the federal level and to uncertainties concerning the future. Although positive effects on balance of payments might result from the influx of funds, substantial interest payment commitments will cause unfavorable results in the future. Moreover, in the long run, high interest rates will weaken the economy and the currency because the eventual repayment of the principal amounts and accumulated interest invested will create a serious negative balance of payments problem. The same applies to long-term capital movements or investments of a duration longer than one year, as discussed earlier. Normally, long-term capital movements include government loans, private portfolio investments, and private direct investment including transactions in foreign bonds and securities.

As a final point, some additional comments must be made regarding errors and omissions, officially known as *statistical discrepancy.* Now that flexible rather than fixed exchange rates are most commonly used, the degree of uncertainty concerning actual balance of payment data has increased. This includes the category of errors and omissions. Factors that contribute to the degree of unreliability include methods of shipment and payment. For example, exports of one country need not be the imports of another country in the same year. Shipments to distant countries may be dispatched in one calendar year, yet arrive in the following year. Some shipments of goods are made against long-term credit. The shipment shows up in the balance of trade, but payment of principal might be received only years later. It is also possible that some shipments will be transported without going through customs, such as military or government aid shipment. Some transactions, such as purchases and sales of short-term financial claims, are difficult to monitor; yet they form a major component of the errors and omissions category. Depending upon the types and numbers of such statistical discrepancy entries, this category may become significant. The indicator by which we may judge the true significance of the errors and omissions category is an analysis of the strength of the nation's currency relative to the world market.

Aside from governmental analysis, balance of payments figures are used for projection in international banking activities especially in the areas of foreign exchange and international lending. For example, the credit risk involved in making a loan to a foreign government is assessed by analyzing balance of payment figures. A nation's ability to meet demands for the repayment of foreign currency borrowed depends on its foreign reserves—which in turn depends on the balance of trade and balance of services. Similarly, in assessing the future trend of a particular currency, balance of payment figures should also be analyzed. In particular, trends in capital movements, as well as the requirements or supply of foreign currency connected with international trade and business transactions, are reflected in these figures. Naturally, other sources of data are used in the decision-making process of international bankers and investors. This does not, however, lessen the importance of the balance of payments data. The point to keep in mind, though, is the variable degree of confidence that should be accorded to a particular nation's statistics. For example, some countries have a practice of preparing different figures for balance of payment statistics depending upon who the ultimate viewer will be. Thus, to avoid significant errors in judgment, one should be aware of the different accounting and statistical guidelines in various countries.

Conclusion

In summary, the balance of payments provides an overall reflection of a nation's internal and external economic condition. Its elements are balance of trade, balance of services, short-term capital movements, long-term capital movements, and errors and omissions. We have examined these elements in order to show their impact upon various sectors of the economy. Repercussions created in response to economic activity were shown to influence the value of a nation's currency. Therefore, the balance of payments should be viewed as a measure of economic vitality that prompts political, economic, and monetary decisions affecting everyday life.

Bibliography

Cairncross, Sir Alexander. *Control of Long-Term International Capital Movements*. Washington, D.C.: Brookings Institute, 1973.

Fieleke, Norman. *What Is the Balance of Payments?* Boston: Federal Reserve Bank of Boston, 1976.

International Monetary Fund. *Balance of Payment Concepts and Definitions.* Pamphlet No. 10, 1969.

Johnson, Harry G. "Money, Balance-of-Payments Theory and the International Monetary Problem." *Essays in International Finance*, 124. Princeton, New Jersey: Princeton University Press, 1977.

Kredietbank. "Exchange Rate Determinants." *Weekly Bulletin*, 22(May 29, 1981), pp. 1–5.

Luckett, Dudley G. *Money and Banking*, 2nd ed. New York: McGraw-Hill, 1980.

Machlup, Fritz. *International Payments, Debts and Gold*, 2nd ed. New York: New York University Press, 1975.

Mathis, F. J., ed. *Offshore Lending by U.S. Commercial Banks*. Washington, D.C.: Bankers Association for Foreign Trade, 1975.

Morgan Guaranty Trust Company of New York. *World Financial Markets*. 1982.

Rendell, Robert S., ed. "International Financial Law—Lending, Capital Transfers and Institutions." *Euromoney*, 1980.

2

International Banking Entities

In recent years, commercial banks have expanded their presence in markets around the world, and they are continuing to find new ways to serve the growing needs of their customers involved in international commerce. This expansion has been largely responsible for the trend toward diversification in banking operations throughout the industry and the application of old forms of doing business to new problems. For the bank customer, the result has been a new availability of services, provided through an increased variety of banking entities. This chapter will focus on the methods by which U.S. banks gain access to international markets and on the major options available to foreign banks seeking to gain a foothold in U.S. banking centers.

U.S. banks can participate in foreign markets directly. They can also participate indirectly through such entities as overseas branches and affiliates, Edge Act and Agreement Corporations, and International Banking Facilities, as well as by establishing foreign correspondent bank relationships.

Similarly, foreign banks seeking access to U.S. markets also have a variety of operational choices available to them. For example, they may establish a representative office, state or federal branches or agencies, an Edge Act Corporation, or a subsidiary bank. In addition, interests may be acquired in domestic banks by merger or acquisition. Furthermore, in New York State, an "investment company" may be formed under Article XII of the New York Banking Law; this is a bank-like entity that is subject to certain restrictions.

Before illustrating the basic differences in the purposes and functions of these various banking entities, let us mention the principal services provided for customers in international markets. Depending upon the type of banking entity chosen, some or all of the following services may be provided.

The *extending of credit* through loans and lines of credit is an important banking function that facilitates international commerce. Import and export trade financing must be available either in local or in foreign currency. In the case of a U.S. bank, foreign currency loans are normally arranged through its overseas branches and affiliates, or with a correspondent bank. In addition, depending upon the required size of the loan and the risk perceived by the lending bank, loans may be syndicated with other lenders. (The principles of loan syndication are discussed in Chapter 8, "Eurodollar Lending.") Other short-term financing is frequently extended either through letters of credit or bankers' acceptances. These topics are also discussed in their respective chapters.

Most banks operating in international markets purchase and sell foreign exchange on both a spot and forward basis, and they often offer foreign currency travelers checks and various bank checks. In conjunction with overseas branches or foreign correspondent banks, banks may transfer funds abroad by draft, airmail, or cable remittance. Collection services (discussed in Chapter 5, "Collections") may also be provided to customers doing business abroad who wish to use the bank as a payment or collection intermediary. This service is particularly important when the collection is made against documents representing title to goods to be released by the bank against either payment or acceptance by the buyer. Finally, other services that generally may be provided for international clients include custodian and trust services, such as for escrow accounts and estates, and local business advisory services offering credit information and investment counseling. Overall, these services provide a comprehensive means for the conduct of international business operations. Frequently, a separate international department will be established within a larger commercial bank to handle these specialized transactions.

International Banking Entities for U.S. Banks

U.S. banks may enter the international market by a variety of methods, including the establishment of Edge Act and Agreement Corporations, of International Banking Facilities, of offshore branches and affiliates, or through the creation of foreign correspondent bank relationships. Incidentally, because foreign banks are authorized to organize Edge Act Corporations ("Edges") pursuant to the International Banking Act of 1978, the following discussion concerning Edges is applicable to them as well. Elements uniquely applicable to the operations of foreign banks, however, will also be mentioned.

EDGE ACT AND AGREEMENT CORPORATIONS

State banks that are members of the Federal Reserve Systems, national banks, and foreign banks may purchase shares in special corporate entities known as Edge Act Corporations, or "Edges," which engage in international banking or financial operations. They are so named after the sponsor of the enabling legislation, Senator Walter Edge of New Jersey. The Federal Reserve Board charters and regulates Edges as provided by Section 25(a) of the Federal Reserve Act and by Regulation K promulgated thereunder. In addition to these federally chartered entities, state member banks and national banks may also purchase, subject to the approval of the Federal Reserve Board (FRB), stock in international banking corporations, which are chartered by state banking authorities and known as *Agreement Corporations*. Agreement Corporations are so named because the purchasing bank must enter into an agreement with the Federal Reserve Board to adhere to certain restrictions imposed on their operation prior to receiving FRB approval of the acquisition. In this respect, the FRB, rather than state law, defines the scope of operations of Agreement Corporations.

Both Edge and Agreement Corporations are subject to organizational requirements, investment restrictions, and liability limits, which are found in Regulation K of the FRB and in applicable statutes such as the Federal Reserve Act. Edges must have a minimum capital stock of $2 million when organized; no such minimum is set for Agreement Corporations but is subject to FRB approval. Furthermore, national banks are permitted to invest in either Edge or Agreement Corporation stock in an amount not exceeding 10% of the bank's capital stock and surplus; this limit is raised to 15% for corporations engaged in banking.

Although certain limitations previously had been imposed on foreign ownership of Edge Corporations, the International Banking Act of 1978 substantially revised those provisions so as to permit foreign acquisition and control of Edge Act Corporations and to allow them to branch domestically across state lines. This enables both foreign and domestic banks to engage in certain kinds of business in states that do not permit nonresident banks to establish branches and agencies.

Another important distinction between Edge and Agreement Corporations is the range of activities in which they are permitted to engage by the Federal Reserve Board. As a general matter, Edges are permitted to enter into foreign financial transactions as well as international banking operations, while Agreement Corporations are limited to activities of a banking nature. As a result, Agreement Corporations can be said to be limited to those activities permitted an Edge that is "engaged in banking," and they may not exercise any banking powers other than those granted to Edges under Regulation K.

Regulation. Several banking-related powers are listed as permissible by the Federal Reserve Board, and FRB Regulation K should be consulted for a specific listing of activities permitted to Edges. Some of those listed include:

- issuance of long-term subordinated debt that does not qualify as a "deposit" pursuant to Regulation D;
- financing international export and import transactions as well as costs of production of goods and services for export;
- issuance of certain guarantees related to import/export transactions;
- overseas collection services;
- issuance of letters of credit;
- acting as paying agent for certain foreign securities;
- making private placements of participations in Edge investments and extensions of credit, with the condition that no Edge may engage in the business of selling or distributing securities in the United States;
- purchase and sale of spot and forward foreign exchange;
- acting as an investment or financial adviser, provided such services are related to foreign assets only.

Permitted activities are included in Regulation K, including a provision listing those for which Board approval may be obtained.

Not surprisingly, restrictions are imposed on activities that are not incidental to international or foreign business. Thus, Edges may accept deposits only from foreign governments and persons principally doing business internationally or residing abroad, including demand, savings, and time deposits (such as negotiable CDs). Similar deposits may be accepted from other persons provided that certain conditions imposed by Regulation K are met. For example, if deposits are to be transmitted abroad, or if they consist of the proceeds of collection abroad used to pay for exported or imported goods or costs related hereto, the Edge is permitted to accept the funds. Furthermore, deposits of an Edge Act Corporation are subject to the reserve requirements of Regulation D and the interest rate limitations of Regulation Q to the same extent as if the Edge were a member bank, unless otherwise provided by the Federal Reserve Board.

An Edge must secure all acceptances outstanding in excess of twice its capital and surplus as well as any acceptances outstanding for any one person in excess of 10% of Edge capital and surplus. Certain exceptions to these limitations are included in Regulation K. Lending limits are also imposed on the amount of liabilities that may be incurred by any one person, which may not exceed 10% of the Edge's capital and surplus. These figures are subject to change by the Federal Reserve Board. In fact, it is expected that Regulation K investment limitations will be amended to reflect increased lending limits granted to national banks in 1982; that is, limits will be increased to 15%.

In addition to restrictions imposed on domestic banking-related activities, the authority given to Edges to acquire and hold shares in certain types of foreign and domestic corporations is also limited. For example, an Edge may not purchase stock of any company that is engaged in the business of buying or selling merchandise or commodities in the U.S., nor of any company that transacts any business in the United States unless such business is considered by the Board to be incidental to the corporation's international or foreign business. An exception is made for stock held to prevent loss on a debt previously contracted. However, Edges may take an equity position in both foreign and U.S. corporations not engaged in business in the U.S., including participations in banks, financial institutions, and certain nonbank entities. Therefore, substantial investment opportunities may still be realized by Edges. Regulation K contains investment procedures and limitations that may either call for prior Board approval or for simple notification regarding the proposed investment, depending upon whether the proposed investment is on the list of permissible activities. Overseas investments by Edge and Agreement Corporations up to 10% of the U.S. investor's capital and surplus are permitted after giving the FRB 45-day prior notification.

Another important power granted to Edges allows them to establish both domestic and foreign branches. Edges are not subject to the branching limitations imposed on member banks by state and federal laws. Agreement Corporations enjoy similar powers. Regulation K currently permits domestic branching for Edges under a 45-day prior notification procedure. This revised procedure calls for publication of the notice of the proposal to establish an Edge branch to be published in a local newspaper before making applications to the FRB. A 30-day comment period must be provided therein. Thereafter, if the appropriate Federal Reserve Bank does not receive any adverse comments from the public, and if it finds that the proposed branch meets certain criteria, the Edge may establish the branch 45 days after the FRB has received the notification. Thus, both foreign-owned and domestic Edges possess the opportunity to expand their operations in the U.S. An Edge Corporation may also establish branches abroad in accordance with the branching procedures outlined in Regulation K for member banks. Unless the conditions for exemption are met that could permit branching with—or in some cases without—prior notice, approval of the FRB must be obtained prior to establishing a foreign branch.

Investment in an organization not engaged in business in the United States or formation of a financial or banking subsidiary abroad is also viewed as consistent with the underlying purposes of the Edge Act, that is, stimulation of international commercial activity. In this regard, the FRB indicates certain listed activities in Regulation K, which it has determined to be acceptable in connection with the transaction of banking or other financial operations abroad. In comparison with the activities listed as permissible for domestic investment, foreign Edge operations are less restricted. Among these permissible activities are included:

- commercial banking;
- certain financing services;
- leasing activities equivalent to an extension of credit;
- fiduciary services;
- underwriting certain types of insurance;
- servicing operations of a U.S. banking organization;
- insurance brokerage;
- data processing;
- managing offshore mutual funds subject to certain restrictions;
- underwriting;
- distributing and dealing in debt and equity securities outside the United States subject to commitment limitations; and
- engaging in activities determined by the FRB to be closely related to banking under Section 4(c)(8) of the BHCA.

The proposed investment must be made in accordance with Regulation K investment procedures, which are categorized according to whether general consent, prior notification, or specific consent must be obtained from the Federal Reserve Board.

As a result of these various provisions, Edges are engaged in a wide variety of international banking and foreign financial activities, which are frequently expanded through the establishment of affiliates and branches. Finally, stock and certificates of ownership in another Edge or in a corporation organized under U.S. or foreign laws may be invested in, provided that the corporation complies with the restrictions on doing business in the United States.

In order to assure compliance with applicable regulations, examiners are appointed by the FRB to examine Edges once a year. In addition, the Edge must itself make sufficient information available for the examiner's assessment of condition and operations, and it must comply with periodic reporting requirements covering foreign as well as domestic operations.

INTERNATIONAL BANKING ACT

Foreign interests in Edge Corporations have proliferated since the enactment of The International Banking Act of 1978 ("IBA") revised certain provisions of the Edge Act. Particularly affected were the provisions that had formerly imposed requirements of citizenship on those acquiring majority interests and control of Edge Corporations. As a result, foreign interests in Edge Corporations have proliferated since its enactment. Overall, the IBA has the objective of establishing uniform national treatment and parity between domestic and foreign banks. Therefore, restrictions formerly placed solely on domestic institutions now apply to foreign institutions as well, while certain barriers formerly applicable only to foreign institutions have been removed. For example, Section 3 of the IBA amends the Edge Act by removing the requirement that corporate directors be American citizens and permits majority ownership by foreign-controlled entities. On the other hand, Section 5 restricts the ability of foreign banks to establish branches outside their "home state" and allows them to accept only such deposits as an Edge Corporation would be permitted to receive under Federal Reserve regulations.

Certain activities, prohibited under the IBA but established prior to its effective date, are "grandfathered" to allow foreign entities to continue operations in the U.S.; nevertheless, it is generally perceived that the IBA results in fairer competition between foreign and domestic entities. Edges themselves may not become members of the Federal Reserve or gain access to its discount window, although required to meet the reserve (and other) requirements of the FRB. This prohibition does not extend to banks holding shares of Edge Corporations.

INTERNATIONAL BANKING FACILITIES (IBFs)

In a development affecting American institutions seeking easier access to international banking markets, the Federal Reserve Board announced the creation of the International Banking Facility ("IBF") on December 3, 1981. IBF operations are located in the United States and permit both domestic and foreign institutions to engage in international activities within FRB guidelines. An institution organizing an IBF need not establish a separate physical entity; the IBF may be simply a segregated division within its sponsor, required to maintain separate recordkeeping functions in order to enjoy privileged regulatory treatment similar to that of an offshore branch. In addition, several states such as New York, California, Illinois, and Florida have since encouraged the establishment of IBFs within their jurisdictions by offering substantial tax relief. For federal income tax purposes, however, the IBF is taxed as part of the sponsoring organization, rather than as a separate entity. IBF deposits are exempt from FDIC insurance requirements; however, to insure compliance, IBFs are subject to examination and reporting requirements of the FRB.

To establish an IBF, actual application to, or approval of, the FRB need not be obtained by the sponsoring institution. Instead, a written notice of intent must be given to the Federal Reserve Bank within the institution's district at least fourteen days prior to forming the IBF. The notice must state that the new IBF intends to comply with the restrictions imposed by Regulation D regarding source and use of funds as well as recordkeeping and accounting requirements.

It is intended that an IBF will function as a quasi-offshore branch since it is not subject to the reserve requirements or interest rate limitations imposed by the FRB on domestic institutions. For this reason, the authorization of IBFs represents a major step in the deregulation of the U.S. banking industry's participation in international financial markets. The basic purpose of IBFs is to give to U.S.-based domestic and foreign banking operations the advantages enjoyed by offshore shell-branches, and thus to attract international financing business from offshore locations in the United States. Since nearly all major U.S. banks opened foreign branches in response to Federal Reserve regulations and controls, authorization of IBFs marks an attempt to return these operations to the U.S. and to improve the domestic market's competitive position as an international banking center. Nevertheless, examination of the range of the activities permitted to IBFs, as well as the scope of their limitations, reveals that important differences, as well as similarities, exist between the powers of an IBF and a typical offshore branch. For example, all IBF funds are exempt from Regulation D reserve requirements and Regulation Q interest rate limitations. Permissible IBF transactions are generally limited to foreign customers. Credit extended by and deposits received by IBFs must be related to non-U.S. activities. Therefore, borrowers and depositors must be foreign residents or certain domestic residents provided that funds are for the use of operations outside the U.S. In addition, certain restrictions are imposed on IBF services. No demand deposits may be accepted. No negotiable instruments, including negotiable CDs and bankers' acceptances, may be issued by an IBF. These activities are prohibited due to the fact that such instruments could easily be transferred to U.S. residents in contravention of IBF regulations.

The residency limitations imposed on deposit taking credit activities have not been interpreted to cover purchases or sales of IBF-eligible assets to or from third parties in the secondary market if such transactions are arranged at arm's length and without recourse. Indeed, IBFs may engage in bankers' acceptance financing, provided that the draft accepted and discounted for a qualifying IBF customer is held until maturity. Such transactions are generally regarded as loans since the accepted draft is held in the institution's own portfolio until maturity.

Aside from extending credit to foreign residents, an IBF may also make loans to other international banking facilities or, subject to Euro-currency reserve requirements, to U.S. offices of parent banking organizations. This limitation prevents the funds from being returned to the U.S. banking system unless required reserves are set aside. This reflects concern for U.S. monetary policy and the negative effects upon the reserve base of the domestic dollar system if these limitations are not properly observed.

The form and type of acceptable deposits are also defined. IBFs may accept time deposits only from foreign sources, to be held in the form of deposits, borrowings, placements, or any other equivalent instruments that may be issued. Negotiable, or bearer, forms of ownership are not permitted. The foreign source requirements found in IBF regulations may be satisfied in a number of ways by institutions such as another IBF, a foreign subsidiary of a domestic corporation, or a foreign government. Strictly speaking, the citizenship of the depositing organization alone is not the key to qualification. IBFs may borrow from foreign offices of depository institutions or other IBFs, as well as from foreign or domestic offices of the establishing institution. When eligible time deposits are accepted by an IBF, they are subject to certain requirements that vary according to their classification.

A distinction is made between the treatment of nonbank and interbank deposits. Nonbank time deposits have a minimum maturity requirement calling for a two-day notice to the IBF prior to deposit withdrawal. Interbank transactions, on the other hand, have a minimum one-day (or overnight) maturity. This includes deposits made by:

- a foreign office of a domestic or foreign depository institution;
- an Edge or Agreement Corporation;
- a foreign or domestic office of the entity that established the IBF;
- another IBF; or
- a foreign governmental entity or an international organization of which the U.S. is a member.

Although IBF time deposits made by bank customers are not subject to minimum transaction amount requirements, no deposit or withdrawal of an IBF time deposit by a nonbank customer is permitted in an amount less than $100,000. Note, however, that this minimum requirement does not apply to withdrawal of interest earned on an IBF since it is not regarded as withdrawal of principal from the account. This minimum transaction amount was adopted in order to limit IBF activities to wholesale international banking.

IBF time deposits and extensions of credit may be booked in either U.S. or foreign currency. As noted earlier, any deposits by or loans to foreign nonbank customers must be related to their foreign business and not used for domestic purposes. Failure to comply with these requirements triggers severe penalties, including imposition of interest and reserve requirements and revocation of IBF authority. In order to assure compliance, the IBF is regularly supervised and examined during the establishing or parent institution's regular examination.

The successful integration of IBFs into existing financial markets is in part dependent upon differences between funding costs and loan spreads in U.S. and other Euromarket centers. During the first-year operations of 1982, four hundred IBFs were established by domestic chartered banks and their Edge Act Corporations, and by U.S. branches and agencies of foreign banks. Assets over $125 billion were booked and deposits over $100 billion were made during the first eight months of operation. Nevertheless, the impact of IBFs on world banking and financial systems appears to be less than expected in terms of the development of superior international financial centers. For institutions seeking freedom from political and currency risks, however, IBFs seem to be a useful alternative to traditional offshore branches.

OFFSHORE BRANCHES

Despite the availability of Edge and Agreement Corporations and IBFs, vehicles through which institutions may engage in international banking, several banks still maintain overseas branches. Compared to agencies or representative offices, branches are used more widely by domestic banks seeking to establish and maintain a presence in overseas markets to permit the offering of a full range of banking services. Once the initial requirements for establishing a foreign branch are met in the United States, the branch will also be obliged to comply with applicable laws within the foreign country, such as obtaining any needed authorizations from foreign bank supervisory authorities.

Before beginning an overview of the permissible powers of foreign branches of American banks and limitations imposed on their operations, it is important to distinguish between foreign branches and foreign subsidiaries. In most respects, branches are considered part of the domestic parent office; subsidiaries, however, are separate legal entities, the stock of which is held by the domestic bank. However, for purposes of general accounting and the treatment of payment obligations on accounts payable only at a foreign branch, the foreign branch is treated as a distinct entity.

Foreign branching is authorized for member banks by Section 25 of the Federal Reserve Act. The actual foreign branching procedures are contained in Regulation K of the Federal Reserve Board, which generally requires that approval of the Board of Governors must be obtained prior to the establishment of foreign branches. However, in order to qualify for application to the Federal Reserve, the institution must possess sufficient capital and surplus. Detailed information must be provided as required on member bank applications. Prior approval of the Board of Governors is not necessary in instances where the member bank has already established branches in other foreign countries. For example, if the bank has branches in two or more foreign countries it may establish other branches in additional foreign countries after giving 60-day advance notice to the Board. In addition, a member bank may establish additional branches in any foreign country in which it already operates one or more branches, without prior approval of, or notice to, the Board of Governors. Other notification requirements are also imposed when certain changes in the foreign branch operation occur. National banks must also notify the Comptroller of the Currency of the intention to establish a foreign branch.

If an uninsured state nonmember bank wishes to establish a foreign branch, it must first obtain the prior written consent of the Federal Deposit Insurance Corporation (FDIC). Application procedures must also be followed for the establishment of an initial branch in another foreign country. A 30-day advance notification requirement is the sole condition, however, when the state nonmember bank wishes to establish additional branches or relocate existing branches in a particular country.

The Federal Reserve Act allows the FRB to issue regulations concerning the powers of foreign branches of member banks. In this regard, the FRB permits foreign branches to engage in activities that are common practice in the place where the branch is located, in addition to the general banking powers granted to domestic institutions. Thus, in order to increase the competitive ability of foreign branches in the local marketplace, the FRB permits banking activities beyond those normally permitted to domestic institutions. Among these additional powers described in Regulation K are the ability to:

1. Guarantee debts or to make payments on the occurrence of readily ascertainable events, if a maximum monetary liability is specified. (Unless it is fully secured, however, the amount may not exceed the permissible lending limits imposed on U.S. institutions.)
2. Accept drafts or bills of exchange drawn upon it, provided that such acceptances shall be subject to the amount limitations provided therein and are of the type described in paragraph 12 of Section 13 of the Federal Reserve Act.
3. Invest in certain types of securities including eligible debt securities subject to limitations.
4. Underwrite, distribute, buy, and sell obligations of the local government or of any agency, instrumentality, or municipality thereof. (However, when

purchasing for its own account, such holdings shall not in the aggregate exceed 10% of the member bank's capital and surplus.)

5. Take liens or other encumbrances on foreign real estate in connection with its extensions of credit.
6. Extend credit up to $100,000 or its equivalent to an officer of the bank for living quarters, if such credit is promptly reported to the branch's home office.
7. Act as insurance agent or broker.
8. Pay employees a higher rate of interest on deposits as part of employee benefits.
9. Engage in repurchase agreements involving commodities and securities that are the functional equivalent of extensions of credit.
10. Any other activities that the Board finds it permissible to engage in upon application.

Thus this list indicates that the powers of a foreign branch are more extensive than those normally permitted for domestic institutions.

Similarly, the foreign branch operations of insured nonmember state banks are regulated by the FDIC. These regulations, in addition to authorizing general banking powers, enable the foreign branch to exercise other powers, as long as they are consistent with the charter of the branch and country practices. As a general matter, these powers are similar to those granted member banks in Regulation K.

Although foreign branches of member banks are considered part of the parent bank for purposes of reserve requirements pursuant to Regulation D, certain exemptions are included for designated deposits. For example, reserves must be maintained against transaction accounts, nonpersonal time deposits, and Eurocurrency liabilities as defined in Regulation D. At the present time, reserves must be maintained in an amount equal to 3% of the institution's Eurocurrency liabilities. However, an exemption is made for deposits payable only at an office outside the United States. A deposit is "payable only at an office outside the United States" when: (1) a U.S. resident has a deposit in a denomination of $100,000 or more subject to an agreement whereby payment may only be demanded outside the United States; or (2) a nonresident of the U.S. has a deposit subject to an agreement whereby payment may only be demanded outside the United States. Note that in the case of a deposit by a U.S. resident, a $100,000 minimum is imposed to prevent evasion of reserve regulations contained in Regulation D. Similarly, foreign branches of member banks do not have interest rate limitations imposed on deposits payable only outside the United States as already defined. In addition, the FDIC exempts insured state nonmember banks from interest rate limits on deposits payable outside the U.S. These exemptions free foreign branches to offer higher returns on funds to deposits and increase the branch's competitive position overseas.

CORRESPONDENT BANKS

In order to adequately provide needed international banking services, commercial banks establish a network of foreign correspondent banks to supplement their own facilities worldwide. Frequently, the expense of establishing a related banking entity, such as an overseas branch, is not warranted due to the low volume of transactions concluded for the bank's international clients. Therefore, to provide service while keeping costs minimal, account relationships are developed with foreign banks to facilitate international payment mechanisms between the institutions. Deposit accounts are opened at the correspondent banks, which enable them to make direct payments overseas by means of debiting and crediting the respective accounts with settlement to be made at a later date. Such accounts are termed *due to* (or *nostro*) accounts and *due from* (or *vostro*) accounts on the banks' books. In addition to payment accounts, correspondent bank relationships facilitate transactions such as letters of credit, documentary collections, foreign exchange services, and loan services for a bank's international clients. Thus, the correspondent bank relationship gives the domestic bank a presence in overseas markets, which permits international transactions to be concluded.

Foreign Banks in the U.S.

Foreign banks seeking U.S. market entry have a variety of operational choices available to them, in addition to entering into correspondent relationships with U.S. banks. Their choices include:

- the formation of an Edge Act Corporation or IBF (discussed earlier);
- the establishment of either state or federal branches or agencies, or of a representative office; and
- the creation of a subsidiary through merger or acquisition.

In New York, a foreign institution also has the option of forming an investment company under Article XII of the New York Banking Law, which must operate in accordance with certain statutory limitations. Each of these major options will be explored with an emphasis on the permissible activities for each option.

Foreign banks generally gain access to the United States banking market either by establishing their own U.S. offices or by acquiring interests in existing financial institutions. Foreign individuals and non-banking entities can also acquire interests in existing American financial institutions or invest in new ones. The predominant method by which foreign banks have gained access to the U.S. banking market is through the establishment of new banking entities, such as branches, agencies, and subsidiaries, or by acquiring U.S. banks. Currently, branches are the dominant organizational form, accounting for slightly over half of all the standard assets and commercial loans of foreign-controlled banks in the U.S. The following discussion describes the choice of business forms from which a foreign bank may choose in establishing a presence in the U.S.: a representative office, an agency or branch, or an acquired subsidiary bank.

REPRESENTATIVE OFFICES

A representative office is both the most commonly used and the most limited in function of all foreign banking operations in the United States. Neither a branch nor an agency, it is a U.S. office of a foreign bank, and it functions mainly as a liaison between correspondent banks and the parent bank. Representative offices are prohibited from engaging in general banking activities, although they may receive checks for forwarding to the home office, solicit loans for the home office, and develop customer relations. However, they may not receive deposits or make loans. These offices, which are regulated by state law, must be registered with the Secretary of the Treasury, normally within 180 days after opening. The International Banking Act of 1978 (IBA) does not authorize foreign banks to organize a representative office in violation of state laws. Generally, representative offices serve as the preliminary step to other forms of banking activity since they are a relatively inexpensive means of establishing a presence in a new location.

BRANCHES AND AGENCIES

Depending upon the extent of services that the institution wishes to offer, either a branch or an agency may be established. The basic definition of "branch" and "agency" may be found in the International Banking Act of 1978. A *branch* is any office of a foreign bank at which deposits are received. On the other hand, an *agency* is any office at which deposits may not be accepted from citizens or residents of the U.S. if they are not engaged in international activities, but at which credit balances may be maintained. Thus, the principal difference between branches and agencies is that agencies cannot accept deposits from U.S. citizens or residents and can only maintain credit balances related to their international activities. In addition, agencies cannot engage in either fiduciary or investment advisory activities with the exception of acting as custodians for individual customers. Agencies do engage in a variety of activities to finance international trade, such as the handling of letters of credit.

Both agencies and branches are principally active in international markets. The IBA has significantly changed the treatment of foreign banks wishing to establish a branch or agency in the U.S. Prior to enactment of the IBA, foreign banks could only establish state-chartered branches or agencies. If a foreign bank has established a state agency, the permissibility of accepting nondomestic deposits is determined by state law. Currently, however, foreign banks also have an option to obtain a federal license from the Office of the Comptroller of the Currency (OCC). Nevertheless, a federal branch or agency may not be established in a state that prohibits foreign bank branches or agencies by law.

As extensions of the foreign parent bank, branches are generally subject to more stringent state regulation than agencies due to the more extensive nature of their operations. The powers of a federal branch are similar in scope to those of a national bank: These branches possess full deposit-taking, loan, and commercial banking powers in addition to other trust powers. They are also subject to duties, restrictions, and limitations similar to those of a national bank organized in the same area. Federal branches and agencies are not required to be members of the Federal Reserve System, but they are subject to certain reporting and interest requirements. In addition, federal branches and agencies of foreign banks are required to maintain a so-called capital equivalency deposit with a Federal Reserve System (FRS) member bank as well as an asset maintenance requirement. Furthermore, federal branches accepting retail deposits in amounts under $100,000 must be insured by the Federal Deposit Insurance Corporation (FDIC), unless the OCC grants an exemption, while federal agencies and federal branches that do not accept such retail deposits from U.S. citizens or residents are not required to obtain FDIC insurance. Similarly, a foreign bank may not establish a state branch that accepts deposits of less than $100,000 wherever state bank deposits must be insured, unless it first obtains FDIC insurance or the FDIC makes a determination that the branch is not engaged in domestic retail deposit activities. However, if the state branch agrees to accept only deposits permissible for Edges, it can be an uninsured branch. It should be mentioned that, prior to the IBA, foreign banking institutions could not obtain FDIC insurance.

LIMITED BRANCHES

Pursuant to the IBA, an additional means by which a foreign bank may participate in U.S. banking markets is through a so-called *limited federal branch*. Basically, this is an office chartered by the Comptroller of the Currency subject to the condition that the foreign bank enter into an agreement with the Federal Reserve Board restricting the branch's deposit-taking activities to those permitted an Edge Act Corporation. However, limited federal branches differ from Edges to the extent that their lending powers are parallel to those of a national bank; that is, unlike Edges, they are not limited to international or foreign lending activities. Since these offices may be established outside the foreign bank's home state, they are restricted to deposit-taking activities of an international nature. Furthermore, before establishing out-of-state operations, permission must be sought from the OCC and the state in the case of a federal license, or from the state bank regulatory authorities in the case of a state license. By way of contrast, Edges may branch upon FRB approval. In all other respects, a limited federal branch may generally exercise the powers of a regular federal branch. Due to the nature of the restrictions on their operations, a limited federal branch is not required to be insured by the FDIC, nor is it required to become a member of the FRS; it need only maintain eligible assets on deposit with a FRS member bank, as must all federal branches and agencies.

Restrictions on the operation of federal branches and the creation of limited federal branches came about with the passage of the IBA, which extended federal regulations to the operations of branches and agencies of foreign banks in the U.S. Before its passage, foreign banks were not subject to restrictions on interstate banking or nonbanking activities. However, in an effort to equalize the competitive position between domestic and foreign institutions, prohibitions against retail deposit-taking activities were imposed on both branches and subsidiary banks. As mentioned previously, operations established as of July 1978 were "grandfathered." After this date, a foreign bank may not engage in deposit-taking activities outside its home state, thus applying the principle of the domestic McFadden Act to foreign banking institutions and restricting foreign banks to a limited range of activities, through limited branches as well as through agencies or Edge Act Corporations.

Generally speaking, the International Banking Act imposes upon foreign banks operating in U.S. markets federal regulation as extensive and complex as that applicable to domestic banks. State banking departments formerly enjoyed sole responsibility for the chartering, supervision, and regulation of foreign branches, agencies and representative offices. As a result of the IBA, the Comptroller of the Currency (OCC), the Federal Reserve Board, and the Federal Deposit Insurance Corporation now all have their own respective supervisory prerogatives, which may be exercised depending upon the type of charter held by the institution and the activities in which it is engaged (such as retail deposit taking). In general, the primary regulator of federal branches and agencies is the OCC. The FDIC holds responsibility for the appropriate regulation of an insured office. The Federal Reserve Board supervises operation of a limited federal branch, in accordance with its agreement to operate within guidelines similar to those prepared for an Edge Act Corporation in certain respects.

The impact of the International Banking Act of 1978 upon the permissible activities of foreign banking institutions operating in U.S. markets is significant; in particular, it reduces their ability to function freely across state lines. For example, IBA Section 8(a) places on a foreign bank with a branch, agency, or commercial lending company subsidiary in the U.S. the restrictions on nonbanking activities contained in the Bank Holding Company Act. Such restrictions, by way of contrast, are not imposed on foreign banks engaging in banking through Edge Act Corporations alone. Furthermore, Section 5 of the IBA limits out-of-state expansion by foreign banks by restricting the deposits that may be accepted by branches established outside the "home state" to those of the type allowed to be taken by Edge Act Corporations. The effect of these provisions is to prevent a foreign bank from exercising full deposit-taking powers in any state but its home state and those states where prior operations were "grandfathered." Agencies, on the other hand, may not accept "domestic" deposits under provisions of the IBA. The location of additional out-of-state offices is also restricted by the IBA in that, while the foreign bank may establish a federal branch or agency in any state (or D.C.) in which it is not already operating a state branch or agency, it may not have both a federal branch and agency in the same state. Finally, federal branches or agencies may establish additional branches or agencies in that state if the foreign bank complies with the requirements applicable to branching by a national bank in the same local (that is, reference is made to state law). If a federal branch accepts domestic retail deposits in amounts under $100,000, FDIC insurance must be obtained to protect such deposits, though the OCC or the FDIC may in some circumstances grant an exemption from this insurance requirement. Generally, if deposits under $100,000 are accepted, they are accepted only from large business enterprises.

The trend of foreign banking institutions operating in the U.S. has changed significantly in recent years. In 1972, agencies, which are not permitted to accept domestic deposits, controlled over half the standard banking assets as well as commercial and industrial loans of foreign banking offices in the United States. Since that time, large banks from Western European nations have opened many branches in the U.S. In addition, Japanese banks, eager to increase their deposit base, have converted many of their agencies to branches.

SUBSIDIARY BANKS

Foreign banks gain control of subsidiary banks by establishing new institutions or by acquiring existing domestic banking institutions, and these subsidiaries generally may engage in a full line of banking activities. With respect to the designation of a foreign bank subsidiary, the terms "bank" and "subsidiary" have the same meaning as those provided by Section 2 of the Bank Holding Company Act (BHCA). A subsidiary bank of a foreign bank may be either a national or a state bank. State banks are governed by the laws of the state in which they are located, while national banks are chartered by the Comptroller of the Currency under the National Bank Act. Although foreign ownership is not restricted, non-U.S. citizens may not form a majority of a national bank's Board of Directors. If chartered by the OCC, the bank must be a member of the Federal Reserve System and maintain FDIC insurance, as must all national banks. State banks have the option of becoming members of the Federal Reserve.

ACQUISITIONS

We have seen that domestic or foreign investors can enter the U.S. banking market by establishing new banking organizations (agencies, branches, representative offices, Edge Act Corporations, or IBFs) or by acquiring existing banks. Between the Bank Holding Company Act, the Bank Merger Act, and the Change in Bank Control Act, federal regulators also have the authority to review and approve attempts to acquire control of banks by holding companies, banks, and individuals.

Under the Bank Holding Company Act, the Federal Reserve Board must approve the acquisition of direct or indirect control of a U.S. bank by a domestic or foreign bank holding company. Various factors are considered in the approval or denial of a BHC application. These include analysis of the competitive effects of the acquisition, the acquirer's financial and managerial resources, future prospects of the bank being acquired, community needs, and the applicant's organizational structure. Often, the lack of complete access to information regarding the acquiring foreign BHC will result in the review procedures used by the Federal Reserve differing somewhat between foreign and domestic applicants. Thus, more extensive information may be required from foreign applicants regarding their direct and indirect ownership of other organizations and the financial condition of all direct and indirect subsidiaries. In addition, the Federal Reserve may solicit the views of the institution's home country regulator while assessing the role and standing of the holding company in its own country. Finally, the staff of the FRB will conduct the analysis and render a decision on acquisition for first-time foreign applicants.

The previous gap in BHCA regulation of acquisitions made by a subsidiary bank of a BHC was alleviated by the Bank Merger Act. Basically, this act prohibits any bank with deposits insured by the FDIC from merging, consolidating or acquiring assets, or assuming the liabilities of another bank, without first obtaining the approval of the appropriate federal agency. Standards for approval of acquisitions are the same as those contained in the BHCA.

Prior to the passage of the Change in Bank Control Act, bank supervisory agencies did not have authority to regulate acquisitions of an insured bank by one or more individuals not acting as a partnership. No distinction is made between domestic and foreign acquirers.

The Change in Bank Control Act authorizes federal banking regulators to review and, if warranted, reject an application by foreign individuals for acquisition of U.S. banks. If the regulators disapprove the acquisition application, the investor may request a hearing before the appropriate federal banking authority. If the regulator again disapproves acquisition plans, the investor may request a review by the appropriate United States Court of Appeals. Various reasons for disapproval of proposed acquisitions of U.S. banks by regulators may include the following:

1. The acquisition would have a monopolistic effect or would lessen competition in any part of the United States.
2. The bank's ability to serve the convenience and needs of the surrounding community would be adversely affected.
3. The competency, experience, or financial integrity of any potential investor might place the stability of the bank or the interests of depositors in jeopardy.
4. The proposed investor neglects, fails, or refuses to furnish all the information required.

Thus, certain acquisitions of bank shares not covered by the Bank Merger Act or the BHCA are covered by the Change in Bank Control Act. Procedures implemented by supervisory agencies seem to treat foreign and domestic applicants equally. The Comptroller reviews acquisitions of national banks, the Federal Reserve reviews those of state member banks and BHCs, and the Federal Deposit Insurance Corporation reviews applications submitted by all nonmember insured banks.

Although federal laws require foreign investors seeking acquisition of domestic banks to submit comprehensive biographical and financial information with their applications, federal bank regulators have a very difficult task in verifying information provided by the applicants in many instances. Frequently, supervisory agencies are forced to rely on the data supplied by the foreign applicant because they have no independent information such as that obtained from on-site examinations, other regulatory agencies, customers, or interested groups. Furthermore, federal bank regulators do not require financial statements provided by foreign investors to be prepared in accordance with U.S. standards known as Generally Accepted Accounting Principles. Differences in accounting principles create difficulties for those seeking to determine the financial strength of foreign investors. Similarly, language barriers, differences in local law and customs, inaccessibility of information, and lack of contact with individuals working with the institution add to the burden of those determining whether or not to approve foreign acquisition of a U.S. banking institution.

If the bank being acquired is a "failed" or "failing" U.S. institution, abbreviated or emergency applicant review procedures may be implemented by federal regulators attempting to save the bank. In order not to have to use the Federal Deposit Insurance Fund to pay deposits and to maintain some assurance of continuity of bank service, the FDIC may seek a foreign- or domestic-owned bank, holding company, or individual to purchase the assets and assume the liabilities of a failed bank.

Bank Mergers

The Bank Merger Act, referred to earlier, makes the federal supervisory authorities responsible for examination and approval of proposed bank merger applications. There are several reasons for a foreign bank merging with a domestic bank. For example, this provides an expedient and economical means of expanding into new markets; it becomes easier to establish an identity on a state-wide basis; and the bank is able to continue smooth operations with experienced management and personnel.

Procedures for review of the merger application are similar for domestic and foreign applicants. When the resulting or surviving bank is a national or District of Columbia bank, this authority is given to the Comptroller. The Federal Reserve has approval authority for surviving state member banks, and the FDIC must approve mergers where state nonmember insured banks survive.

The Comptroller and the FDIC allow a review of the regional level to the extent of a preliminary evaluation of the application's technical completeness. In addition, they permit their regional officials to meet with the management of the merging banks to discuss the proposed transaction and to determine the potential for formal approval. The Federal Reserve Board allows Federal Reserve banks to fully review a merger application prior to formal filing, and to approve the merger application unless a local conflict of interest exists or the transaction raises policy issues. Some of the factors considered by bank regulatory agencies include: the financial condition of the merging banks, management capabilities, future prospects of the surviving institution, community needs, and the surviving bank's effect on competition.

In the event that regulators decide to deny a merger application, they must promptly send a written notice to the applicants specifying the reasons for the denial. After receipt of this notice, the applicants can file a written request to amend their application. Regulators must then provide the applicant with an additional 30 days to amend the application or prepare a presentation in defense of the merger.

Conclusion

We have examined in this chapter various entities through which domestic and foreign banks may pursue their respective international banking activities in domestic U.S. markets. Each of the possible forms brings with it numerous requirements and conditions for operation. Most important is the fact that limitations imposed by supervisory authorities may significantly curtail certain activities, particularly those affecting U.S. domestic markets. Nevertheless, banking institutions have a wide range of choices available to them, each with its own set of advantages and disadvantages. The following chapters will explore the functions of international banking institutions.

Bibliography

Bellanger, S. "Unfair? Or Just Foreign?" *Euromoney* (December 1981), p. 122.

Board of Governors of the Federal Reserve System. Federal Reserve Press Release. December 17, 1981. (IBF purchase/sale of financial assets in the secondary market.)

C.F.R. 12, Part 211 (effective November 8, 1982). Amendment to Reg. K—International Banking Operations (procedures for establishing a U.S. branch of an Edge corporation).

Cacase, L. M. "Foreign Banks Swelling the Edge Act Ranks." *American Banker* (May 24, 1982), pp. 1, 12.

The Edge Act. 12 U.S.C. §§611–632. 1976.

Glidden, W. and J. Shockey. "U.S. Branches & Agencies of Foreign Banks: A Comparison of the Federal and State Chartering Options." *U. Ill. L. Forum*, 65.

Gruson, M. and P. Jackson. "Issuance of Securities by Foreign Banks and the Investment Company Act of 1940." *U. Ill. L. Forum*, 185(1980), pp. 185–229.

International Banking Act of 1978. Pub. L. No. 95-369, 92 Stat. 607 (codified in scattered sections of 12 U.S.C.).

International Banking Act of 1978. Report of the Committee on Banking, Housing and Urban Affairs to Accompany H.R. 10899. 95th Congress, 2nd Session, 1978.

Izlar, William H. *New Banks and New Bankers.* New York: Practicing Law Institute, 1981.

Kelly, D. E. "Edge Act Corporations after the International Banking Act and New Regulation K: implications for foreign and regional or smaller banks." *Va. J. Int. L.*, 20(1979), pp. 37–59.

McPheters, R. D. "Formation of Edge Act Corporations by Foreign Banks." *Bus. Law*, 37(January 1982), pp. 593–612.

Mendelson, M. S. "First Anniversary of IBFs Finds Much Ado About Little." *American Banker* (December 9, 1982), p. 2.

"The Regulation of Interstate Bank Branching Under the International Banking Act of 1978: The Stevenson Compromise." *N. W. J. of Int. L. and Bus.*, 1(1979), p. 284.

Spero, Joan. *The Failure of the Franklin National Bank.* New York: Columbia University Press, 1980.

Taran, D. A. "The International Banking Facility." International Bureau of Fiscal Documentation Bulletin (1982), p. 554.

Washington Financial Reports, 39, No. 19(November 15, 1982), p. 872.

Weeramantry, L. G., Schlichting, W. H., Cooper, J., and J. Sexton. *Banking Law.* Albany, New York: Matthew Bender, 1982.

3

Letters of Credit

Periods of expansion in international and domestic trade invariably increase the demand for methods of facilitating payments between trading partners. The customary response of bankers is the development of even more modern service techniques. As a result, international payment and credit transactions are handled almost exclusively by banks or through their intermediaries. As a general rule, these payments are not made through actual shipment of cash (using currency, banknotes, gold, or other coins) but rather by recorded transfer mechanisms and/or documents, that is, through accounting entries of the institutions involved. Actual payment is completed only when the chosen transfer procedure is concluded by the bank or its correspondent.

As a principal method of transfer, the letter of credit plays a central role in the world of international banking and finance. An understanding of the basic features of this device and its potential uses is of great importance.

Several terms are used interchangeably when referring to letters of credit. For example, "documentary letter of credit," "documentary credit," and "commercial letter of credit" are all terms used to refer to basically the same type of instrument.

Definition

Although there have been numerous attempts to define the *letter of credit*, a simplified definition will illustrate its basic character. A "letter of credit" is an instrument issued by a bank at the request of its customer by which it promises to pay an indicated amount to a beneficiary upon receipt of certain documents in accordance with some specific terms. Therefore, the documentary credit represents the bank's commitment to put a specified sum at the customer's disposal on behalf of a beneficiary under precisely defined terms and conditions. It is important to note that the bank's commitment to pay is enforceable only when the seller (or beneficiary) fulfills all of the conditions stipulated in the letter of credit.

The letter of credit differs materially from other means of transfer in the rights and duties conferred upon the parties. These differences determine the appropriateness of one method of transfer over another, and they warrant brief mention at this point.

The *remittance* (or *transfer*) abroad is made at the order of the party making the payment through a debit of his or her account in one bank and a corresponding credit in the bank of the payee. This is accomplished by means of a cable, wire, telex, or other written message conveyed to the location where it is desired that the payment be made. Protective procedures, such as the use of codes in the messages to prevent unauthorized transfers, are often employed. The foreign exchange regulations of several countries severely impact upon the cross-border use of transfers.

Using a transfer remittance, direct payment to a named payee may be accomplished without the use of unnecessarily protective conditions and with a minimum of intervening steps. By contrast, payment under a letter of credit assures the payee of the availability of funds but restricts access to them until the agreed protective conditions have been met. Furthermore, by assuming the obligation to carry out payment exactly in accordance with its customer's instructions, the bank's role as a representative of its customer is expanded, since payment made without closely following the customer's instructions can result in liability for the bank.

Another means of receiving payment from abroad is by the use of the collection method, discussed in another chapter. The bank, usually located in the buyer's vicinity, collects the creditor's claim for the seller and releases documents conferring title to the goods purchased to the buyer upon payment. This method assures safe delivery of both the title documents and payment through the use of the bank as intermediary.

Checks, as well as bills of exchange, are instruments that are themselves delivered. If properly executed, they represent an undertaking to pay the amount for which they are drawn. The use of a clearing account for the settlement of debts and claims is another means of payment, useful for trade with countries where payment restrictions prevail.

Although prohibited in several countries, such as the United States, Japan, and others, a bank guarantee may be obtained to secure the payment of its customer. In the event that payment is not made through anticipated methods, the bank will be liable for payment under the terms and conditions of its guarantee.

History

The highest level of development in the area of letters of credit was achieved by England before World War I. The practical monopoly on international letters of credit held by England was broken after the war, and the United States penetrated and became dominant in this particular market, quickly learning the "know-how" from London bankers. The Federal Reserve Act of 1913 permitted member banks to issue letters of credit. In the 1930s England went off the gold standard, which, together with her loss of domination of world trade to the United States, further enhanced the worldwide importance and recognition of the American dollar as a world currency.

After World War II, America became the most important supplier of goods in international trade and the largest buyer of foreign goods. This accelerated the development of letters of credit in the United States, and American banks today play a leading role in the field of issuance of letters of credit.

Since various customs and practices developed in the United States and in foreign countries concerning the interpretations and usages surrounding letters of credit, the International Chamber of Commerce in Paris, in cooperation with various national Chambers of Commerce and banks, developed the Uniform Customs and Practice for Documentary Credits. The rules were published in 1962 and since July 1, 1963, the American banks, through their various associations, have subscribed to them and are governed by these rules. Virtually every country and territory in the world has accepted these rules.

Reflecting the numerous changes in international trading and transport techniques occurring since 1962, the rules were amended in 1974, and a further revision has been approved by the International Chamber of Commerce to become effective on October 1, 1984.

Applications

Letters of credit were originally used to facilitate transactions involving sales of merchandise by assuring payment for goods. By obtaining the obligation of a bank whose credit was considered more valuable than that of a distant purchaser, the seller knew that an independent party (the bank) would make payment as soon as the goods were shipped and the documents prescribed by the credit were delivered. On the other hand, the buyer knew that the amount of the purchase price would only be released against receipt of the documents specified in the credit.

The use of letters of credit for this purpose continues today. For example, if an American exporter receives an order from a foreign buyer, he wants assurance, before making shipments or before starting to manufacture the goods ordered, that he will be paid upon the shipment of the goods. He will require the foreign buyer to open a letter of credit in his favor, which will be payable to him upon proof to the bank through which the letter of credit is opened, that the shipment has been made in accordance with the order. Upon presentation of such proof, the bank will then pay the exporter. The exporter thus has obtained the promise of the bank to make payment for the buyer upon fulfilling the order, without having to depend on the reliability or willingness of the foreign buyer directly.

Conversely, if an American importer wants to buy goods abroad, the foreign seller will want to know that payment will be made when shipment is made to or received in America. Therefore, he will require the American importer to open a letter of credit through his bank, possibly through an intermediary of an American bank and the foreign bank, in favor of the foreign exporter before shipment is made. The advantages and benefits for both the buyer and seller lie in the assurance that payment will be made for the goods shipped.

Letters of credit are not confined to international trade and are used domestically. Their use is not confined to financing importation or exportation of merchandise, but includes assuring payment by domestic parties as well. Variations in local laws, customs and usages, together with the peculiar demands of foreign trade, however, make for distinctions between domestic and foreign, or international, documentary letters of credit, which are explored in a later section.

Letters of credit can be required not only for delivery of goods, but also to assure the performance of certain services. A broker, for example, may wish to assure payment of his or her commission by means of a letter of credit, payable upon proof of having obtained funds for financing a certain enterprise. Similarly, a letter of credit arrangement could assure payment of a real estate commission upon proof of services connected with the sale or purchase of real estate. Finally, a fixed sum may be paid under a letter of credit upon delivery of a document to the bank waiving certain rights.

When issued for payment of services instead of for delivery of goods, the credit is called a *financial letter of credit*. This is because the nature of the documents required to be presented as a condition for payment is different from that of trade documents, though still of a financial character. Furthermore, the underlying transaction does not involve the exchange of goods, but nevertheless involves a financial transaction of some kind.

The benefits of establishing a financial letter of credit include the elimination of the need for credit investigation as well as the prevention of default due to possible cancellation of an order by the buyer. In this respect, financial letters of credit also support a promise of payment.

Many variations of the basic letter of credit are available. As will be discussed, each type has specific characteristics and uses to accommodate the desired results of the parties. However, before examining the mechanics involved in the choice and establishment of specific types of credits it will be useful to examine in a general fashion their unique legal character.

As was mentioned earlier, virtually every country has adopted the rules of the Uniform Customs and Practices (UCP) for documentary credits. This collection of customs and practices forms the framework that guides everyday transactions. For example, letters of credit issued in the United States usually stipulate that unless otherwise expressly stated, the credit is subject to the UCP. Although the UCP is not law and is mandatory only if the terms of the credit so stipulate, it is proof of custom when disputes arise. Therefore, it is important to be familiar with its terms and conditions.

Perhaps the most significant principle expressed in the UCP is that credits by their nature are separate transactions from the sales or other contracts on which they may be based. The independent character of the letter of credit prevents the bank from being placed in the position of party to the underlying sales contract and potentially assuming the buyer's debt. Instead, when undertaking to effect payment to the beneficiary, the bank is concerned only with the documents required to be presented under the credit rather than with the goods themselves. In effect, a separate letter of credit contract between the issuer (bank) and the beneficiary (seller) is established by the customer (buyer). The relationship between the parties creates certain legal rights and obligations, which are more fully discussed later.

It is important, therefore, to realize that the bank undertakes a direct and primary promise to make payment to the beneficiary. Payment is made by the bank exclusively upon performance by the beneficiary (rather than by the customer) of all of the conditions defined in the credit.

A letter of credit should be distinguished from a guarantee since, unlike the guarantee, it is independent of the underlying contractual arrangement; consequently, its terms and conditions are interpreted separately. A letter of credit is also distinguishable from a negotiable instrument because it is not an unconditional promise to pay a certain sum to bearer or to the beneficiary, despite the fact that other elements of a negotiable instrument may be present. Note, however, that the drafts or bills of exchange drawn by the beneficiary under the credit do remain subject to the rules regarding negotiable instruments and must be examined separately.

The solutions to questions and disputes involving letters of credit and the drafts that may be drawn under them call for reference to applicable provisions of local law in addition to the UCP. For example, in the United States, a codification of fundamental legal principles governing credits is found in the Uniform Commercial Code, Article 5 (Letters of Credit). This code has been enacted in most, if not all, states. If a credit states that it is governed by the UCP, the potential exists for conflict between the two. For example, in New York, Article 5 of the Uniform Commercial Code is explicitly inapplicable to letters of credit that state they are governed by the UCP. Nevertheless, in *United Bank Ltd. v. Cambridge Sporting Goods Corp.*, the Court of Appeals ruled that Section 5–114 codified common law and was therefore applicable in instances where it is neither inconsistent with the UCP nor concerns a subject provided for in the UCP. Consequently, both the UCP and the UCC must be read in conjunction to determine which provisions may apply in case of dispute. Interpretation of the words of the credit may differ depending upon which provisions apply, as will be illustrated in the discussion of various types of credit available to the parties.

Mechanics of Establishing a Letter of Credit

This brings us to an examination of the mechanics of opening a letter of credit. An applicant who makes a request to open a letter of credit is known as the *account party* or the *customer*. In a trade contract, this individual may be the buyer of goods. The *issuer* is the party who provides the credit and is in most instances a bank. The third party is the *beneficiary* of the issuer's promise and is usually the seller of the goods. The term "beneficiary" implies no interest in a fund or other property, nor the existence of any fiduciary duties owed by other parties under the letter of credit contracts. The commercial letter of credit is issued directly in the name of the beneficiary.

Other parties may be involved in a letter of credit transaction. The *advising bank* gives notification of the issuance of a credit by another bank to the beneficiary. In addition, a *confirming bank's* services might also be engaged. If this is the case, the confirming bank gives a commitment to the beneficiary either that it will itself honor a credit already issued by another bank, or that such a credit will be honored only by the issuer or a third bank. The advantage of choosing to have a confirming bank over an advising bank is that the beneficiary will have an equal claim for payment against either the issuing or confirming bank. An advising bank is not liable for payment. The rights and obligations that arise when either of these additional parties are involved in the transaction will be further analyzed in a later section.

Types of Letters of Credit

Letters of credit may initially be differentiated according to three broad functional categories:

1. revocable v. irrevocable,
2. clean v. documentary, and
3. sight v. time.

When filing an application for the credit, it is of the utmost importance to precisely state the functional type of credit desired. The application itself is similar to an application for a loan and is often evaluated in the same manner.

IRREVOCABLE/REVOCABLE CREDITS

Irrevocable letters of credit are instruments that may not be revoked, cancelled, or changed without the consent of all parties involved, especially of the beneficiary. Conversely, *revocable letters of credit* may be altered or withdrawn by a party up to the moment of presentation for payment. In cases involving ancillary financing by intermediary banks, the consent of the participating banks may also be required to change the terms of the credit.

Since a credit that does not specify whether or not it is revocable is assumed to be revocable, the text of every credit should always state which type it is. A revocable letter of credit is not an ironclad guarantee to the beneficiary, since it can be revoked at any time, even minutes before the required documents are presented. Furthermore, prior notice to the beneficiary would not be necessary in case of amendment or cancellation. For this reason, it is most unusual for a credit to be issued without the word "irrevocable" being mentioned. If the revocable credit can be revoked or amended at any time without notice, the seller has no assurance that payment is protected because of the lack of a legally binding agreement between the bank and the seller.

CLEAN/DOCUMENTARY CREDITS

Clean and documentary credits are another broad functional type. A *clean credit* calls only for presentation of a draft or other demand in order to obtain payment; no accompanying documents are necessary. On the other hand, a *documentary credit* calls for payment to be made against presentation of specified documents proving compliance with the terms of the credit. These may include documents of title to goods or documents certifying performance of a service.

If the documents refer to a sale of merchandise, the letter of credit is considered a commercial documentary credit. Depending upon whether the opening of the credit is initiated by the American exporter or the American importer, the document is called a *documentary export letter of credit* or a *documentary import letter of credit*. Although there is basically no difference between the two credits, banks often differentiate between them because sometimes they are handled by separate departments.

SIGHT/TIME CREDITS

Once performance by the beneficiary has been established, the terms of payment will distinguish sight from time letters of credit. A *sight letter of credit* is payable upon presentation of required documents. The stipulated amount is released as soon as the prescribed documents have been submitted and checked by the bank. Consequently, the exporter may receive money for the goods shortly after shipment and will be able to finance further transactions.

A *time letter of credit* defers payment to a certain date subsequent to the presentation to the bank of the required documents. The text of a time letter of credit authorizes the beneficiary to draw a draft on a specified bank if certain documents are also submitted. In return for the documents surrendered, the beneficiary will receive the draft back "accepted" by the drawee bank. (See Chapter 4, "Bankers' Acceptances.")

The originator of the letter of credit frequently arranges with the beneficiary that payment will be made only 30, 60, or 90 days, and occasionally six months, after the date of presentation of the documents or other specified date. The wording of the letter of credit names the bank on which the draft is to be drawn (that is, advising or confirming bank) and states the length of time that must run before actual payment is made.

With acceptance of the exporter's draft by the bank, payment by that bank at a later date is assured. The accepted time draft is returned to the exporter and the letter of credit continues to be a binding obligation of the bank, with a maturity fixed on a specified future date.

Discounting

If the beneficiary wishes to receive payment prior to the future date specified in the letter of credit and stated in the draft or in the acceptancs, it may request the bank to discount the draft. Since an accepted draft represents the bank's own obligation, it will normally discount it, with the interest cost of discounting borne by the exporter. Under certain conditions the bank can rediscount its time drafts originating from import/export transactions with the Federal Reserve Bank, if it is a member. Such drafts can be easily discounted since they represent an unconditional banking commitment for future payment. Such drafts should state that the transaction creating this instrument is the consequence of an importation of goods. Thus, the time letter of credit implies an extension of credit by the issuing bank beyond the date when documents are supposed to be presented. In effect, there is an extension of credit on a trust receipt during this time period.

Since a sight letter of credit is payable upon presentation of the sight draft, no credit transaction is involved between the beneficiary of the letter of credit and the bank.

A letter of credit represents the bank's commitment to honor a demand for payment by a named beneficiary upon compliance with the terms and conditions stipulated in the letter of credit. An important feature is that it conveys no commitment or obligation to persons other than the beneficiary. The documents called for under the letter of credit must be presented to the bank that is committed to honor the draft and supporting documents submitted by the beneficiary. No legal obligation arises on the part of the bank to honor the letter of credit if someone else negotiates the documents or if the documents are presented to another bank for negotiation.

If the fact of establishment of the credit is conveyed to the beneficiary by an intermediary bank, rather than directly by the issuing bank, it is called a *letter of credit specially advised.*

The letter of credit may be readily adapted to provide financial support for a great variety of transactions. For example, the letter of credit may be used to procure financing for the production of goods. With the letter of credit promising payment, an exporter requiring funds to manufacture or assemble export goods can seek financing from the bank, especially if the exporter is a manufacturer in good standing. Upon shipment of the goods, proceeds of the transaction, secured by the letter of credit, will be applied to the loan.

Skeleton Letters of Credit

When the goods to be delivered under the documentary letter of credit have not been specified in the terms of the credit, the term *skeleton letter of credit* may be used. The seller is authorized to deliver any kind of goods listed (such as, wearing apparel) in the letter of credit up to the limit of the amount of the credit.

Red-Line Clause

In connection with the shipment and export of commodities, the bank is often required to include a red-line clause in the letter of credit, so-called from the common law business practice of printing the clause in red ink. Such provisions permit advance partial payments of the credit in order to facilitate performance by the beneficiary. For example, an exporter may purchase goods from various sources, including minor manufacturers who assemble the shipment. If payment for these goods is due when the goods to be shipped are purchased, the exporter may not have funds available for this purpose; he or she is, of course, prevented from drawing from the letter of credit to alleviate the situation until shipping documents are presented.

To overcome this problem, if the importer has faith in the exporter, he or she will permit the bank to make an advance partial payment to the exporter against presentation of draft and/or other papers, and pending the presentation of the final documents. Thus, the red-line clause permits the exporter to assemble the goods to be shipped from various sources and make payments on the spot before shipping documents can be presented. Use of such a clause entails the risk that the seller of bad faith may draw the advance without ever shipping the goods to the buyer and so disadvantages the buyer and the buyer's bank. Therefore, a letter of credit containing a red-line clause will be issued only when the bank is assured it will receive reimbursement from the buyer.

Green Clause

A variety of the red clause offering more protection to the buyer is the green clause letter of credit. Its terms require the merchandise to be stored under the bank's control until shipment is made. This practice, used in countries such as Australia, reduces the buyer's risk of no-delivery.

Assignable/Transferable Credits

Sometimes there is an intermediary between the buyer and the seller of goods. For example, the broker might decide to purchase goods from several producers or manufacturers for export to the buyer. The suppliers might in turn require a domestic letter of credit from the broker to secure payment. With a letter of credit from the foreign buyer, the broker can instruct his or her bankers to split up the letter of credit in favor of various suppliers. The banker is permitted to do so, however, only if the letter of credit stipulates that the credit is indeed assignable and divisible. If the letter of credit does not so specify, then the bank would not be allowed to divide or assign the letter of credit. Therefore, if there are several intermediaries the letter of credit should be made *assignable* and *reassignable*.

An important distinction is made between an assignment of the right to payment under the letter of credit and transfer of the credit itself. Both the Uniform Commercial Code and the Uniform Customs and Practices recognize the right of the letter of credit beneficiary to dispose of the proceeds to which he or she has become entitled under the letter of credit. The basic principle behind an assignment is the alienation of the right to receive monies due or to become due under the letter of credit contract. However, regardless of the manner in which the assignment of the proceeds is accomplished, no independent contract rights in favor of the assignee are established against the issuer. This applies to a situation where the assignee is designated as payee or endorsee of the beneficiary's draft as well as where a separate agreement of assignment is entered into. Therefore, the asisgnee acquires the right to the proceeds, but not the right to perform or enforce payment under the credit. This means that the assignment is of value *only* if the beneficiary actually presents documents in compliance with all of the stipulated terms and conditions of the letter of credit. If the beneficiary does not draw a draft under the letter of credit, the bank need not honor the assignment of the proceeds.

An assignment of the right to receive payment is not a transfer of the letter of credit and thus is not prohibited by a designation that the credit is not transferable. A transferable letter of credit is a distinct variety. It entails a substitution of the parties and includes the transfer by the beneficiary of both the right to perform and receive payment under the terms of the letter of credit to a third party. The beneficiary's right to substitute a third party in his or her place is limited in several respects. First, the ability to transfer the credit is limited by its actual terms and conditions. The letter of credit must expressly state that it is transferable. Second, a transferable credit may be transferred only once unless otherwise specified. That is, the party to whom the beneficiary transfers the letter of credit cannot transfer it again. Fractions of the original letter of credit, up to an amount not exceeding the total amount of the credit may be transferred separately, however. The sum of the fractions transferred constitutes one transfer. Third, the beneficiary of the credit is also limited by the fact that any transfer of the credit might require the consent of the issuing bank. Such consent is not required for an assignment of the right to proceeds, which was already discussed. However, once consent has been obtained from the issuing bank the new beneficiary will be able to present documents and drafts under the terms of the transferred credit. With the exception of the ability to reduce the amount of the credit, the stated price per unit and the period of validity or period of shipment, the original terms and conditions of the credit apply in the transferred credit.

Transferable credits are often used by an agent for the buyer, who transfers the credit to the actual seller or supplier. This allows the agent to avoid calling on the bank for credit to open a second credit in favor of the seller. Payment of the original credit is obtained on the strength of documents presented under the transferred credit. Therefore, if the first beneficiary fails to substitute his or her own invoices within a reasonable time, the bank usually reserves the right to apply the invoices received under the transferred credit against the original credit.

A potential problem of interpretation may arise when the word "assignable" is used in a letter of credit. Under the Uniform Commercial Code, Section 5–116(1), the words "transferable" and "assignable" are interchangeable in designating a credit of either type. However, the Uniform Customs and Practice permits the use of only the word "transferable" to designate a transferable credit. Although the text of the Uniform Customs and Practice is incorporated by reference into the letter of credit agreement, one should be aware of the potential for misinterpretation, which could lead to loss. The parties involved in a letter of credit transaction must carefully choose the terms included therein.

Negotiation Credit

If the letter of credit contains an extension of the issuer's obligation to third parties who purchase the beneficiary's draft or other demand, it is called a *negotiation credit*. Language to this effect must be included in the terms of the letter of credit if so desired; without the engagement of the bank to endorsers and bona fide holders of a draft drawn according to the terms of the letter of credit, it will be assumed that the credit is not a negotiation credit. Therefore, if the party opening the letter of credit wishes to provide the endorsers and bona fide holders of drafts drawn with the same rights as the named beneficiary of the credit, a negotiation credit should be opened.

Another feature of negotiation credits is that they provide for negotiation of the beneficiary's drafts and documents at banks other than the confirming bank. The bank that purchases drafts drawn under a negotiation credit is called the *negotiating bank*. The negotiating bank will have recourse to prior endorsers and to the drawer (beneficiary) to the same extent as any other purchaser of negotiable instrument. This refers to the draft drawn under the letter of credit only. As mentioned earlier, the letter of credit itself is not a negotiable instrument.

Revolving Letter of Credit

It may arise that the shipment of goods is to be made over a period of time or for an amount larger than any bank or buyer desires to have outstanding. To solve the problem, the buyer may open a *revolving letter of credit*. When opened, the revolving credit covers merely a portion of the entire quantity of goods; however, the bank undertakes an irrevocable obligation to restore the amounts drawn once a portion of the delivery is made and paid for up to a fixed maximum. The advantage of using a credit that may be reinstated up to a specified amount is that only a single letter of credit is used instead of issuing a new letter of credit for every shipment. The bank notifies the beneficiary that the letter of credit is reinstated with a revised date of expiration if all of the conditions stipulated are met.

Back-to-Back Credits

A second credit opened on the strength of a nontransferable (or transferable) credit is called a *back-to-back credit*. It can be arranged only by agreement between the applicant for the second credit and his or her bank. Such credits might provide the beneficiary of the subsidiary credit with a better assurance of payment than an assignment of proceeds. The back-to-back credit consists of two letters of credit that have similar documentary requirements. Different prices to be shown in the invoice and draft, as well as a possibly curtailed expiration date, would be provided for. If an agent whose own credit is weak is acting between buyer and seller, the first credit opened by the buyer in favor of the agent will be deposited with the bank to facilitate issuance of a credit in favor of the ultimate seller. In this way, the credit issued in favor of the first beneficiary (the agent) serves as cover for the one issued in favor of the actual supplier. To protect the parties involved in a back-to-back credit transaction, certain safeguards should be considered.

For example, Section 5–116 of the Uniform Commercial Code, Official Comment 1, discusses the issuing bank's potential for loss when establishing a back-to-back letter of credit. Specifically, it risks nonpayment if an effective advance assignment for the exporter of his or her rights under the initial credit issued on behalf of his foreign buyer was not obtained. To guard against such a possibility, Section 5–116 of the Uniform Commercial Code provides that the assignability of proceeds cannot be prohibited in advance of performance. Note, however, that this safeguard has significant limitations. Namely, the assignment of the right to proceeds under a letter of credit is only as good as the rights of the party assigning his rights to payment under the letter of credit.

A recent case that illustrates the limitations of back-to-back credit transactions is the one involving Creditanstalt Bankverein in Vienna, Austria's largest bank, and a British banking consortium headed by Singer and Friedlander. A beneficiary assigned to the consortium its right to proceeds under nontransferable letters of credit opened with Creditanstalt. When the alleged fraud by the beneficiary was discovered, an injunction against payment was obtained. Therefore, no right to payment was held by the party who took that assignment. Because the fraud vitiated the obligation of the bank under the letter of credit, the injunction was held effective not only against the beneficiary, but also against any party, in this case, the consortium, whose right to receive proceeds was dependent on the right of the original assignor. The court stressed that, although a claim for payment under even a nontransferable documentary letter of credit may be assigned, a beneficiary may not transfer his right to present the documents upon which payment must be made unless express permission is given in the credit. Thus, an assignee of rights to payment bears a risk that the presentation of the documents that creates a right to payment may be stalled indefinitely.

An additional problem may arise in a back-to-back credit transaction whereby one bank may receive documents that appear to be in order but that, when presented to the other bank, may be rejected. Since payment depends upon presentation of conforming documents, rejection of documents leads to delay and, most likely, suit for payment. For these reasons, it is said that banks often prefer to avoid issuing a back-to-back credit.

Stand-By Letter of Credit

When a party to a transaction wishes to have assurance that a contract for goods or services or other "performance-type" obligations will be satisfactorily completed, it may require the establishment of a *stand-by letter of credit* by the performing party with itself as beneficiary. Also known as "guaranty" or "performance" letters of credit, these instruments generally have a fixed expiration date. They are generally payable upon presentation of a draft accompanied by a simple written statement from the beneficiary stating that the applicant for the credit has not performed the contract or obligation and is in default.

This form of credit is used by United States and Japanese banks, which are not authorized by law to issue ordinary guarantees or suretyships. Since the demand for payment usually consists of presentation of a draft and a written statement of default, rather than third-party paper such as shipping documents, insurance policies, certificates of origin, or certificates of inspection of quality, the beneficiary's business reputation becomes even more important. The bank undertakes the obligation to honor a properly drawn draft and statement of default upon presentation without any investigation of the nonperformance of the underlying contract or obligation. Therefore, the beneficiary has the assurance that he or she may draw on the stand-by letter of credit in the event of nonperformance.

There is a risk that a beneficiary will fraudulently notify the issuing bank of default. Although certain remedies may exist in such a situation, they entail considerable delay and expenses for the client who opened the stand-by letter of credit. In addition, since the bank also faces the danger of nonpayment from its customer, United States regulatory agencies require all stand-by letters of credit to be counted with other direct lending to any borrower when the legal lending limit is being calculated.

Since banks in the United States are not authorized to enter into guarantee or suretyships agreements as a general rule, if the stand-by letter of credit is characterized as an unenforceable guarantee, the bank's obligation to pay under it becomes void due to the fact it is *ultra vires.* As a result, banks seeking to avoid stand-by letter of credit commitments raise this *no-guaranty defense.* Consequently, when the issue is raised, a court must determine whether the instrument is an unenforceable guaranty or a valid stand-by letter of credit. Without entering into a detailed comparison of guarantees and stand-by letters of credit, it is important to note that their distinction lies in the documentary nature of the letter of credit. The bank, unlike a surety who issues a guaranty, must pay the beneficiary when it receives proper documents notifying it of default, rather than when the fact of default is actually established. Furthermore, the form of the document itself presented for payment is important since inclusion of the words "letter of credit" normally establishes that the instrument is indeed a letter of credit.

In lieu of raising the no-guaranty defense, it has been suggested that banks should issue stand-by letters of credit only upon satisfaction by the customer of the same conditions necessary for the granting of a loan. For example, the bank may require the customer to deposit a segregated fund to cover the amount of the credit. At a minimum, each party should take steps to protect its interests. The bank should obtain sufficient collateral or assurance of reimbursement for payment, while the beneficiary must be certain that a proper documentary form is used to make the stand-by letter of credit enforceable.

Foreign Currency Letters of Credit

Banks in the United States issue a substantial number of letters of credit that are expressed in the national currency of the country of the seller or of a third country. Although the basic documentary characteristics of a letter of credit apply to those expressed in a foreign currency, certain procedural differences are entailed. The additional risk of foreign exchange fluctuation is normally borne by the buyer or importer of the goods.

However, in addition to a letter of credit expressed in United States dollars, a credit may be expressed in Swiss francs, German marks, Japanese yen, or any other readily negotiable currencies agreed upon. If located in the United States, the exporter will probably want to receive final payment in dollars regardless of the currency of the letter of credit. Therefore, at the time of negotiation of the documents under a foreign currency letter of credit, he or she most likely will instruct the confirming or conveying bank to convert the foreign currencies into United States dollars, and make those dollars available to him. The conversion takes place at the rate of exchange of the day when the documents are negotiated. Of course, the exporter has assumed an exchange risk if he does not cover himself with a *forward contract* in due time when the letter of credit is not expressed in his home currency. A forward contract insures delivery at a future date of a specified amount of one currency against payment of another, thus fixing the exchange rate for purposes of payment at the time the contract is made by the exporter.

An example of a foreign currency credit is a letter of credit expressed in Swiss francs under which the drafts are drawn on the Swiss correspondent bank of the American bank that issues the credit. The issuing bank has to follow a different procedure as well as face a foreign exchange situation not present in a U.S. dollar credit. For example, drafts expressed in a foreign currency are drawn on a bank in the country of that currency. The issuing bank may have an account and a correspondent relationship with the foreign bank, thus allowing payment to be made by means of accounting entries. However, it is also possible for a reimbursement credit to be used. In this situation, the paying bank will be authorized to draw on another bank to reimburse itself for payments made under the letter of credit. Thus, a credit relationship is established between the paying and issuing banks.

In order to cover the drafts drawn, the customer is expected to purchase the necessary foreign exchange. Usually the American bank buys and sells foreign exchange for spot or future delivery while trying to maintain a balance between purchases and sales. The bank often sells the customer the required amount of foreign exchange by charging a fee, which is used to cover the purchase of the foreign exchange. Banks often earn an exchange profit on such transactions. Note that, since the conversion of a sight draft occurs at the time of presentation to the foreign bank, the settlement of foreign exchange transactions is postponed until maturity of the letter of credit. The customer may fix the price of foreign exchange in terms of dollars by entering into a futures or forward contract to cover the amount of foreign exchange owed.

Several other types of letters of credit are occasionally encountered. These include:

1. the authority to pay,
2. the authority to purchase,
3. the letter of credit with previous notice, and
4. the nonoperative letter of credit.

The *authority to pay* actually signifies an advice with regard to the proper place for payment of the letter of credit, rather than a bank's obligation to make such payment. It may be revoked any time before the presentation of documents. Furthermore, a draft paid under an authority to pay is extinguished by payment whether or not it is drawn on the party authorized to pay.

The *authority to purchase* is encountered principally in the Far East. Although similar to a letter of credit, the draft is drawn on a foreign buyer. Unlike the authority to pay, it can be either revocable or irrevocable.

The buyer often desires to be reassured that the seller actually intends to enter into a sales contract before tying up its assets in a letter of credit that may never be used. Therefore, it may cause an issuing bank to inform the seller than an irrevocable letter of credit will be issued in his favor, at a future date, provided that the seller/beneficiary delivers or presents specified documents to the designated bank within a definite time. A penalty for nonuse of the credit by the beneficiary will often be provided for. This letter of credit *with previous notice* may include additional conditions, such as requiring the necessary export license to be presented with other documents. Failure to present the necessary documents within the time specified results in a lapse of the bank's or buyer's obligation to issue the letter of credit.

A similar release from payment obligation is provided by the so-called *nonoperative letter of credit.* The irrevocability of the payment obligation is dependent upon presentation of specified documents within a short time period.

Advised/Confirmed Credits

The use of advising and confirming banks greatly facilitates letter of credit transactions, particularly in the international export-import field, where they are almost exclusively used. Aside from their role as informants, these intermediaries may provide additional credit assurance between parties unfamiliar with each other or with one another's legal system and financial customs.

An *advising bank,* as the name implies, notifies a beneficiary of the opening of a letter of credit in the beneficiary's favor at another bank. The issuing bank is often in another jurisdiction and frequently has a correspondent relationship with the advising bank. Under very limited circumstances does the advising bank incur liability for its activities (such as through error in the making of its advisement), and in no event does liability for payment on the letter of credit shift from the issuer.

On the other hand, in addition to providing notification to the beneficiary, a *confirming bank* assumes both the obligations and rights of the issuer of the letter of credit, including the obligation to make payment according to the terms of the letter of credit. These obligations and rights are assumed as if the confirming bank were the original issuer; however, the actual issuing bank's obligations and rights do not lapse by virtue of the confirmation.

In many instances a bank's confirmation of a letter of credit will be useful to the parties. For example, letters of credit issued by foreign banks are often unacceptable to a seller located in the United States because of the risks of nonpayment. Numerous factors indicate the need to obtain a confirmed letter of credit such as foreign exchange restrictions existing in the importer's country, political and/or economic uncertainties, or the possibility of war. Typically, the importer is located in a remote or unstable country or is unknown to the exporter. The exporter requests an additional assurance that payment will be made against presentation of the documents giving title to the merchandise. Therefore, at the importer's request, the payment obligation will be assumed by the correspondent of the importer's bank located in the exporter's country in the form of a confirmation. The correspondent bank located in the exporter's country assumes a separate obligation to make payment under the terms of the letter of credit established by the foreign issuing bank. In that way, the exporter has the independent promise of both banks to make payment upon presentation of the documents. The obligation of the confirming bank is added to that of the issuer and relieves the exporter of the risk of nonpayment due to circumstances existing in the foreign country.

A further example will best illustrate the mechanics of an advised and confirmed letter of credit. First assume that a letter of credit is opened by the importer's bank in his own country. The bank will ask one of its correspondent banks in the foreign country from which shipment is to be made, to transmit the letter of credit in favor of the exporter. The correspondent bank will convey the letter of credit commitment of the importer's bank to the exporter. Since the exporter might not know the standing of the foreign bank, he might feel more comfortable if the letter of credit conveyed to him by the bank in his country is confirmed by a local bank. If the bank of the country of the exporter adds its own commitment to the conveyance, it is then a *confirmed letter of credit.*

FIGURE 3–1

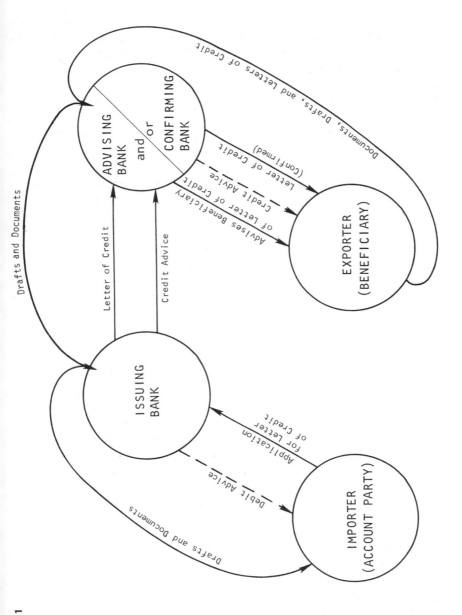

Commonly, the foreign bank issues a letter of credit and conveys it to the beneficiary through its banking correspondent in a major city located in the country of the beneficiary (or exporter). If the beneficiary does not live in the city in which the bank is located, he may wish to have a letter of credit "issued" by his local bank. This may be accomplished by a request that the letter of credit be confirmed not only by the correspondent bank of the originating bank, but also by a local bank in his city. In this case, the letter of credit is issued and conveyed to the correspondent bank, which confirms the letter of credit and instructs the local bank in the city where the exporter is located to reconfirm it to the exporter. Hence, the beneficiary has a *confirmed and reconfirmed letter of credit.* The exporter now has the legal commitment of his local banker who is covered by a commitment from the correspondent bank which, in turn, is covered by the commitment of its foreign correspondent bank. This is because a bank that confirms a letter of credit in favor of a beneficiary upon request of its correspondent foreign bank adds its own commitment to that of the issuing bank. Furthermore, it undertakes the obligation to honor drafts and is thus directly obligated as though it were the issuer of the letter of credit to the extent of its confirmation. The confirming bank therefore acquires the rights of the issuer when it undertakes its obligation.

If the exporter is satisfied with the standing of the bank in the foreign country, the confirmation of his local bankers might not be sought. For example, the local bank may be asked merely to "advise" it. In this situation the local bank merely advises the beneficiary of the fact that the credit has been opened in his favor by the foreign bank. When the local bank advises a beneficiary of the letter of credit, it merely conveys the commitment of its foreign correspondent bank and assumes no obligation to make payments to the beneficiary under the credit. Therefore, unlike a confirming bank, the advising bank is under no obligation to accept drafts and negotiable documents. It may elect to do so nevertheless. Since the advising bank assumes no obligation under the letter of credit, any incorrect statement of terms it may make does not change the obligation undertaken by the issuer. Finally, banks often disclaim liability for the acts of correspondent banks to which a letter of credit transaction has been entrusted. Therefore, the parties to a letter of credit transaction should verify the standing of all banks that assume the payment obligation.

Terms and Conditions

The bank customer opening a letter of credit seeks to cover his risk of loss arising from nonperformance of the underlying contract. It is of the utmost importance to precisely spell out the terms and conditions of the letter of credit when it is being established. The utmost care should be employed in examining the terms chosen, taking care to make them simple and clear. Since the credit is independent of the underlying contract between the buyer and the seller, it is useful to include reasonably detailed terms that parallel those of the contract. For example, a listing of documents proving that the seller has complied with the agreements should be included, instead of mere reference to clauses in the outside contract. By listing the documents that the bank is to receive in exchange for the payment, the parties have a means independent of the underlying contract for measuring compliance. Additionally, the application signed by the originating bank's customer will incorporate an agreement describing the rights of the issuing bank and the obligations of the customer on whose behalf the credit is issued. Finally, a deadline should be included for the establishment of the required type of letter of credit, with a provision that the underlying contract automatically terminates if the letter of credit is not established by that date. In this way, the buyer is less likely to postpone issuance of the desired credit. This is especially useful when it is possible that foreign exchange restrictions or other regulations may delay the issuance of a letter of credit.

Regardless of the type of letter of credit, certain terms must be included. For example, the amount of the credit, the expiration date for presentation of drafts and documents and the names and addresses of the parties thereto must be stated. All credits must stipulate an expiry date for presentation of documents for payment, acceptance, or negotiation, notwithstanding the stipulation of a latest date for shipment. If the applicant lacks sufficient financial rating to obtain a credit, it is possible to add another party's name either as a guarantor or as someone jointly liable. Since a guarantor is not normally involved in the underlying contract, the letter of credit will not refer to him. Instead, the credit will state that it is issued *for account* or *by order* of the originating party.

In addition, the documents to be presented under the credit should be specified. Payment is made only if the seller submits the required documents on time. Usually these documents indicate that goods have been delivered in accordance with the terms and time limits agreed upon.

Bills of Lading

In the import/export trade a bill of lading is usually required. Several copies are often required to assure an alternate in case of loss. The bill of lading represents title to the goods. It is a contract between the exporter and the shipper that requires the delivery of goods from port of shipment to port of destination. In addition, it specifies who is entitled to possession of the merchandise upon arrival and serves as the shipper's receipt for the goods.

Bills of lading may be issued in various forms to cover diverse modes of transportation. For example, an ocean bill of lading may be issued in straight (non-negotiable) form, that is to say, consigned directly to the consignee, or to order (negotiable) form. (The straight form is infrequently used in connection with a commercial letter of credit.) A bill of lading can be a simple bill of lading or an on-board bill of lading. The latter means that the bill of lading is issued by the shipping company and signed by the captain of the ship to confirm that the merchandise has actually been loaded onto the ship. This might be of significance because several problems could occur if the merchandise is delivered to the pier but left alongside the ship. For example, a strike may occur before the goods are loaded, or the ship may develop problems or burn. In these situations the simple bill of lading does not give complete protection to the importer. Therefore, it is usually specifically requested that an on-board bill of lading be presented. If a received-for-shipment bill of lading is converted into an on-board bill of lading, the on-board notation must be dated and signed or initialed by the carrier or his agent to qualify.

Certain bills of lading may be required under a documentary letter of credit. For example, banks usually require the clean bill of lading, meaning that the shipper received the goods in apparent good order. When speaking of letters of credit, the expression full set on-board bills of lading is frequently used. Steamship companies usually issue these bills of lading in one to six originals, any one of which can be used for the purpose of collecting under the credit. Once collection is made, all the other copies become void. The letter of credit usually states how many copies were issued, and that any of them is suitable for collection. This policy gives protection to the paying bank or to the exporter in case some of the copies are lost. In general, a letter of credit should state that the bill of lading may be issued by the forwarding agent, by the shipping company, or by other parties. In addition, it should also state whether the bill of lading is a through bill of lading or a bill of lading that permits trans-shipments.

Under a documentary commercial letter of credit, the required bills of lading usually mention the category of merchandise, the port of shipment, the name of the consignee, and the name of the party to be notified. These details must correspond to the requirements expressed in the application for a letter of credit. The bill of lading should show that the goods are loaded on board the ship unless the letter of credit specifies otherwise. It must also show whether the freight has been prepaid or is collectible at the destination. It is important that the bill of lading not show any defective condition of the packaging or of the goods loaded. If the letter of credit calls for clean shipping documents, any documents showing defective packing cannot be accepted. Furthermore, the bills of lading can also state that the merchandise has been loaded *on deck* (as opposed to being loaded in the hold of the ship). This is permissible only if the letter of credit provides for it. Furthermore, the credit must state the time after the date of issuance of the bill of lading during which the documents must be negotiated with the bank. If no time is stipulated, banks will require documents to be presented not later than 21 days after the date of issuance of the bill of lading or other shipping document because they would be considered *stale*.

Invoices

In addition to the bill of lading, invoices are documents usually required to be presented for payment under a letter of credit. The invoice is a statement of the seller to a buyer describing what has been sold, with price and details included. It is a non-negotiable document that does not convey title to the holder. Customs authorities and intermediary banks process the data found on such an invoice. Unless otherwise specified, banks may refuse invoices issued for amounts in excess of the amount provided for the credit, even though no payment in excess of the amount specified in the letter of credit is requested.

In addition, a letter of credit can call for presentation of consular invoices with the bill of lading. A consular invoice is presented to the nearest foreign consular official for examination where it is stamped and signed, or *consularized*. In some countries, customs practices may require such an invoice (also called a *customs invoice*) for price or exchange control and statistical purposes. When required, the customs invoice is a document that is vital for customs clearance of the goods. Although it does not convey title and is non-negotiable, even trivial discrepancies between the consular invoice and the commercial invoice, bills of lading, and any insurance certificate might delay customs entry and subject the importer to fines.

Insurance

Frequently, a letter of credit calls for a document showing that insurance has been obtained in accordance with the stipulation contained in the letter of credit. Of course, in most transactions involving a shipment of merchandise, it is certain that an insurance policy covering the risks of transit will be procured by one of the parties. Insurance is necessary not only for the purpose of covering the exposure of the parties during shipment; it may also be a condition of bank financing for either the buyer or the seller. Policies issued on goods in transit are viewed by lenders in the same light that a bank granting a mortgage on a house requires the property to be covered by proper fire insurance, designating the mortgagee-bank as beneficiary.

Because letter of credit transactions will often place an issuing bank in the position of extending credit to the parties, the bank must be satisfied that insurance protection is available. Unless otherwise specified, insurance documents covering goods must be expressed in the same currency as the credit. The documents must also bear a date prior to the shipping document date, unless expressly confirmed that the goods are covered no later than the date of shipment.

Insurance covering shipments of merchandise between a port of embarkation and a port of destination is called *marine insurance.* Specialized insurance firms handle these policies.

When insurance documents are required, the document must be issued by an insurance company and not by a broker, unless specifically permitted. Finally, the letter of credit must expressly state the type of insurance required. Expressions like "usual risk" or "customary risk" should not be used because they are subject to numerous interpretations.

Certificate of Origin

In order to benefit from possibly lower custom duties and also for statistical and political purposes, the *certificate of origin* is a useful addition to the list of required documents. Its main purpose is to certify the country where goods were produced. It can be issued by a local Chamber of Commerce showing that the goods are indeed of origin of the exporting country and not in transit from a third country.

Other documents useful in verifying the character of shipments include a *weight list,* indicating the weight of the shipment, and a *packing list,* showing the contents of individual packages. If the importer is concerned with receiving goods of a certain quality, it is best to require presentation of an *inspection certificate,* issued by an independent third party; this will insure, additionally, that the packing is exactly in accordance with the type and quality stipulated. Since the banks are governed only by the documents required by a letter of credit and are not concerned (indeed, they cannot be concerned) with the quality of examination of the merchandise, the importer frequently requests a so-called *inspection firm* to inspect the goods before they are shipped, and to confirm that they are in accordance with the requirements of the importer. In such cases, the importer will specify in the letter of credit that an inspection certificate of a certain firm is required as part of the documents presented under the letter of credit before payment will be made. Once the inspection firm issues the inspection certificate, it is responsible for the findings conveyed therein. As a result, inspection firms are usually of international reputation.

Finally, to avoid delays in the shipment of goods from some of the exporting countries that have exchange or export/import control, it should be stipulated in both the letter of credit and in the underlying contracts that, if an export license is required, it must be obtained and presented as a document required for payment under the credit.

When requesting the issuance of a letter of credit, the customers of the bank agree that the bank cannot be held responsible for the genuineness of the documents required. The bank is not responsible for the actions of the parties involved, for the quality of the goods, or for the representations made in the documents so long as they comply with the requirements of the letter of credit. Although certain less vital documents, such as a certificate of origin or warehouse receipt, are generally accepted in whatever form tendered, other documents such as the bill of lading must be what they purport to be. That is, the issuer is entitled to reimbursement from the beneficiary for payments it makes under a letter of credit only if payment was made against documents conforming to specified terms. Therefore, payment will be made by the issuer after careful examination of the documents in accordance with the requirements under the letter of credit.

The terms of the credit will further stipulate the currency of payment and the manner in which drafts are to be drawn under the credit. In addition, the banks on which the beneficiary is allowed to draw drafts will be indicated. A brief description of the merchandise to be shipped is normally contained in the letter of credit. This description must match that found in the documents later presented for payment, as we will examine further.

Shipment terms must be clearly specified to anticipate situations that may arise in the transit of goods. For example, full or partial shipment of merchandise may be desired depending upon the necessity of having the entire order arrive at one time. Machinery without a vital part, for example, would be of little use until the entire machine arrived. Generally, partial shipments are allowed unless the credit specifies clearly that partial shipments are not permitted; payment, however, will only be made when delivery of the goods is completed. Partial shipments made in such a way that the shipments are loaded on the same ship are not regarded as partial shipments. If the intention of the buyer is to permit partial shipments, then he may specify "partial shipment permitted," which will make the letter of credit divisible, that is, payable in installments as partial delivery is made.

A letter of credit can also specify that the shipments have to be made without trans-shipment, which means that the shipment must be placed on a ship that goes directly to the destination without transferring the merchandise to another ship. Trans-shipment would mean that the merchandise is unloaded at an intermediate port and reloaded onto a new ship headed toward the final destination. The bill of lading prohibiting transshipment is called a *through bill of lading*. Since this often has significance, it is something of which the exporter should be aware. For example, if the letter of credit calls for direct shipment and the shipping schedules offer only trans-shipment, the exporter would not be entitled to payment unless the documents presented showed that a direct shipment had been made. That is to say, if the documents presented do not show direct shipment when the credit specifies a bill of lading indicating direct shipment, then the documents might not be in compliance with the requirements of the letter of credit. As a result, no payment could be obtained by the exporter. It is therefore desirable that the exporter examine the shipping situation carefully before accepting the terms of the letter of credit.

It should be emphasized again that banks do not assume responsibility for the genuineness of documents, nor do they assume any liability for the description, quantity, weight, quality, conditions, or even existence of the goods represented in the documents.

Use of Trade Terms

When preparing the terms of a letter of credit, certain terms and abbreviations should be avoided. One should avoid the use of abbreviations as much as possible. Conditions should be spelled out whenever possible, even though certain abbreviations are generally accepted in the trade.

If the terms of the letter of credit specify FOB (Free on Board), then the seller must deliver the goods free of charge on board the carrier. When FOB terms are used, this can be specified FOB and the name of the vessel, or FOB and the name or type of the carrier. Of course, it should be specified whether the transportation should be by truck, railroad, ship, barge, aircraft, or the like. Also, any possible transfer from one type of carrier to another should be stated, if possible.

Frequently, the expression FAS (free alongside or free alongside ship) is used. Usually, the name of the vessel is also mentioned. In this case, the exporter or the shipper is not responsible for loading the goods onto a ship, but only for delivery alongside the ship, in which case a clean dock or ship receipt will be provided. The exporter is not responsible for the loading onto the carrier. Other terms commonly used indicate which costs are included in the price and responsibilities of the seller. For example, CIF (cost insurance freight), CIFC (cost insurance freight and commission), CIFCI (cost insurance freight commission and interest), and so on.

The expressions "ton" or "hundredweight" should also be avoided. This is because a ton can be a long ton of 2,240 pounds, a metric ton of 2,204.6 pounds, or a short ton of 2,000 pounds. A hundredweight can be either 100 or 112 pounds. All types of measurement should be defined clearly. If an inspection certificate is required under the terms of the letter of credit, it should state whether the cost of same should be to the account or for the account of the buyer or the seller.

Prices can be quoted ex-factory, ex-plantation, ex-warehouse, ex-mine, or ex-any other place (ex meaning "out of" or at point of origin). The seller will have to carry all the risks up to the point of delivery or cost. Thereafter, the buyer must take delivery of the goods as soon as they have been placed at his disposal at the agreed place on the agreed date.

The buyers and sellers must agree on who will pay export taxes, if any, or other taxes and fees applicable to export shipments. They must also agree on who will pay for any costs incurred in the procurement of documents required under the letter of credit, and whether the freight charges are prepaid or to be collected at destination.

Terms that are open to dispute should not be used. For example, the use of ambiguous terms such as "first class" and "qualified" should be avoided.

If expressions are used concerning the quantity of goods or amount such as "about," "circa," or similar expressions, then it is assumed that differences of plus or minus 10% are allowed.

If expressions are used such as "immediately," "as soon as possible," or "prompt," the bank will assume that performance should be made within 30 days.

The term "first half of the month" means from the first to the fifteenth of the month, inclusive. The term "second half of the month" means from the sixteenth to the end of the month. If the letter of credit mentions "beginning," "middle," or "end" of the month, then the interpretation is from the first to the tenth, the eleventh to the twentieth, and twenty-first to the end of the month, respectively.

When an issuing bank's cable or telex states that a mail confirmation will make the message operative, the receiving bank can so advise the beneficiary and make the credit effective only subject to receipt of the mail confirmation.

Banks utilizing the service of another bank for the purpose of giving effect to the instructions of the applicant for the issuance of a letter of credit do so for the account and at the risk of the applicant. This applies even in cases where the bank itself has chosen the other bank.

Since the chosen terms of the letter of credit become binding once the application for its establishment is approved and transmitted, proper instructions will avoid subsequent difficulties. Furthermore, subsequent modifications and amendments to the letter of credit that entail additional delay, expense, and inconvenience may be avoided.

The letter of credit is established when the beneficiary receives either the credit itself or an *authorized* advice that the credit has been issued. Without receipt thereof by the beneficiary, the issuer's liability to the beneficiary is not established. No acceptance of its terms by the beneficiary is necessary for a binding obligation to be formed. A contract is thus formed by establishing a letter of credit.

Under an irrevocable letter of credit, the issuer may not terminate or modify its obligation without the agreement of all the parties involved in the credit transaction. For example, the customer originating the letter of credit may not cancel or change an irrevocable credit without the consent of the beneficiary and all other parties involved. Once the express written agreement of all the parties involved in the credit transaction is obtained, any or all of its terms may be changed, thus altering the rights and obligations of the parties thereto.

An issuer of an irrevocable letter of credit will not consent to any modification or amendment without the written agreement of all the parties involved. This includes the consent of confirming banks as well. This is because the issuing bank's right to reimbursement under the credit would be jeopardized if an unauthorized change were to be made. This procedure is in contrast to termination or modification of a revocable credit, which may be cancelled or amended as long as the issuing or correspondent bank has not negotiated, accepted, or paid under the credit.

There is one exception to the general rule requiring the consent of all parties involved in the letter of credit transaction prior to its modification. Modification by the courts may be sought by a party to the letter of credit transaction when evidence of intentional fraud is present. The additional terms may, in some cases, effectively suspend a bank's obligation to pay under the letter of credit for an indefinite period. Consequently, this remedy is regarded as a highly unusual step, to be taken only under the most unusual circumstances.

The Role of the Bank

Issuance of the letter of credit establishes the issuing bank as a key intermediary in the payment transaction. Its activities are limited, however, to the extent necessary to assure conformity of the documents presented with the requirements of the letter of credit. Nevertheless, the issuing bank exerts an important influence on the underlying transaction. This influence reflects the fact that the bank normally makes no outlay of funds until presentation of a draft together with the required documents; consequently, from the time the letter of credit is issued until the draft and documents are presented to it for payment, the bank is extending its own credit commitment to the buyer.

Payment is made only if the seller submits the stipulated documents to it on time. In general, documents must be presented to the negotiating bank within a reasonable time after issuance of the documents. Banks may refuse documents that in their judgment are presented with undue or unreasonable delay. These documents are called *stale documents*, and it will be necessary to ask for permission from the originator of the credit to accept stale documents. Furthermore, banks are not obliged to accept presentation of documents outside banking hours; if on the day the credit expires the documents are presented after bank hours (usually after 3:00 P.M. in the U.S.A.), the bank has the right to refuse them. The expiration date expressed in the letter of credit is the final date on which drafts may be presented for negotiation.

No deviation from the terms and conditions of the letter of credit, such as the time or place allowed for negotiation or presentment, is allowed. When the expiration date stipulated in the credit falls on a Sunday or public holiday, however, the deadline for presentation of documents is extended to the following business day. Shipping documents must bear a date corresponding to the latest stipulated date for shipment. If none is specified, the shipping date may not be later than the original expiration date of the credit. Bills of lading or other shipping documents must be presented within 21 days after issuance unless otherwise stipulated. Of course, the 21 days must not exceed the expiration date of the letter of credit, as the bank cannot honor documents presented beyond the permissible time limit.

Although the place of presentation may differ from the place of payment, documents will be honored only after it has been established that they were presented on time at the designated place. Negotiation of documents presented according to the terms of the documentary letter of credit usually takes place at the domicile of the bank that originally issued the letter of credit (the original bank), or, if the letter of credit is confirmed, at the location of the correspondent bank that confirmed the letter of credit. This is customary, unless otherwise specified in the letter of credit.

In sum, the negotiation of the documents required under the terms of the letter of credit will occur when they are presented as specified, examined by the bank, and, if found to be in order, honored by the bank either by making payment against the documents or by accepting a bill for future payment (if so provided in the letter of credit).

Upon proper performance, certain obligations arise between the parties to the letter of credit transaction. From the perspective of the issuing bank, it assumes an obligation to both its customer and the beneficiary that it will, after careful examination of the documents, make payment to the specified beneficiary (or accept or negotiate drafts drawn thereunder, if so stipulated) under the terms of the credit, and will forward the documents received from the seller to the buyer. This obligation to honor conforming documents is contingent, however, upon the performance of the beneficiary. That is, although the beneficiary owes the issuing bank no duty to perform, any performance undertaken must be proper. Consequently, only conforming documents can be presented for payment. Once payment is made against conforming documents by the issuing or confirming bank (and, in certain instances, before that time), the buyer is obliged to reimburse the bank for the amount paid. In addition, the buyer usually must pay any commissions agreed upon as well as take over the original and approved documents that the bank had received from the seller.

Legal Disputes

The existence of these rights and obligations often forms the basis for legal dispute when improper performance is alleged. Legal disputes frequently develop due to alleged wrongful dishonor of documents by the issuer. Because such disputes are governed by the terms of the letter of credit and not by those of the underlying contracts, this means that a breach of the underlying sales contract is not a defense to a suit against the issuer for nonpayment. This effectively precludes the bank from becoming involved in breach of contract claims by the beneficiary against the seller. Thus, only the terms of the letter of credit must be examined in case of dispute.

If the issuer wrongfully dishonors conforming documents, the resulting legal action may take the following forms. First, the beneficiary of the credit has a cause of action against the issuer for nonpayment, which is based on the rights created by the letter of credit contract. If the beneficiary can prove the proper presentation of documents stipulated in the credit and the refusal of payment by dishonor of the draft and documents, damages may be awarded in addition to the payment due. Damages resulting from wrongful dishonor by the issuer will be measured by the law of sales under the Uniform Commercial Code.

The customer of the bank who established the letter of credit may bring suit against the issuer based upon the letter's contract to make payment upon compliance with the stipulated conditions. Upon proof that the bank did not make payment when the terms of the credit had been satisfied, the customer is entitled to reasonable and foreseeable damages resulting from the issuer's breach, provided that damages can be proven and documented. Note that a protest or a certificate of dishonor may be necessary to certify dishonor of a draft in compliance with the laws of the places where dishonor of a draft drawn under a credit occurs. Dishonor of a documentary draft or demand for payment falls within provisions of Article 3 of the Uniform Commercial Code governing protest to the extent that a negotiable instrument is involved. This procedure might be necessary on drafts drawn or payable outside the United States by a party who wishes to pursue his rights and remedies for wrongful dishonor.

In addition to suits for wrongful dishonor by the issuer, improper performance may also give rise to legal action. For example, a beneficiary may present a draft and documents to a bank under a letter of credit that do not conform to the terms agreed upon by the parties. If payment is made against such nonconforming documents, the bank has violated its obligation to honor only conforming documents. Under these circumstances the bank's customer escapes liability in the sense that, if he so chooses, he is relieved of the obligation to reimburse the bank for the wrongfully made payment. Namely, if the bank deviates from the stipulation of the credit, it assumes the risk that its customer may refuse to reimburse the payment made by the bank and might even seek damages.

Similarly, the issuing bank may be liable if it waives a restriction in terms by choice or by inadvertence and pays the beneficiary. Once again, the bank jeopardizes its right to reimbursement from its customer. In addition, however, the issuing bank may be held responsible to the beneficiary under the modified terms of the letter of credit despite the fact that such modification is not binding upon the bank's customer without consent. Absence of consent as a defense is available only to the customer; therefore, when a unilateral waiver is made, the bank is bound to make payment to the beneficiary under its terms and is not entitled to reimbursement from a customer who did not agree to the waiver. The waiver can be enforced as against the issuing bank in a suit by the letter of credit beneficiary against the issuing bank, however.

Improper performance by the beneficiary of the credit may also create the need for judicial intervention. For example, the remedy of injunctive relief exists in the case of fraud—either in the underlying transaction or in documents that are demonstrated to be false. As mentioned earlier, banks involved in the credit are not, and should not be, parties interested in the details of the underlying sales contract. Payment is made against documents and not against proof of compliance with the underlying transaction. However, a possible problem may arise where the bank receives a stop payment order from its customer who had established an irrevocable letter of credit. Let us assume that the parties involved discover they are victims of fraud and go to their bankers seeking a stop payment order for the irrevocable letter of credit. Although the bank may be sympathetic toward its client, the bank has an obligation to pay against the presentation of certain conforming documents. However, it is logical to see that presentation of fraudulent or falsified documents is *per se* nonconforming. Consequently, if the bank is satisfied that a fraud is involved or, due to some other compelling reason, wants to cooperate with the originator of the letter of credit, the bank may stop payment. Generally, the client requesting such stop payment must first obtain an indemnification bond for double the amount of the letter of credit. This insures protection for the bank in the event of a claim for breach of contract by the beneficiary, which can involve double indemnity and damages. This situation arises very rarely.

For obvious reasons, an issuing or confirming bank may refuse to stop payment voluntarily. In this event, the party seeking to stop payment—that is, the bank's customer—may apply to the courts for injunctive relief. Under certain extreme circumstances, courts will restrain payment under a letter of credit pending a determination of whether an egregious fraud exists in the underlying transaction. This is the remedy available before an actual breach of the letter of credit transaction has occurred.

Fraud in the transaction is a difficult concept to define in a precise fashion, in no small way because it appears to violate the chief virtue of the letter of credit: the independence of its payment obligation from the underlying transaction. It is precisely because of the potential for abuse that the credit's independence generates, however, that this device for mitigating the rule is available. Section 5–114(2) of the Uniform Commercial Code forms the basis of availability of injunctive relief. The thrust of the principle is as follows: When the misconduct of the party claiming payment under the letter of credit is so egregious as to vitiate the transaction itself, then the issuer is entitled to look beyond the performance required by the credit (which in most cases will be satisfactorily completed) to examine the party's performance of its underlying obligations. Conduct going beyond a mere breach of warranty through forged or falsified documents and constituting *active fraud* must be present (that is, delivery of worthless goods). While any showing of fraud depends on the facts of the particular case, it seems that only *egregious misconduct* or *intentional fraud* by the beneficiary will satisfy the requirement. When the issuer of a letter of credit knows that a document, correct in form, is in fact false or illegal, it cannot be called upon to recognize such a document as complying with the terms of the credit. Meeting the necessary standard, therefore, will be a key determinant in the granting of injunctive relief, and this standard seems to require fraudulent conduct of an aggravated nature. Whenever a party seeks injunctive relief, it must be remembered that courts are naturally hesitant to interfere, except in extreme circumstances, with a payment mechanism that has been established to facilitate commerce.

Rights Between Banks

As between banks, such as the issuing and confirming correspondent banks, the risk of nonpayment is borne by the confirming bank if the documents against which it paid are subsequently rejected by the issuing bank. Naturally, a cause of action would exist for wrongful dishonor if this were proven. However, assuming that payment was in fact made against nonconforming documents, plaintiff bank may be entitled to recover from the beneficiary of the credit on a theory of payment by mistake.

In the same manner, the issuing bank would be liable to a negotiating bank for payment under a letter of credit in the same way as it would be liable to a beneficiary or drawer of the draft, provided that all the documentary requirements of the letter of credit have been met.

Conformity of Documents

Because of the potential liability that may result from inadequate safeguards, any discrepancies in the documents presented can assume major importance. For example, when payment is sought, the terms of the credit must be analyzed word by word, and compliance proven by presenting the documents exactly as required. If minor discrepancies are found between the terms of the credit and the documents presented, they are referred to a discrepancy officer of the bank for resolution. For example, if the invoice presented describes goods as "imported acrylic yarn" as opposed to "100% acrylic yarn" as specified in the letter of credit, payment could not be obtained from the bank despite the fact that a packing list disclosing that packages contained 100% acrylic yarn as specified in the credit may be attached to the invoice, since lists may not be considered part of the invoice by reason of their being appended to it.

If discrepancies are found, they must be referred to the party who originated the letter of credit for written approval. This procedure of obtaining express agreement to accept documents in spite of discrepancies can entail extended periods of time before consent is obtained. It may, in fact, extend beyond the time allowed for presentation under the terms of the letter of credit, a risk of which the seller must be aware. Banks should be aware that previous acceptances of nonconforming documents cannot be construed as a waiver in subsequent instances.

In general, and the exception for fraud notwithstanding, conformity of the required documents is measured by form rather than content unless the wording of the credit states exactly what the documents shall contain. For commercial credits, as mentioned, description of the goods in invoices must match the letter of credit's description. However, in other documents, such as the bill of lading and insurance documents, the goods themselves may be described in general terms. Furthermore, commercial invoices as well as transportation documents need only be consistent rather than correspond to descriptions found in other documents or the letter of credit. Finally, if other documents, such as certificates of origin, weightlists, or warehouse receipts, are called for, they are deemed conforming in whatever form presented unless they are required to contain certain terms.

Despite the fact that the general rule is to require strict conformity to the terms of the letter of credit, some courts seem to allow minor discrepancies in the terms of relevant documents, and they will give effect to the ordinary and sensible meanings behind language. For example, payment by a bank upon presentation of a bill of lading with the word "grapes," where the letter of credit calls for "Alicante Bouchez grapes," may be proper because the parties have the right to use language as they see fit. If the credit requires packing in wooden cases with steel slots, however, and the documents show that the packing is in steel cases, the terms of the credit have not been complied with. If the letter of credit requires steel straps and the documents indicate copper straps around the wooden cases, the documents can be refused and payment denied.

As shown in these illustrations, sometimes the documents presented may not conform 100% to the stipulations of the credit. They may, however, be considered more or less in compliance with the spirit of the letter of credit. The negotiating bank will not take upon itself the responsibility for accepting the documents, but it will take the documents against a *trust receipt*. The bank will forward the documents to the originating bank, which, in turn, will usually inquire of its client whether the variance in the documents presented is acceptable. If they are found to be acceptable despite the variance, then the documents will be returned and the seller will return the trust receipt to the bank in exchange for the documents. Therefore, it is of utmost importance that conforming documents be presented for the parties involved.

Since documents must be carefully examined before payment is made, time may lapse between presentation of the draft and documents and payment in the case of a sight draft or acceptance in the case of a time draft. However, the beneficiary may not wish to wait an undue length of time before knowing whether the documents will be accepted as conforming. The Uniform Commercial Code, Section 5–112 (regarding time allowed for honor or rejection), specifies that the bank has until the third banking day following receipt of the documents to decide whether or not to honor the documents. Furthermore, the Code permits a provision in the letter of credit for payment on notice to the issuer that the required documents are in possession of a correspondent bank or other agent of the issuer, if the issuer does not reject nonconforming documents within three banking days of their receipt. This is useful to parties involved in international transactions in which correspondent banks may have to forward documents to the issuing banks.

Payment

Once the documents are found to be in order, payment will be made by either the issuing bank or the bank to which documents were presented such as a confirming bank. As mentioned earlier, if a sight letter of credit was established, it means that payment will be made as soon as the issuing or other agreed-upon bank receives, examines, and approves the documents. Therefore, sight drafts will be paid, and the client's account will be debited when the documents are found to be in conformity with the terms of the letter of credit.

In the case of foreign currency sight drafts, a basic difference should be noted. Drafts under foreign currency credits must be drawn on a bank in the country of the currency in which the credit is issued. For example, the situation may arise in which an American importer arranges to have a letter of credit opened at his bank in favor of the exporter and denominated in Swiss francs. The drafts under the letter of credit will have to be drawn on a Swiss correspondent bank. Since a foreign currency is involved in the transaction, a foreign exchange operation is entailed in the payment. For example, when the sight draft is expressed in a foreign currency, the bank's customer (importer) will have to pay the dollar equivalent amount of Swiss francs necessary to cover the foreign currency drafts at the rate of exchange existing at his bank for cable transfer to the place of payment on the date the draft is drawn for payment. In effect, this places the risk of exchange fluctuations on the buyer or importer of goods. This situation is in contrast to that of an importer establishing a sight draft denominated in his own currency—there the risk of exchange rate fluctuations is borne by the exporter.

As between the banks involved in this transaction, the foreign bank charges the amount of the credit to the account of the issuing bank if the documents are found to comply with the terms of the credit. For instance, if the letter of credit requires submission of a sight draft no later than the end of the month, and on that date a telex is received by the bank from a correspondent bank confirming the presentation to it of the sight draft, then the beneficiary has failed to comply with the terms of the credit. The wording of the credit may require that the sight draft be actually presented to the negotiating bank and not to a third bank or third party. This is just one example of the many processes and details to which the beneficiary of the credit must pay careful attention. Of course, the banks must rely on the expert knowledge of their staff to see to it that only the documents that are exactly in accordance with the terms of the credit are accepted.

Presentation of a time draft calls for somewhat different bank procedures. The seller presents the draft and conforming documents to the bank. Instead of receiving payment in the form of cash, check, or a credit to his account, the seller will receive his own draft, which is marked "accepted" by the bank. The time draft is accepted by the bank and returned to the seller, the beneficiary of the letter of credit. Once accepted, it becomes a direct and binding obligation of the bank.

The seller now possesses a banker's acceptance, which will be paid by the accepting bank upon maturity on the date indicated. It is likely, however, that the seller may not wish to wait until the acceptance has matured to receive payment. If cash is desired prior to maturity, the acceptance may be discounted through market sale at a slightly lower price than the face amount of the acceptance. In fact, the seller might want the bank to discount the draft, which it will gladly do, because the acceptance represents its own unconditional obligation for future payment. The cost of discounting is borne by the seller. The bank can usually rediscount these time drafts originating from import/export transactions with the Federal Reserve Bank, if it is a member. Such drafts should state that the transaction creating this instrument is the consequence of an importation of goods. In addition, it should state the type of commodity and the points of shipment and designation. It is up to the seller-beneficiary to seek discounting of the time draft at a fee, or else hold it until the expiration date, depending upon whether the beneficiary of the time draft wants payment before the due date. The procedures and availability of discounting of banker's acceptance is governed by the Federal Reserve Board's Regulation A (discussed further in Chapter 4, "Banker's Acceptances").

If the amount of the time draft is expressed in a foreign currency, the settlement procedure for the specified amount of foreign exchange follows the same overall pattern as for sight foreign currency transactions. However, the date of settlement of the foreign currency needed to cover the draft can be postponed until maturity of the draft. When this occurs, the exchange rate of the currency needed to cover the time draft and reimburse the bank is the rate effective on the date of payment as opposed to the rate in effect when the credit was first established. Once again, however, the party establishing the credit may avoid this exchange risk through the purchase of a forward exchange contract in the amount necessary to cover the letter of credit on that future date.

Reimbursement

Once payment is properly made, the bank has the right of reimbursement from its customer. The proper fulfillment of its obligation to honor conforming documents as specified in the letter of credit gives rise to this right of reimbursement. This duty to make payment under the letter of credit is not dependent upon the bank's ability to ultimately obtain reimbursement, however. That is, even if it is discovered that the buyer or originator of the letter of credit will be unable to make reimbursement, the bank must still pay the seller under the terms of the letter of credit. Thus, the bank would have to pursue separate remedies against the buyer to obtain reimbursement for payments made.

In addition to pursuing the legal right of reimbursement, it is important to realize that the bank is in possession of the documents of title to the merchandise. These were presented to the bank with the draft for payment by the seller. If a correspondent bank had been used, then those documents are conveyed to the issuing or originating bank to be presented to the buyer so that he can obtain the merchandise. These documents are often good collateral for the bank waiting for reimbursement.

When documents are released against a promise to pay for the merchandise at a later date (that is, time drafts), they are usually released against what is called a *trust receipt*. The trust receipt gives the bank a security interest in the merchandise. All major banks have trust receipt forms. Originally, after many years of work by the National Conference of Commissioners of Uniform State laws, the Uniform Trust Receipt Act was developed. This act has been replaced in most states, however, by several sections of the Uniform Commercial Code. For this reason, any bank officer releasing values against a trust receipt should have a good understanding of regulations prevailing in the state in which he is located.

When releasing the documents under a trust receipt, the bank endorses the bills of lading to its customer and prepares an advice of acceptance with the maturity date indicated. The trust receipt must include the amount of the draft and its maturity; most important, it must describe the goods exactly as they appear on the bills of lading. The trust receipt has to be executed, signed by the customer, and presented to the bank in exchange for the documents that give title to the merchandise. In states that are still governed by the Uniform Trust Receipt Act, it is necessary to file a Statement of Trust Receipt Financing with the proper state office. This becomes public record and is published by various financial newspapers. It is a customer's responsibility to see to it that, when the transaction is finally consummated and liquidated, the Statement of Trust Receipt Financing is withdrawn from the respective registry.

The bank may, instead of releasing the documents against a trust receipt, place the merchandise in a public warehouse and hold a warehouse receipt. It will then decide when to release the warehouse receipt to the buyer. Normally, the receipt is held until payment for the merchandise is received. Alternatively, the bank may reserve a right to have the goods stored for its own account with a stipulation that any sale of such goods may be made only with prior consent of the bank. This stipulation will usually prevent the goods, secured by a trust receipt or their equivalent value, from being drawn into a bankrupt's estate in case of the buyer's insolvency.

Thus, the reasons a bank processing documents in a letter of credit transaction will want the documents to be in negotiable form are clear: Title to the merchandise is obtained between the time it makes payment and the time it is reimbursed. Of course, there is always the risk that the bank is given worthless or fraudulent documents. If no merchandise of value is represented by such documents and payment was already made by the bank, there is no collateral for the bank to levy against. For this reason the reputation of the parties to the transaction should be checked as far as possible, to avoid the delay and expense of suit for fraud.

However, assuming that payment was made and reimbursement was obtained by the paying bank, the letter of credit transaction is now closed for that particular shipment. Thereafter, if additional shipments are ordered, new applications for letters of credit must be submitted. However, as mentioned at the beginning of the discussion of available types of letters of credit, a revolving letter of credit provides for automatic renewal of the letter of credit amount. This allows a series of shipments to be made, each under a renewed letter of credit amount. The revolving letter of credit is frequently used by importers with a large and steady volume of business. This enables them to avoid possible delay, added cost, and inconvenience of filing a new application for each shipment to be covered by a letter of credit.

This concludes our discussion of letters of credit. Although the procedure involved in establishing a credit is not complex, the ability and skill needed to discern whether or not the terms of the credit have been met and confirming documents presented determine the extent of risk in the transaction. Finally, the advantage of having such a payment mechanism independent of the underlying contract, using the bank as intermediary, normally outweighs the risks involved. Except in case of fraud, the protection afforded is significant, especially for international transactions.

Bibliography

American Bankers Association, Credit Policy Committee. *A Banker's Guide to Financing Exports.* New York: American Bankers Association, 1966.

Benedict, Erastus. *Benedict on Admiralty, Carriage of Goods by Sea,* 7th rev. ed. Albany, New York: Matthew Bender, 1977.

Convention for the Unification of Certain Rules Relating to International Transportation by Air. Concluded at Warsaw, October 12, 1919; entered into force for the United States, October 29, 1934. 49 Stat. 3000, T.S. 876.

Curtin, D. "How Safe Are Letters of Credit?" *Euromoney* (July 1981), pp. 28–30.

"Documentary Letters of Credit and the Uniform Customs and Practice for Documentary Credit (1974 Revision): A Selective Analysis." Comment. *J. Corp. Law* (Fall 1977), pp. 147–207.

"Export Financing Part I—Documentary Credits." *Credit Suisse*, 47 1(1978).

Harfield, Henry. *Letters of Credit*. Philadelphia, Pennsylvania: American Law Institute, American Bar Association Committee on Continuing Professional Education, 1979.

International Chamber of Commerce. *Decisions (1975–1979) of the ICC Banking Commission on Queries Relating to Uniform Customs and Practice for Documentary Credits*. Paris: ICC Services S.A.R.L., 1980.

International Chamber of Commerce. *Uniform Customs and Practice for Documentary Credits*. Brochure No. 290 (1974 revision). (See also *International Chamber of Commerce Uniform Customs and Practice for Documentary Credits*. Brochure No. 400, 1984 revision.)

International Convention for the Unification of Certain Rules Relating to Bills of Lading. Done August 25, 1924. 120 L.N.T.S., 120 (1931–32), p. 155.

Kozolchyk, Boris. *Commercial Letters of Credit in the Americas: A Comparative Study of Contemporary Commercial Transactions*. Albany, New York: Matthew Bender, 1966.

Leary, Fairfax, Jr. *Banking Problems Under the U.C.C.* New York: Practising Law Institute, 1979.

"Letters of Credit: Current Theories and Usages." Comment. *La. L. Rev.*, 39(Winter 1979), pp. 581–622.

Lord, R. A. "The No-Guarantee Rule and the Stand-by Letter of Credit Controversy." *Banking L. J.* (January 1979), pp. 46–63.

Meznerics, Ivan. *International Payments: With Special Regard to Monetary Systems*. Alphen aan den Rijn, The Netherlands: Sijthoff and Noordhoff, 1979.

O'Halloran, John L. *ABC of Commercial Letters of Credit*, 7th ed. MHT, 1979.

Oppenheim, Peter. *International Banking*, 3rd rev. ed. Washington, D.C.: American Bankers Association, 1979.

Rendell, Robert. *Exporting: Governmental Assistance and Regulation*. New York: Practising Law Institute, 1975.

Schmitthoff, Clive. *The Export Trade: The Law and Practice of International Trade*, 6th ed. London: Stevens, 1975.

Stevens, Edward F. *Shipping Practice: With a Consideration of the Relevant Law*, 10th ed. London: Pitman, 1978.

Swiss Bank Corp. Documentary Operations. 1976.

Symons, E. L., Jr. "Letters of Credit: Fraud, Good Faith and the Basis for Injunctive Relief." *Tul. L. Rev.*, 54(Fall 1980), pp. 338–381.

Uniform Commercial Code, Arts. 3 and 5. 1978 version.

"Uniform Commercial Code Sections 5-102 and 5-103: A Solution to the Standby Letter of Credit Identity Crisis." *Loyola Univ. L. J.*, 11(Spring 1980), pp. 607–636.

4

Bankers' Acceptances

Bankers' acceptances represent a flexible and efficient means of obtaining credit for short periods of time. They are utilized particularly in instances where the underlying transaction is self-liquidating in nature. This is due to the fact that self-liquidating acceptances are eligible for discount by a Federal Reserve member bank. The transaction financed by this type of acceptance will thus produce the funds necessary to pay off the acceptance. Thus, the bankers' acceptance covers the time normally needed to ship and sell goods. In theory, this eliminates a great deal of risk for the accepting bank since payment will be forthcoming from the transaction. On the other hand, the fact that the bank assumes primary responsibility for payment upon creation of an acceptance eliminates substantial risk from the point of view of the purchaser of the acceptance.

Since World War II, the number of bankers' acceptances that have been created has increased substantially. This expansion reflects the increase in world trade as well as the worldwide use of the U.S. dollar to finance international trade. In the United States, acceptances are generally governed by Article 3 of the Uniform Commercial Code, as adopted by the various states. In addition, Federal Reserve member banks are subject to a combination of statutes, administrative rulings, regulations, and interpretations governing the creation, use, and discounting of acceptances. These are aimed at such factors as the permissible time for which acceptances may be outstanding, as well as the total amount of acceptances allowed to be outstanding at any time. In particular, Section 13 of the Federal Reserve Act will be examined. It is useful to first define a bankers' acceptance and examine the way in which it is created.

Definition

A *bankers' acceptance* is a draft or bill of exchange drawn on a bank (the drawee) by a party (the drawer) and accepted by that bank to pay a third party (the payee) a certain sum at a fixed future date. The bank's acceptance of a draft represents a formal acknowledgement of the bank's unconditional promise to pay the draft at maturity. A distinction should be made between the bankers' acceptance and a letter of credit under which it is often created, since the acceptance is a credit mechanism whereas the letter of credit is a security device. Furthermore, the difference between the acceptance and the cashier's or certified check is the fact that it is payable at a fixed future date. The steps followed in the creation of an acceptance involve a presentation of the draft signed by the drawer to the drawee for acknowledgement or acceptance of its payment obligation on the face of the draft along with the drawee's signature. Any words of acceptance that accompany the signature can create a valid acceptance. If the drawee is a bank, the draft is called a bankers' acceptance. Since these actions are taken prior to the due date of the draft, all that remains is to await its maturity for payment of the draft. If funds are desired prior to maturity, the holder may be able to sell it at a discount as an alternative.

An acceptance is evidenced by an authorized signature appearing on the face of the draft and must be accompanied by delivery or appropriate notification to the holder. Liability on an accepted instrument is primarily that of the accepting bank and is unconditional. The drawer of the draft is now secondarily liable unless his signature was accompanied by the words "without recourse." For this reason, acceptances drawn on and accepted by a well-known bank (or *prime acceptances*) are both desirable credit instruments and, in certain instances, a favored source of short-term financing. Furthermore, the creation of acceptances may be preferable to the bank as well since it does not entail the use of its own funds and is normally offered at lower cost than that of a loan. Section 13 of the Federal Reserve Act offers a guideline as to which banks may create acceptances eligible for discount. These include member banks of the Federal Reserve System as well as their foreign branches, if the acceptances are payable in the United States. In addition, branches and agencies of foreign banks may also create acceptances eligible for discount by a Federal Reserve bank if they maintain adequate reserves with the Federal Reserve Bank.

Currently, legislation has increased overall limits on the issuance of acceptances by member banks from 50 to 150 percent of paid-in capital and surplus (an aggregate of 200 percent with prior Federal Reserve approval) and has extended these limits to include U.S. branches and agencies of foreign banks.

Why Acceptances Are Created

Acceptances may be created for reasons related to trade and for nontrade reasons.

TRADE-RELATED ACCEPTANCES

Trade-related acceptances may be created in the buyer's and seller's attempt to finance their deal. Typically a buyer of goods does not have cash to pay to the seller. The buyer will seek out a bank to act as his intermediary and provide the credit he needs until he has the cash (such as when he has sold the goods that he is now seeking to buy).

If a bank is willing to provide its assurance that payment will be made, it notifies the seller that he may draw a draft on the bank for an indicated dollar amount payable at a future date. The bank then stamps "ACCEPTED" across the face of the draft and places an authorized bank signature on the draft.

If the bank takes no further action, it has simply provided its commitment to the seller that payment for the goods will indeed be made. The seller, however, may desire to receive payment of the draft immediately. Since acceptances are negotiable, they can be sold before maturity at a discounted price. In this event, the bank will discount the acceptance, that is, purchase the acceptance for its own account. The acceptance may also be discounted with a bank other than the accepting bank. The seller is paid the current market value of the time draft by the bank. The discount factor is heavily influenced by the credit standing of the parties. The bank in turn will either hold this instrument or rediscount the acceptance. The rediscount rate is normally lower than the discount rate. When rediscounting an acceptance, the bank will seek to earn the spread between the bid and asking rates on acceptances in the secondary market. In any event, the bank will earn a commission, which is the fee for the use of its name in the extension of credit through the creation of an acceptance.

From the perspective of the bank creating the acceptance, its initial guarantee to its customer is not a reservable liability. If the bank discounts the acceptance and continues to hold the draft in its portfolio as an investment, the bank in effect has made a loan to its customer. This loan must be funded like any other loan. Holding acceptances may be attractive if the bank has reached its limit on sales of certain types of acceptances.

Finally, the acceptance may serve as a medium for the bank to fund itself as well as to advance credit. This is accomplished through the bank's discounting and subsequent rediscounting of its own acceptances. The funds raised through rediscounting acceptances are exempt from reserve requirements, providing the acceptance is of the type described in Section 13(7) of the Federal Reserve Act and the total number of outstanding acceptances are not greater than 50% of a member bank's paid-up and unimpaired capital stock and surplus.

Creating, buying, and selling an acceptance from the bank's viewpoint is akin to issuing a negotiable certificate of deposit to fund a loan to a customer. However, because the funds raised from the sale of an acceptance that meets the regulatory standards, as discussed, are exempt from reserve requirements, they will be less costly to a bank than those raised through issuing a certificate of deposit.

NONTRADE-RELATED ACCEPTANCES

The uses of acceptances are not limited to the needs of trade. One type of nontrade-related acceptance is known as a *finance bill*. This type of bill raises working capital for the firm drawing the draft, and it is a corollary to commercial paper. Another type of nontrade-related acceptance is known as a *dollar exchange bill*. Both finance bills and dollar exchange bills are discussed below.

Finance bills raise working capital for the firm drawing the draft. Such acceptances are close substitutes for commercial paper. Indeed, in 1969, severe restraints on credit, together with the limiting effect of

FIGURE 4–1

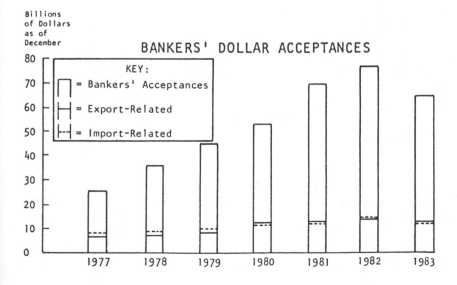

Billions of Dollars as of December

BANKERS' DOLLAR ACCEPTANCES

KEY:
☐ = Bankers' Acceptances
⊢⊣ = Export-Related
⊢⋅⋅⊣ = Import-Related

Regulation Q, led some banks to create "working capital" acceptances—that is, finance bills—in order to continue their loan expansion. Innovative banks turned to these finance bills because the funds received from their sale were not reservable at the time. The volume of such bills increased rapidly, from average levels of $300 to $400 million in the early 1970s to almost $1.5 billion in June 1973, or equal to about one-fifth of all other acceptances of that time.

In mid-1973 the Federal Reserve Board amended Regulation D to impose reserve requirements on funds raised through the sale of finance bills, and only negligible amounts have been created since then. This reflected the Board's concern that finance bills would be used instead of certificates of deposit in order to fund bank loans for purely financial (and possibly speculative) purposes. Certificates of deposit were and always had been "deposits" and thus required reserves under Regulation D. Under the amendment, the definition of deposits includes a bank's liability on acceptances used by it to obtain funds for its banking business. However, the Board excepted from the definition of deposits a bank's liabilities on acceptances of the kind described in Section 13 of the Federal Reserve Act and eligible for discount by the Federal Reserve banks.

Dollar exchange bills, another type of nontrade acceptance, are used to finance the extension of dollar exchange credits to foreign countries. This type of financing is especially attractive to foreign banks in countries whose exports to the U.S. are highly seasonal. Through the dollar exchange acceptance, a bank seeks to provide itself with dollars to finance its customers' imports during seasons when export earnings are low and dollars are in short supply. In later months, when exports expand, the acceptance is paid off.

Agriculturally dependent countries, mostly in Latin America, have turned to dollar exchange bills to alleviate their seasonal shortage of dollars. In recent years, however, these countries have tried to stabilize their foreign trade earnings through crop diversification and industrial development. Therefore, their need for this form of financing has become negligible.

Acceptances drawn for the purpose of furnishing dollar exchange are eligible for discount by a Federal Reserve Bank if they have not more than three months sight to run. Although eligible for discount, dollar exchange acceptances have been removed from the Federal Reserve list of acceptances authorized for its open market purchase operations.

Some experts in the field of international banking believe that, although trade-related acceptances perform a most useful function, they are sometimes misused. Specifically, the credits obtained may not be used for financing transactions of a self-liquidating character but instead are employed in providing working capital that should have been obtained through the issue of securities or by other methods.

This misuse of acceptance credits is cited as being dangerous especially to the lender but also to the borrower. The lender suffers because funds that are supposed to be liquid and easily withdrawn become frozen. The misuse of acceptance credits also constitutes a danger to the individual debtors and may jeopardize the foreign exchange position of their country. The debtor banks operate under the constant threat that the credits granted to them may be withdrawn. In order to meet these withdrawals, the banks must call the loans of their debtors, and, since the credits are not based on self-liquidating transactions, it is obvious that they might not be repaid. In fact, the use of foreign short-term credits to finance long-term transactions was considered one of the principle causes of difficulties experienced by several European banks. When foreign banks began to withdraw their credits, European banks were unable to liquidate some of their own loans and were therefore unable to obtain cash with which to buy foreign exchange.

Liabilities Arising from the Creation of an Acceptance

Creation of an acceptance renders the bank liable, as a principal, to make a payment and enables a third party to enforce that liability.

Acceptance of a draft puts the value (the bank's commitment) in the hands of the holder or beneficiary, rather than in the hands or at the disposition of the borrower. The engagement made in the acceptance is independent of the arrangement between the bank and its customer or borrower. An alteration in the circumstances of the customer does not excuse the bank from honoring the commitment embodied in its acceptance.

The bank thus interposes itself between its customer and a creditor as the debtor of first resort. Consequently, a prudent banker will create an acceptance for its customer only pursuant to a written agreement from the customer to put in the bank funds to meet maturing acceptances or to reimburse the bank for payments under the acceptance as well as for related charges. The agreement between the customer and the bank normally contains covenants securing the customer's obligation to the bank. These covenants protect the bank against the risk of deterioration of the bank's assets (its customer's assurances) when the bank cannot reduce its own obligation on the acceptance. They generally include provisions for collateral, mandatory prepayment, and acceleration of the customer's obligation.

The Role of the
Federal Reserve System
in Acceptance Financing

The primary function of the Federal Reserve Bank is to extend credit to member banks to accommodate commerce, industry, and agriculture. Consequently, it plays an important role in the acceptance market.

Federal Reserve credit is available on a short-term basis to enable member banks to meet temporary requirements for funds. Federal Reserve credit can also be seasonal to meet a member bank's changing deposit and loan portfolio. Seasonal credit may be extended for a period of up to 90 days.

If a Reserve Bank should conclude that a member bank would be better accommodated by the discount of paper than by an advance on bonds that serve as the underlying security, it may discount papers endorsed by that member bank.

Trade-related and nontrade bankers' acceptances are eligible for discount by a Federal Reserve Bank if they are drawn in accordance with Section 13 of the Federal Reserve Act. While discount by a Federal Reserve bank is seldom necessary as long as an active private trading market exists, it serves as protection for a bank. The real advantage of creating an eligible acceptance, however, is that the bank does not have to maintain reserves on such acceptances.

Eligible bankers' acceptances must grow out of transactions involving one of two things:

- the current shipment of goods between countries or within the United States;
- the storage within the United States of goods under a contract of sale or expected to move into the channel of trade within a reasonable time that are secured throughout their life by a warehouse receipt or similar document conveying title to the underlying goods.

Furthermore, these trade-related acceptances must be no more than six months from maturity to be eligible for discounting.

An acceptance drawn for the purpose of furnishing a dollar exchange that has no more than three months to maturity is also eligible for discount under the Federal Reserve Act. It should be mentioned that the acceptance relating to the shipment of goods may be created any time prior or subsequent to actual shipment. In addition, there is no limitation concerning the actual jurisdiction in which the goods are stored, meaning that goods properly stored abroad or in the U.S. may satisfy the requirements if properly secured.

Discount Eligibility
of Domestic Acceptances

In 1978 the Board of Governors of the Federal Reserve System reexamined the discount eligibility of acceptances that finance the storage of goods within the United States. The outcome of this examination was the adoption of an interpretation of former Regulation A, which effectively extended the eligibility for rediscounting to bankers' acceptances backed by field warehouse receipts financing the storage of goods. The earlier rule had held such acceptances to be ineligible for discount by a Federal Reserve bank due to the impaired nature of the lending bank's security inherent in the field warehouse arrangement.

In a *field warehousing arrangement*, a field warehouse is created by segregating an area inside the borrower's premises or outside in a field yard. The area is fenced off, is subject to limited access, and is leased from the borrower by the warehousing company. A sign is posted indicating the warehouseman's control of that portion of the premises, which gives notice to creditors that the debtor does not have unencumbered title to the merchandise in the enclosure.

Central to the Board's position that such acceptances were ineligible was the practice in the field warehousing arrangements of detaching one or more employees of the borrower from the borrower's payroll to act as custodians of the goods. The workers technically become employees of the warehouse company, and they are paid by the warehouse company, which ultimately is reimbursed by agreement with the borrower. The lending bank's security was thought to be impaired due to the close identity between the custodian of the goods and their owner.

The Board has determined that, in cases where the custodian of the goods was a current or former employee of the borrower, acceptances secured by such warehouse receipts would be ineligible for discounting because:

> Such receipts do not comply with the requirements of section 13 of the Federal Reserve Act that a bankers' acceptance be "secured at the time of acceptance by a warehouse receipt or other such document *conveying or securing title* covering readily marketable staples. . . ." [paragraph 1443 Published Interpretations 1933 Bulletin 188]

The Board's 1978 decision took into account the changes in commercial law since 1933. If the field warehousing operation is properly conducted, a security interest in the goods is perfected when a warehouse receipt is issued in the name of the secured party (the lending bank). The Uniform Commercial Code now refers to "perfecting security interests" rather than "securing title" to goods. As a result, if, under State law, the issuance of a field warehouse receipt provides the lender with a perfected security interest in the goods, the receipt should be regarded as a document "securing title" to goods for the purposes of Section 13 of the Federal Reserve Act. Therefore, warehouse receipts issued pursuant to a bona fide field warehousing operation currently satisfy the requirements of Section 13.

Investors in the Acceptance Market

An impressive record of safety and liquidity makes acceptances attractive short-term investments. Yields of 90-day acceptances are closely in line with rates on 90-day certificates of deposit. Since late 1977, the yields on both acceptances and 90-day CDs have been higher than those of Treasury bills of comparable maturity.

Acceptance investors include state and local governments, governmental agencies, savings institutions, foreigners, foreign central banks, industrial corporations, insurance companies, investment funds, accepting banks, and individuals. In addition, banks may join together to syndicate eligible acceptances.

Nonbank investors play a limited role even though, as mentioned previously, acceptance yields are comparable to commercial paper yields. This is so because it is difficult to obtain large blocks of bankers' acceptances with the maturity desired. Initial investors usually hold acceptances to maturity.

Federal Reserve Bank data on dealer sales to investors in the acceptance market reflects the following market distribution. During 1980, dealers reporting to the Federal Reserve Bank of New York made about 19.8% of their sales (exclusive of those to other dealers and through brokers) to commercial banks; 18.5% to industrial corporations; 18.5% to federal, state, and local government agencies; and 8.7% to foreigners, including the foreign central banks for whom the Federal Reserve Bank of New York acts as agent.

Conclusion

In summary, therefore, the widespread use of the bankers' acceptance as a means of providing credit shows that they represent an important financing instrument. Furthermore, the laws and regulations to which banks creating or discounting acceptances are subject are aimed at preserving market stability.

Statutory Appendix:
Section 13 of the Federal Reserve Act

Section 13(7):

Any member bank may accept drafts or bills of exchange drawn upon it having not more than six months sight to run, exclusive of days of grace, which grow out of transactions involving the importation or exportation of goods; or which grow out of transactions involving the domestic shipment of goods provided shipping documents conveying or securing title are attached at the time of acceptance; or which are secured at the time of acceptance or which are secured at the time of acceptance by a warehouse receipt or other such document conveying or securing title covering readily marketable staples.

Section 13(12):

Any member bank may accept drafts or bills of exchange drawn upon it having not more than three months' sight to run, exclusive of days of grace, drawn under regulations to be prescribed by the Board of Governors of the Federal Reserve System by banks or bankers in foreign countries or dependencies or insular possessions of the United States for the purpose of furnishing dollar exchange as required by the usages of trade in the respective countries, dependencies or insular possessions. Such drafts or bills may be acquired by Federal Reserve banks in such amounts and subject to such regulations, restrictions, and limitations as may be prescribed by the Board of Governors of the Federal Reserve System.

Bibliography

"Bankers Acceptances." *FRBNY Quarterly Review*, 6, No. 2(Summer 1981).

Board of Governors of the Federal Reserve System. Press Release. March 26, 1974.

"Fed. Proposes Regulations on New Bankers Acceptances Limits," *Foreign Bank Focus* (February 1983), p. 4.

"Federal Proposal on Bankers Acceptances Criticized." *Foreign Bank Focus* (March 1983), p 4.

Federal Reserve Act. 12 U.S.C. §§611–631. 1981.

Harfield, H. *Bank Credits and Acceptances*, 5th ed. New York: John Wiley and Sons, Inc., 1974.

Harfield, H. "Credit Mechanisms and Security Devices." In *Proceedings of the 1961 Institute on Private Investments Abroad and Foreign Trade*. New York: Matthew Bender, 1961.

Madden, John T. and Marcus Nadler. *International Money Market*. New York: Greenwood Press, 1968.

Oppenheim, Peter. *International Banking*, 3rd rev. ed. Washington, D.C.: American Bankers Association, 1979.

Prochnow, Herbert V., ed. *Bank Credit: An In-Depth Study of Credit and Loan Practices by 30 Outstanding Banking Authorities.* New York: Harper & Row, 1981.

Ryan, R. H., Jr. "Bankers Acceptances and Bank Credits—Selected Problems." In *Banking and Commercial Lending Law.* ALI, 1980.

White, James. *Teaching Materials on Banking Law.* St. Paul, Minnesota: West Publishing Co., 1976.

Willis, Parker Brown. *Federal Funds Market: Its Origin and Development,* 4th ed. Boston, Massachusetts: Boston Federal Reserve Bank, 1970.

5

Collections

Several methods are available to those wishing to effectuate international payments using banks as intermediaries. In Chapter 3, the letter of credit method was discussed, through which the bank's credit is added or substituted for that of a party to the transaction. In this chapter, the collection process is examined. This method of payment minimizes the bank's responsibilities concerning payment when the standard procedures of presentation and acceptance, such as those outlined in the Uniform Rules for Collection, are followed. More importantly, the bank's liability for payment of the draft is eliminated, since the credit of the bank is not substituted for that of the buyer. In a typical case, a seller of goods will rely upon his buyer to satisfy his payment obligation when the bank presents the agreed-upon papers required for payment to the buyer since the draft or bill of exchange is drawn directly on the buyer. Therefore, the party on whom the draft is drawn must be sufficiently creditworthy to justify the risk. At the same time, when the bank serves as agent for collection, the degree of risk that would be encountered when shipping on open account is eliminated, since title to goods shipped will be secure up to the point when the bank releases documents of title to the buyer.

Before outlining the basic steps in a typical collection procedure, a differentiation should be made between terminology used to identify parties to the transaction. These include:

- the *principal* or customer requesting the bank to handle the collection,
- the *remitting bank* coordinating the collection,
- the *presenting bank* presenting the documents to the buyer (*drawee*), and

- the *collecting bank*, which is any other bank involved in carrying out the collection order.

In a typical import-export situation, the collection procedure entails the delivery of a collection order by the principal (a seller of goods) to the remitting bank with specific instructions to have them presented through a collecting bank to the buyer (drawee), wherever he may be located, through a presenting bank. The bank will arrange for presentation of the draft to the importer for payment or acceptance, depending upon the seller's instructions, in conformity with its role as collector for the principal. The most important bank in the collection process is the presenting bank because it is responsible for the release of documents against payment or acceptance. The bank is frequently designated by the exporter since it controls the funds paid by the importer until receipt by the exporter's bank. However, if the principal does not choose a collecting bank, the remitting bank may choose any bank in the country of payment or acceptance in order to carry out the instructions of the principal.

Significantly, the intermediary banks involved in the collection process act as agents for collection. As agents for collection, banks would not normally have the authority to sell goods in the case of nonpayment by the initial buyer. However, the seller should be aware of the fact that this issue may arise if the bank has advanced funds or discounted drafts on behalf of the seller.

We will now proceed to a discussion of collection methods.

Types of Collections

It is possible to distinguish between the *documentary collection* method, in which documents of title accompany the usual draft being presented to the drawee by the presenting bank for collection, and a *clean collection*, in which documents are not presented. It is also possible for exporters to sell on *cash against documents*, in which case a draft will not be sent. These distinctions have a pervasive effect on the subsequent collection process and on the rights of the parties in case of suit for nonconforming goods.

Assuming that in most situations the importer will be receiving documents of title from the presenting bank, three basic documentary collection procedures are available to the exporter. These include: (1) documents against payment (D/P), (2) documents against acceptance (D/A), (3) collection with acceptance or acceptance (D/P). Important differences exist between these procedures.

If a *documents against payment* (D/P) is specified, the documents may be released by the presenting bank only against full cash payment. Furthermore, documents may be released only if the sum paid is immediately and freely available. Consequently, a potential difficulty encountered with use of this procedure is the interference and delay in prompt payment of funds when a currency is subject to exchange control restrictions. In the absence of these exchange control restrictions, however, this method affords a large degree of protection since the buyer may not obtain possession of the goods until actual cash payment has been made.

In a *documents against acceptance* (D/A) transaction, the bank may release the title documents only after the buyer has accepted the bill of exchange (draft) for future payment at the agreed-upon maturity and only if the collection order so provides. Thereafter, the only assurance of payment the seller has is the draft accepted by the buyer. Thus, it can be seen that the seller accepts a greater risk of nonpayment when goods are released against acceptance of this draft. If a draft payment at a future date is sent to the remitting bank for collection, the collection order should state whether the documents are to be released D/A (documents against acceptance) or D/P (documents against payment) because they will ordinarily be released D/P if such instruction is lacking.

The third type of documentary collection is the *acceptance D/P or collection with acceptance method*. This method is a combination of the D/A and D/P collection. A draft is sent with the documents of title to the presenting bank requiring acceptance by the buyer. However, unlike the D/A, the documents are not released until the date of actual payment of the draft accepted by the buyer. This two-stage process permits the seller to have an early indication that the buyer will not make payment, and it serves as additional protection for the goods until such time as payment is made.

Procedure

After agreement on the desired collection method by the parties, it is necessary for the seller to deliver any necessary documents to the remitting bank for collection. As previously mentioned, these normally include a draft as well as documents. Documents may be of a financial or commercial character. Financial documents include bills of exchange, promissory notes, receipts, and similar instruments. On the other hand, commercial documents include invoices, shipping documents, documents of title, and any nonfinancial documents. Documents of title will most often accompany the draft. The document most commonly used, however, is the negotiable bill of lading, which is a receipt representing title to the goods as well as a contract for shipment by the carrier. The delivery of a negotiable bill of lading completes a transfer of title between seller and buyer.

As regards the draft, if the seller draws the draft to his own order, it will typically be indorsed for collection by the bank. However, several forms of indorsement are available. These include restrictive or nonrestrictive indorsements, indorsements in blank, and indorsements with or without recourse. This choice of form offers the seller some flexibility in obtaining payment of the draft drawn on buyer as drawee.

Regarding shipment of the goods, it is generally not advisable to send goods directly to the buyer. Instead, they should be sent to the presenting bank's disposal (if a prior agreement to accept delivery has been reached) or to a forwarding agent at the disposal of the presenting bank. This will avoid a situation where the buyer, having already obtained possession of the goods, will delay or avoid payment therefore. Note that, without prior agreement, the bank has no obligation to take delivery of the goods.

Since banks forward the documents received for collection without examination, it is important for the seller to have assembled a complete set of the documents called for by the terms of the sales contract or else by trade usage. Thereafter, all the documents will be forwarded by the remitting bank to a presenting bank, which will notify the buyer of receipt of the documents. In addition, the buyer will be notified of the conditions to be met for release of such documents.

Uniform Rules for Collection

Over the years, uniform terms, rules, and procedures have evolved and are now routinely applied by banks when handling documents for collection of payments. The Uniform Rules for Collection Brochure No. 322 (URC), prepared by the International Chamber of Commerce, is one of the more comprehensive codifications of these principles; for that reason, it is recognized and used by most banks in the United States and abroad.

The articles of the Uniform Rules for Collection are divided into subsections governing particular phases of the collection process. These include:

1. liabilities and responsibilities of the parties,
2. presentation of documents,
3. payment,
4. acceptance,
5. promissory notes, receipts, and other instruments,
6. protest,

7. case-of-need and protection of goods,
8. advice of fate,
9. interest charges, and expenses.

Responsibilities of the Bank

As a general matter, the responsibilities, as well as the limitations on the collecting bank's liability, are contained in the Uniform Rules for Collection (URC). Normally, an agreement for collection entered into with a bank is made subject to the URC. In addition, however, certain provisions of the Uniform Commercial Code (UCC) may otherwise be found applicable to a bank collection. The application of the UCC to bank collections may be varied by agreement of the parties, such as by reference to the URC in an agreement. Nevertheless, no agreement can disclaim a bank's responsibility to deal in good faith and exercise ordinary care. Furthermore, damages resulting from the bank's failure to exercise such duties may not be limited.

The duty to act in good faith and exercise reasonable care is also contained in the URC which, as previously mentioned, governs most collections. In addition to these duties, banks subject to the URC have a duty to verify that documents received appear to be those required in the customer's collection order. Furthermore, in the event that any documents are missing, the bank must so advise the party from whom the collection order was received.

In addition to outlining duties, the URC provides for limitations on the bank's liability for events occurring during the collection process. No liability is incurred for consequences of interpretation, loss, or delay in communications. Similarly, no responsibility is assumed for consequences of Acts of God, riots, wars, insurrections, strikes, or other events beyond the bank's control.

Concerning delivery and/or storage of goods, the URC states that goods may not be sent to a bank without its approval first being obtained. This does not mean that the bank is obliged to grant such approval. This effectively relieves the bank of an obligation to conserve, protect, or otherwise oversee the condition of the goods for which the collection is being made. Banks assume no liability for the acts and/or omissions of third parties having custody of such goods. Finally, the bank need not be concerned with whether the goods conform to the terms of the contract.

Regarding promissory notes, receipts, and other instruments, the presenting bank does not assume responsibility for the genuineness of signatures, or for the actual authority of signatories to such documents.

As between the various collecting banks, a collecting bank is entitled to prompt payment from the bank sending the collection order for costs incurred, whereas the remitting bank must seek payment from the principal. These costs may be recovered regardless of the fate of the collection.

Collection Order

The procedure for presentation of documents is contained in the *collection order* issued by the principal, which defines the permissible actions of the bank and, in so doing, establishes additional rights and obligations between the parties. The collecting banks have the responsibility to comply with the specific instructions for collection contained in the order; in the event that these instructions cannot be complied with, the bank must immediately advise the party who initially submitted the order of any difficulties.

Typically, banks have forms for use by the principal outlining useful instructions to be provided and suggested wording for those instructions. In particular, the appointment of a case-of-need agent to handle such problems as delays that may arise during collection may be provided for. This appointment of a local agent prevents delays due to lack of rapid communication with a distant principal.

Additional items that may be included in the collection order are terms concerning who will pay costs, conditions to be met for release of documents, methods of transferring payment, procedures to be employed in case of nonpayment, and protection of goods against loss. It is vital that the collection order contain instructions regarding the conditions necessary for the release of the documents to the buyer. The order, as well as the documents, will eithre be sent directly to the presenting bank or through an intermediary collecting bank. However, the principal assumes the risk of using an intermediary bank. For this reason the seller should obtain the services of a local agent to handle problems such as delays if the need arises. It should be noted that instructions regarding interest costs and expenses incurred must specifically mention that such payment obligations of the drawee may not be waived, if this is desired by the seller. Otherwise, such charges may be waived and documents released even if the buyer refuses to pay them. Furthermore, such details as the rate and period of time during which interest is incurred must be included. If such collection charges and expenses are waived, they are then charged to the account of the principal. Finally, if the seller wishes to be immediately advised regarding events occurring during the collection, such as nonacceptance of the draft by the buyer, instructions regarding form of advice must also be given. Another important option is provision for protest.

Protest

Frequently, the protest procedure or formal demand for payment is a legal prerequisite to suit in foreign jurisdictions for nonpayment of an accepted draft or bill of exchange. The presenting bank, on behalf of the principal, will arrange for the necessary notification form to be completed. It requires that a local notary public substantiate the presentation of the accepted instrument for payment and refusal of payment by the drawee. Thereafter, the notary public will notarize the required documentation establishing nonpayment of the accepted draft. When submitted to the proper authorities, this official protest satisfies the formal prerequisite to suit for payment on the accepted instrument. In the case of the buyer's refusal to accept the draft, a suit for breach of contract is the most likely legal remedy.

Presentation

Once the presenting bank is in possession of the collection order, drafts, and/or documents, presentation will be made to the buyer as drawee. Therefore, the bank notifies the buyer of the arrival of the draft and documents.

The bank is required to make presentation for payment without delay if the documents (including drafts) are payable on sight. Presentation for acceptance must also be made without delay and before the specified maturity date. Advice of nonpayment or nonacceptance may be called for if difficulties arise.

The draft will be presented to the buyer as drawee. The drawee only has the right to examine the collection documents held by the bank; that' is, actual delivery of the documents to the buyer may occur only after the buyer has satisfied the seller's conditions. Nevertheless, at the risk of the collecting bank, it is possible for the drawee to obtain documents in trust for inspection off bank premises. Naturally, the release of documents in trust implies that the buyer may not use the documents before payment. For this reason responsibility for loss remains with the bank if documents are released before the stipulated payment or acceptance.

Assuming that the buyer finds the documents in order, the accompanying draft will be paid at sight if a D/P collection was stipulated. In the case of a D/A collection, the buyer will "accept" the draft when presented. It is the duty of the presenting bank to verify that the form of the acceptance appears to be complete and correct. However, as previously discussed, no responsibility is assumed for the genuineness of the signature or the authority of the party signing such an acceptance. When a time draft requiring acceptance is used, the instrument serves as a short-term extension of credit, which facilitates international trade. Once it appears that the buyer has fulfilled the conditions of the collection order, the bank will release the documents or goods as the case may be. The drawee is entitled to receive documents in the form in which they are received by the bank.

In the case of dishonor of the presented draft or other difficulties, it is prudent practice to report the circumstances to the seller for decision. In that way, the bank will avoid liability incurred by reason of having acted on its own initiative. This assumes, of course, that instructions covering the particular situation were not included in the collection order.

Payment

The currency of payment is an important factor to consider when international collections are being handled. Potential problems may be caused by local foreign exchange regulations and interfere with the immediate transfer of proceeds to the seller. If local currency is called for by the collection order, the presenting bank must release the documents only against payment in local currency that is immediately available for disposal according to the terms of the order. If the collection order requires payment to be made in foreign currency, the bank must only release documents against payment in that foreign currency provided it may immediately be remitted according to the terms of the collection order. Although banks in certain countries frequently release documents against a deposit of local currency equivalent to the amount of foreign currency required to be paid, this practice typically occurs only when the required foreign exchange permit has not yet been procured.

Needless to say, a long period of time may pass before the desired currency is finally remitted to the seller.

Assuming that permits for the transfer of funds are not required, the presenting bank transfers the amount collected to the remitting bank, which in turn credits the account of the principal for the amount collected, less costs and expenses. Other methods of payment include certified check, cashier's check, and bank drafts. In the case of a D/A collection, the bank will follow the customer's order and typically will: either return the accepted draft to the remitting bank for forwarding to the principal or hold the accepted draft in trust until maturity and transfer the proceeds to the remitting bank once the amount has been collected from the buyer. Alternatively, the seller may make arrangements with the bank for a provisional credit to be established for the collection amount or a portion thereof. In addition, the seller may arrange financing for goods by discounting the documentary draft before maturity with the bank. However, such amounts will be added to the account of the seller in case of dishonor of the draft by the buyer. Purchasers of the draft possess the right to payment as well as a security interest in the underlying transaction. As mentioned earlier, however, the same rights that could permit a sale of the underlying goods in case of nonpayment would not accrue to a bank serving merely as agent. A question concerning the right of resale exists where an extension of credit is involved. Because no active market exists in trade acceptances, discounting is normally done on a "with recourse" basis.

Partial Payment

A situation may arise where the buyer wishes to make partial payment of his obligation. The URC specifies that partial payment may not be accepted as a condition for release of documents unless authorized by the principal. Consequently, in the case of documentary collections, the presenting bank may release documents only against full payment. Unless authorized, partial payment need not be accepted. If partial payment is acceptable, any amounts collected are to be promptly made available to the bank from which the collection order was received.

Thereafter, all proceeds of payment are remitted to the seller's bank (the remitting bank) for forwarding to the principal. An advice of payment including the details of the collection will be sent by the collecting bank to the bank from which the order was received. Thus, the seller will be able to dispose of the sales proceeds after payment has been made by the buyer. Despite the fact that collections might involve a longer time factor, overall costs are usually lower than those incurred in the establishment of a letter of credit. Additional factors, such as the buyer's financial integrity and the political climate of the countries involved, also influence the choice of payment methods.

Conclusion

Banks occupy an important role in the orderly collection of international payment obligations. They greatly facilitate transactions covering great distances by providing a measure of security over documents and/or goods.

Bibliography

American Bankers Association, Credit Policy Committee. *A Banker's Guide to Financing Exports.* New York: American Bankers Association, 1966.

Beckman, Theodore and Ronald Foster. *Credits and Collections, Management and Theory,* 8th ed. New York: McGraw-Hill, 1969.

Clark, Barkley and Alphonse Squillante. *The Law of Bank Deposits, Collections and Credit Cards.* Boston, Massachusetts: Warren, Gorham & Lamont, 1970.

Clarke, John, Bailey, Henry, and Robert Young. *Bank Deposits and Collections,* 4th ed. Philadelphia, Pennsylvania: Joint Committee on Continuing Legal Education of the American Law Institute and the ABA, 1972.

"Export Financing Part I—Documentary Credits." *Credit Suisse,* 47 1(1978).

International Chamber of Commerce. *Uniform Rules for Collection.* Brochure No. 322. New York: U.S. Council of the International Chamber of Commerce, 1979.

Kammert, James. *International Commercial Banking Management.* Am. Mgmt, 1981.

Meznerics, Ivan. *International Payments: With Special Regard to Monetary Systems.* Alphen aan den Rijn, The Netherlands: Sitjhoff and Noordhoff, 1979.

Meznerics, Ivan. *Law of Banking in East-West Trade.* Leiden, Sijthoff; Dobbs Ferry, New York: Oceana, 1973.

Murphy, John C. *The International Monetary System: Beyond the First Stage of Reform.* Washington, D.C.: American Enterprise Institute for Public Policy Research, 1979.

Oppenheim, Peter. *International Banking,* 3rd rev. ed. Washington, D.C.: American Bankers Association, 1979.

Uniform Commercial Code, Art. 4. 1978 version.

6

Checks

Checks, drafts, and money orders are an integral part of the payment mechanism in use both in the United States and around the world. Numerous resource books are available that present a detailed technical analysis of the Uniform Commercial Code and its application to questions concerning negotiable instruments. Thus, the aim of this chapter is to examine the basic functional characteristics of various types of checks and to illustrate the problems frequently encountered with their use.

Initially, a distinction should be made between a check and a note. A *note* is a two-party instrument by which the maker of the note promises to pay a specific sum of money on demand, or on a definite future date, to a named payee. A *check,* on the other hand, is a three-party instrument drawn on a payor bank (the drawee) by its customer (the drawer) ordering a specific sum to be paid to a payee.

The fact that the check is drawn on a bank distinguishes it from an ordinary draft. A *draft* is an instrument whereby the drawer orders the drawee to pay a specified sum of money on the indicated date or on demand to the order of a payee. Therefore, checks are simply a specialized form of draft drawn on a bank, which are payable upon demand unless postdated. In effect, the check represents the drawer's instructions to the bank to pay money held in the drawer's account to the specified third party. If drawn in conformity with statutory requirements, particularly Article 3 of the Uniform Commercial Code, the check may also be a negotiable instrument. As will be seen, only a valid authorization for payment makes a check properly payable.

Two basic types of checks are used commercially: personal checks, which include checks drawn by business and other establishments, and bank checks. The most important distinction between personal and bank checks is the identity of the party having primary responsibility for payment of the check. In the case of a bank check, the bank is primarily liable as the drawer thereof, whereas in the case of a personal check, the bank typically serves merely as drawee without assuming primary liability for payment of the instrument. Liability for a personal check may be shifted onto the bank as regards third parties through the procedure of *certification*.

The following section defines and describes the various types of bank checks most frequently encountered in commercial use.

Certified checks and cashier's checks are the most commonly used forms of bank checks. Other types of bank checks include those issued by savings and loan associations, teller's checks, and travelers checks. Due to their widespread use, Eurocheques and bank and personal money orders will also be mentioned.

Certified Checks

When a check is presented and *certified* by the drawee bank, three important factors are established. First, the bank certifies that the signature of the drawer is genuine, thus precluding a subsequent refusal of payment by a bank claiming forgery of the drawer's signature. Note, however, that the genuineness of any other endorsement, such as that of the payee, is not being certified. Consequences resulting from improper payment on a forged endorsement will later be examined. Second, certification establishes that funds sufficient for payment of the check are in the drawer's account. This is accomplished through segregation from the drawer's account of an amount adequate for payment of the certified check, thus removing it from his control. Third, and perhaps of most significance, is the fact that certification of a check constitutes an acceptance by the bank. By accepting the check without actually paying for it at that time, the bank converts the check into its own primary obligation, enforceable by the payee.

The certification must be in writing (which is typically in the form of a rubber stamp) and signed by an authorized officer of the certifying bank. Furthermore, certification does not become effective until the issuance and delivery of the check (or notification) to the payee or to the beneficiary. Once effective, certification legally binds the bank to pay the check to the individual rightfully entitled to the funds. There is no obligation on the part of a bank to certify a check, however.

Regarding the drawer's liability to third parties, certification at the request of the drawer does not discharge the drawer from liability; rather, the certifying bank becomes liable for payment along with the drawer. As between the bank and the drawer, however, certification has the same effect as payment since the funds are effectively removed from the drawer's control. Finally, if a payee or holder of a check has it certified rather than receiving cash in payment, the drawer and all prior endorsers of the check are discharged from liability.

Overall, one of the most attractive features of certification is the added assurance of payment brought by the bank's assumption of the payment obligation. This feature accounts for its wide acceptability by payees. The drawee bank will be liable to a bona fide holder (known as a *holder in due course*) of a check it has certified regardless of the state of the drawer's account.

A party who takes an instrument by negotiation in good faith, for value and without notice of any defense or claims against it, or that it is overdue or has been dishonored, is known as a holder in due course. The holder in due course acquires good title to the instrument, free from all claims and defenses except those known as *real defenses*.

This does not mean, however, that by certifying a check the bank admits that the holder of the instrument is a holder in due course. Nevertheless, it is possible for a bank to revoke a certification it has made by mistake if the rights of others have not intervened and the holder of the certified check has not acted in reliance on the bank's certification (or, in the vernacular, "changed his position"). It should be understood that, unlike an ordinary check, the ability to stop payment of a bank check or to revoke certification is quite limited.

In summary, certification indicates that: the check is drawn on sufficient funds in the hands of the drawee bank; these funds have been set aside for the satisfaction of the check; and that the funds will be paid to a holder entitled to the funds when the check is presented for payment since certification constitutes an acceptance by the drawee bank. Because the customer's account is charged for the amount of the check when it is certified, the bank is obliged to make proper payment even when it is presented for payment more than six months after its date. This differs from the general rule governing ordinary checks whereby the drawee bank is under no obligation to pay a check that is considered "stale" (that is, one that is presented for payment more than six months after its date).

Cashier's Checks

Cashier's checks are one of the most frequently encountered forms of bank checks. A *cashier's check* is a draft or bill of exchange that is drawn by the bank on itself and that is issued by an authorized officer or employee of the institution. Thus, a cashier's check differs significantly from an ordinary check drawn by a customer on an account, as well as from an ordinary bank or banker's check. The banker's check is a draft drawn by one bank upon another bank. For this reason, the banker's check is subject to the general rules governing ordinary checks including those permitting stop-payment orders.

Regarding the use of the terms "draft" and "bill of exchange," note that these terms are used interchangeably to signify the same type of instrument. The term "bill of exchange," however, is encountered more frequently when reference is made to international rather than domestic drafts. In addition, one may find that the term "bill of exchange" sometimes includes reference to orders, checks, drafts, and trade acceptances.

When the bank issues a cashier's check, a direct payment obligation is created. Furthermore, this obligation is said to be accepted by the mere issuance of the cashier's check. The bank has an independent and direct obligation to the holder to honor the instrument.

One who takes a cashier's check in good faith and for valuable consideration holds good title to the instrument. Nothing short of actual notice that the instrument is defective (that is, stolen, lost, or forged endorsement) will defeat a holder of a cashier's check. If circumstances indicate that the holder or payee of a cashier's check has acted in bad faith in procuring the instrument, the issuing bank may be able to assert a defense against payment such as lack of consideration given for the cashier's check. However, once the check is delivered to the payee, it is assumed that it was issued for value and enforceable. Therefore, with extremely limited exceptions, the purchaser of a cashier's check may not have the bank cancel the check if a valid delivery thereof has already been made. The fact that a valid cashier's check is not subject to countermand is the main reason for its acceptability. Under the Uniform Commercial Code, a customer may stop payment only on an "item payable for his account." Consequently, the purchaser of a cashier's check cannot order payment to be stopped because such checks are for the account of the drawer bank rather than for the account of the purchaser/remitter. As mentioned earlier, this differs from the ordinary bank check upon which payment may be stopped since, unlike a cashier's check, it is not accepted by the mere act of issuance.

A savings and loan association may also issue its own checks drawn on itself. Such an instrument is substantively the same as a cashier's check, in that, once issued, the transaction is complete and not subject to cancellation.

Teller's Checks

Instruments drawn by savings banks and savings and loan associations on commercial banks are known as *teller's checks*. In effect, the institution draws a check on its account held at a commercial bank. Such a check is not issued by the commercial bank as in the case of a cashier's check. For this reason, the act of issuing such a check does not in itself constitute acceptance of a primary payment obligation. Although courts are in disagreement on this point, several instances have occurred where a stop payment order was effectively placed by the drawer institution, making such a check resemble a personal check rather than bank check in this regard. However, as in the case of a cashier's check, the purchaser of a teller's check ordinarily cannot order payment to be stopped because, under the Uniform Commercial Code, a customer may stop payment only on an "item payable for his account." A teller's check is for the account of the drawer bank and not for the account of the purchaser/remitter.

Traveler's Checks

Traveler's checks are instruments having the features of a cash substitute, which offers the security of a cashier's check. In fact, when issued by a bank, traveler's checks are essentially equivalent to cashier's checks once a proper endorsement in the form of a countersignature is placed upon the instrument. The check form typically provides a space for the signature of the purchaser, which is used for comparison with the countersignature at the time of payment. Thus, the countersignature requirement provides security against loss or theft subsequent to the purchase of the instrument since the check is properly payable only if a valid countersignature is placed on the instrument at the time of payment.

Money Orders

A money order is an instrument calling for the payment of money to a named payee or to bearer; generally, it provides a safe and convenient means of remitting funds for persons not having checking accounts.

Bank money orders are issued by banks and, like cashier's checks, are obligations of the issuing bank. It evidences the fact that the payee may demand and receive the amount stated on the face of the instrument upon endorsement and presentation to the bank. They must contain the signature of an officer or employee of the issuing institution. Such instruments are paid from the bank's funds, and liability for payment rests solely on the issuing bank.

Similar to ordinary checks and bank money orders in form, personal money orders are most frequently viewed as ordinary check obligations because, while they are purchased for an amount deposited with the bank, they are usually issued without an authorized signature of a bank officer. In addition, they are often issued with unfilled blanks for the name of the payee, the date and the signature of the purchaser. Only the name of the drawee bank and the amount are filled in at the time of the personal money order's issuance. Personal money orders are not viewed as bank obligations since they are not signed by authorized representatives of the bank. Furthermore, payment may be stopped by the purchaser if the money order is lost, even if in an uncompleted form. This includes loss of an instrument without a payee's name. Due to their resemblance to an official bank check, one should be aware of the fact that personal money orders are subject to the same exposures as ordinary checks.

Eurocheques

The Eurocheque is a blank check issued in a uniform format and color by any of the member banks of the ten European countries that formed the Eurocheque system. Despite their official appearance, the Eurocheque is like an ordinary check even when cashed with what is called the Eurocheque Guarantee Card. The Eurocheque guarantee of payment extends only to European countries and to some North African countries bordering on the Mediterranean Sea. Therefore, a Eurocheque should be treated like an ordinary check since the guarantee does not extend to the United States.

Foreign Checks

Laws governing checks in most foreign countries are more stringent and give greater protection to the acceptor of checks than those in the United States. For example, various countries (particularly in Latin America) require checks to be deposited and cashed fairly promptly in order to prevent the checks from losing certain characteristics. After a certain amount of time, checks are treated like ordinary instruments without the protections afforded by the stringent laws governing the proper issuance of checks. These protections will vary depending upon the particular legal system involved.

All Checks Are Risky

Whether a cashier's check, a certified check, or a personal check is used, all checks carry certain risks regardless of their classification. For example, even a certified check or a cashier's check can be stolen, counterfeit, or altered, or it can contain forged signatures. Therefore, all instruments require careful examination before they are paid despite the fact that some are less risky than others. A few preliminary inquiries as to whether or not the instrument is valid can prevent unnecessary financial loss. In particular, a certified check endorsed to a third party may be an indication that the instrument was lost or stolen and the endorsement forged. Therefore, as a general matter, all third-party checks should be handled with extreme care. It will be useful to examine the major problems encountered with the use of checks, namely, forgery, alteration, and counterfeiting.

Forgery

Forgery consists of falsifying or altering an instrument, with fraudulent intent, in such a way that, if it were genuine, would make the instrument legally effective. Forged checks may be classified into two basic categories: those where the signature of the maker has been forged, and those where the endorser's signature has been forged.

Since the bank must be authorized by the drawer to make payment on a check, checks paid on a forged drawer's signature are not properly payable. Because the bank is charged with knowing the signature of its customer/drawer, it must bear any loss resulting from improper payment. The bank is not permitted to charge the drawer's account for the sum paid since the drawer's signature is a nullity and of no effect. A bank paying a check bearing a forged drawer's signature is required to recredit the drawer's account. If final payment is made on a forged check, the bank cannot recover the funds paid to a holder in due course or from a party who in good faith acts in reliance on the payment. This is known as the *finality of payment rule*. However, this rule does not apply if the check is presented with knowledge of the forgery since actual knowledge both defeats the holder in due course status and constitutes a breach of the presentment warranty. Note, furthermore, that the Uniform Commercial Code is ambiguous with regard to whether the finality doctrine may only be claimed by a holder in due course or by a party who changed his position in reliance on final payment.

The loss of benefits resulting from accepting a forged signature obliges the drawee bank to verify the drawer's signature with the signature card prepared for that purpose. With regard to certified checks upon which the drawer's signature has been forged, the same principle applies, that is, the amount paid by the drawee bank may not be recovered from the drawer's account. However, an important distinction is made for holders of the instrument. When a certified check has a drawer's signature that was forged prior to certification, the holder thereof possesses the obligation of the drawee bank to pay the amount of the check as accepted through its certification. Therefore, unless a stop payment procedure or injunction has been successfully procured, the drawee bank would suffer the loss incurred and be obliged to honor its payment commitment. Once again, the bank is charged with verifying the signature of its customer/drawer prior to accepting the payment obligation through certification of the check, which includes a guarantee that the drawer's signature is valid for payment purposes. The duty to verify the drawer's signature exists whether the signature is handwritten or a facsimile, such as printed signatures used for payroll checks.

The second type of forgery frequently encountered is forgery of the payee's endorsement. As with the forgery of a drawer's signature, a forged endorsement prevents the check from being properly payable. Consequently, as a general rule, the drawee or payor bank will be precluded from charging the check against the drawer's account.

A certified or cashier's check may also contain a forged endorsement. The general rule is that a bank is obliged to make payment only when the check is properly endorsed at the time it is presented for payment. It is incumbent upon the institution to verify the authenticity of endorsements prior to payment in order to avoid loss. It should be realized, however, that, in order for an assessment of liability to be made against the drawee bank, the drawer must show injury due to the improper payment. For example, if it can be shown that payment in fact properly reached the intended payee despite a forged endorsement, no damages were incurred as a result from the improper payment.

Only under circumstances involving negligence on the part of the drawer and an absence of negligence by the drawee bank will the bank be able to assert a defense against liability for payment on either a forged drawer's or payee's endorsement. Examples include failure to examine statements or report forgeries which may result in a denial or limitation of recovery from the drawee bank. However, if the bank itself was negligent, it may be precluded from asserting such a defense against payment.

If the bank debits the client's account and subsequently it is proven that an endorsement was forged, the bank must recredit the drawer's account and claim the amount involved from the unauthorized endorser, since that signature is enforceable only against the actual endorser. Thus, when a check contains a forged endorsement, the loss is passed along to the party who first took the forged instrument based on a warranty theory. Needless to say, since the identity of the forger is usually unknown, the bank typically bears the loss in such a situation. Finally, as between the party accepting a check with a forged payee's endorsement and the final holder, there is no right to enforce payment against the drawer.

Finally, the operation of the finality of payment rule differs when a forged payee's endorsement is established. That is, without a proper payee's endorsement, no transfer of an instrument occurs. This means that the party in possession is not a holder protected by the rule and is not entitled to payment.

Imposter Rule

The ordinary consequences of paying a check with a forged endorsement are altered in situations covered by the so-called *imposter rule*. The Uniform Commercial Code shifts the burden of loss from the drawee bank to the drawer where an imposter payee obtains payment on a check. When a maker or a drawer is induced to issue a check in the name of the imposter payee or where a person signing as (or on behalf of) the drawer intends for the payee not to have an interest in the instrument, the drawer bears the loss. Under these circumstances, the bank is relieved of liability for improper payment since the drawer is charged with knowing whether or not the transaction for which he issues a check is authentic. Thus, if an imposter pretends to be a certain payee and fraudulently induces a drawer to issue a check to him, the drawer cannot claim that payment was improperly made by the drawee bank because of that fraud. The imposter rule shifts the loss onto the drawer in such a situation. Furthermore, the imposter's endorsement is not classified as a forgery so as to relieve the drawee bank of the consequences of improper payment of a forged instrument.

Alteration

Problems are also frequently encountered when an instrument that is negotiated or presented for payment has been altered from the form in which it was originally issued by the drawer. Examples include raising or lowering the amount of the check, changing the name of the payee or of the drawee bank, or filling in an incomplete instrument without authorization. However, any unauthorized change in the writing is an alteration. Additional factors, such as whether the party seeking payment is a holder in due course and whether the alteration was material or made with a fraudulent intent, will have an effect upon the liability of the parties to the instrument including the drawee bank that makes payment on the instrument as altered.

An alteration is material if it changes the contract of any party thereto in any respect. A material alteration will render the instrument void, except against a holder in due course, in any amount above its original tenor. That is, the drawee bank may only charge the drawer's account for the amount of the check as originally drawn. However, if the check has been materially altered by a holder with fraudulent intent, any party whose contract is thereby changed is discharged from the payment obligation, unless they asserted or are precluded from asserting, that the instrument was altered. Once again, a subsequent holder in due course may still enforce the check in the form and for the amount originally drawn with the option of enforcing it as altered if it was altered by completion. This allows the drawee bank to charge the drawer's account for the original amount. If there is a discrepancy between the amount payable as shown in figures and as written out, the words control figures unless the words are ambiguous.

If it is found that the alteration is not material or is not made for a fraudulent purpose, then the parties are not discharged and the instrument may be enforced according to its original tenor. The bank is only authorized to pay in accordance with the order originally given by the drawer with the exception of payment to a holder in due course who may enforce payment of an incomplete instrument as it has been completed. Therefore, holder in due course status (such as, in this instance, no notice of alteration) must be established if an altered instrument is to be properly payable.

As in the case of forgery, the drawer may be prevented from avoiding an altered check if the party seeking payment asserts that the drawer's negligence substantially contributed to the alteration of the check or that there was an unreasonable delay in discovering or giving notice of the alteration. The drawee bank, however, must have paid the instrument in good faith to be protected under such circumstances. Thus, a bank that pays an instrument bearing obvious evidence of alteration cannot alleviate its own negligent conduct with that of the negligent drawer. It is therefore important to carefully examine all items prior to payment.

A risk of loss due to alteration of the instrument is also assumed whenever a drawee bank issues a cashier's check or certifies a check that turns out to have been altered. In particular, since certification constitutes acceptance of the payment obligation, the bank is liable for payment in cases where the check has been altered prior to certification. Barring application of the exception for holders in due course or the raising of the negligence defense, the bank may only charge the drawer to the extent of the original tenor of the check. The drawee bank may normally seek the full amount paid or at least the additional amount, from the party improperly paid due to the alteration; however, such recovery is not possible from a holder in due course.

If the alteration occurs subsequent to certification, the bank is liable for payment only according to the original tenor of the instrument as certified. In the case of an improper payment of a subsequently altered certified check, the usual consequences discussed above would apply. The results of payment of a cashier's check are even more clear-cut, as the bank is charged with responsibility for verifying the authenticity of its own obligation. Since cashier's checks, like all checks, can be altered, forged, or completely counterfeit, the party accepting a cashier's check should ensure that it is valid and payable as presented. This includes ascertaining that no stop-payment orders are in effect for the check since payment or even cashier's or certified checks may be stopped in certain instances.

Stop Payment

The availability of a stop-payment order on a check, which will effectively prevent its payment, varies according to several factors. These include: the type of check (that is, ordinary versus bank check), the identity of the party seeking to stop payment (that is, drawer versus payee); the reason for stopping payment and the time the stop payment order is received by the bank (that is, prior versus subsequent to final payment or acceptance).

The effect of a stop-payment order is to cancel the authority and obligation of the bank to pay the check of the drawer. It is a revocation of the drawer's order. In general, a drawer has an absolute right to stop payment of personal checks, but the order must be timely made. Difficulties arise, however, in the case of a certified or cashier's check due to the effect of the bank's acceptance of the payment obligation. The circumstances under which payment of a bank check may be stopped are quite limited; indeed, the circumstances are so limited that it is generally asserted that payment of a cashier's or certified check may not be stopped, although exceptions may be found in instances involving fraud or illegality. Even if an effective stop payment order is made, its actual effect upon the liability of the drawer to third parties may be curtailed. The stop payment order directly affects only the customer's relationship with his bank. Consequently, the drawer will remain liable to a holder in due course on the underlying obligation whereas a payee or subsequent holders may consider the check to be dishonored when a stop payment order is in effect.

The consequence to the drawee bank of a failure to comply with a valid stop-payment order is liability for any loss actually resulting from payment of the check (rather than liability for the face amount of the check). Therefore, if a valid stop-payment order is violated, the bank pays at its own risk and will not be permitted to charge the drawer's account for the amount of the check. On the other hand, the bank that seeks to protect itself against the effects of an executed stop-payment order may require an indemnity bond from the party stopping payment.

The distinction between stop-payment orders affecting domestic drafts and those affecting foreign drafts is significant. Unlike instruments drawn on domestic institutions, foreign drafts present a radically different picture. For example, in Europe there is no uniform banking procedure with respect to the placement of stop-payment orders. Rather, practices and policies differ from bank to bank. With few exceptions, the protection provided by domestic stop-payment procedures is nonexistent in Europe. Therefore, customers who purchase instruments drawn on foreign banks should be aware that it may be difficult or impossible to stop payment on the instrument. Generally, foreign banks that accept stop-payment orders often will do so only after a certain period of time after issuance (such as, 60 to 120 days) or in certain cases where the instrument was lost or stolen. Furthermore, one should be aware of the fact that foreign banks normally will not accept responsibility if the instrument is inadvertently paid despite the entry of a valid stop-payment order.

Generally, the right to stop payment is vested in the drawer to the exclusion of a payee or subsequent holder. However, this right may be limited further where the drawer of the check is also the drawee, by preventing the drawer/payee from stopping payment. Although it may also occur that the payee or holder may attempt to stop payment, such as where the check is lost or stolen, normally the bank will seek instructions from the drawer of the instrument, since only the customer having that account may issue stop-payment orders. In addition, upon death or incompetence of the drawer, a person claiming an interest in an account may seek to stop payment of a check drawn on the customer's account. Examples include surviving relatives and creditors of a drawer's estate. Any order received must give a complete and accurate description of the check to enable the bank to correctly identify the item on which payment is to be stopped. Failure to give an accurate description may relieve the bank of liability if payment is in fact not stopped as requested. In this instance, liability becomes a triable issue of fact. Finally, if permitted by any applicable state law, oral stop-payment orders will be effective for a limited time (usually fourteen days unless confirmed in writing) whereas written orders are effective for six months unless renewed.

The reason for stopping payment and the timing of the order are major factors to be considered when a stop-payment order is sought for a bank check. As mentioned earlier, the general rule prevents a party from stopping payment of either a cashier's or a certified check. Nevertheless, courts have recognized limited exceptions to this general prohibition.

Underlying this prohibition is a basic policy of the Uniform Commercial Code, that acceptance, as well as payment, is final in favor of a holder in due course, or a person who has in good faith changed his position in reliance of the payment. For example, when a holder in due course is involved, a drawer's insolvency or breach of contract are insufficient reasons for revoking payment. Similarly, payment by mistake or negligence will not be recovered, and the drawee will remain liable for payment from its own funds. In contrast, when a check is certified by mistake, it may be possible for the bank to revoke the certification if the holder has not changed his position in reliance on the certification and no rights or other parties have intervened. After valid issuance of a bank check, if it is shown that no value has been given by the holder or if the holder either takes the instrument in bad faith, or with notice of the defective character of the check, then holder in due course status cannot be established and the finality of payment or acceptance rule is inoperative.

As the preceding illustrates, the reason for which the stop-payment order is sought becomes important in the case of a bank check. If the check is not in the hands of a holder in due course or a party who in good faith changed his position in reliance on the bank's acceptance, an effective stop-payment order may be possible. This occurs, for example, when a cashier's check has not been properly endorsed. When a cashier's or a certified check is lost by the payee prior to endorsement, a stop-order payment will be effective since no proper endorsement is thereafter possible, precluding holder in due course status. Stop-payment orders may be obtained when the bank check was given for illegal consideration. Similarly, if there has been a failure of consideration, the issuing bank may resist payment if the instrument is in the hands of one who does not qualify as a holder in due course.

The bank's position in these instances is a tenuous one. Unless the allegation amounts to a claim of fraud or illegality, the bank accepts the stop-payment order in its own risk; that is, stopping payment without sufficient justification will expose the bank to liability toward the holder seeking payment. Conversely, payment in violation of a valid stop-payment order may subject the bank to suit by the drawer. The Uniform Commercial Code does provide for the drawee bank to be subrogated to the rights and defenses of the payee or other holder of the instrument if it pays in such a situation. For example, if a stop-payment order is placed against a holder in due course, the drawee bank will normally be subrogated to the rights of the holder in due course as against the drawer of the bank is sued for making payment against the drawer's wishes. However, if it turns out that no valid defenses are available, the loss incurred due to payment over a valid stop-payment order falls on the bank. Furthermore, if a suit is brought against the bank solely on its acceptor's liability (or in the case of a bank check, on its drawer's liability), the bank may not be able to raise defenses available to its customer.

Regarding the timing of stop-payment orders, it is less difficult to stop payment of a bank check before the transaction is complete. The cashier's check transaction is considered complete once it has been issued by the drawee bank and delivered to the payee. Thus, a stop-payment order will be most effective before the instrument has been delivered to the payee, since the rights of a holder in due course or third party have not yet arisen. Otherwise, the general principles outlined regarding stop-payment orders are applicable.

In summary, there are certain instances in which payment of even bank checks may be stopped, though these are limited to situations involving fraud or illegality, which defeat the holder in due course status of the party seeking payment. Otherwise, the generally accepted rule is that payment on a bank check may not be stopped once the transaction is complete if it is held by a party who has changed his position in reliance on the bank's acceptance or by a holder in due course.

Conclusion

This chapter has illustrated the major features that differentiate several types of checks and money orders used to effectuate domestic and foreign payments.

Depending upon the type of instrument utilized, the parties to the instrument may be able to provide a larger degree of security than is offered by an ordinary check. Nevertheless, certain problems and risks are frequently encountered with the use of all drafts and notes, such as those arising from forgery and alteration of the instrument. This overview hopefully provides a guideline to the presence of such risks, as well as to the basic rights and obligations of the parties involved in such transactions.

Bibliography

Bailey, H. *Brady on Bank Checks*, 5th ed. Boston, Massachusetts: Warren, Gorham & Lamont, 1979.

Clark, Barkley. *The Law of Bank Deposits, Collections and Credit Cards*, rev. ed. Boston, Massachusetts: Warren, Gorham & Lamont, 1981.

Hart, Frederick and William Willier. *Commercial Paper Under the Uniform Commercial Code*. New York: Matthew Bender, 1972.

Leary, Fairfax, Jr. *Banking Problems Under the U.C.C.* New York: Practising Law Institute, 1979.

Mandell, Sidney. *Laws Governing Banks and Their Customers.* Dobbs Ferry, New York: Oceana Publications, 1975.

Reitman, J. and H. Weisblatt. *Banking Law.* New York: Matthew Bender, 1981.

Uniform Commercial Code, Art. 3. 1978 version.

Wallach, G. "Negotiable Instruments: The Bank Customer's Ability to Prevent Payments on Various Forms of Checks." *Ind. L. Rev.,* 11(1978), pp. 579–99.

7

Foreign Exchange

For centuries, people around the world have been exchanging, lending, and borrowing money. However, foreign exchange trading in its present form has developed in only the last hundred years. This transformation is due in large part to the important role that effective communication plays in modern foreign exchange trading. The link of modern communications has produced a worldwide market where 24-hours-per-day trading is available.

Despite these recent developments, the words "foreign exchange" still represent something complex and mysterious to most people. One of the major aims of this chapter will be to dispel these impressions by explaining the transactions encountered in various areas of the foreign exchange industry.

The foreign exchange industry encompasses transactions taking a variety of forms. For example, when speaking of foreign exchange, one may consider trading in physical foreign banknotes. When there is a need for specific foreign paper money and coins, as when one desires to exchange foreign paper money and coins for United States (or other) currency, this particular type of transaction will be used. A physical exchange of currencies will occur at a specific rate of exchange. Currency exchange rates, however, seldom remain stable, but reflect market fluctuations caused by economic, political, and market factors. Market participants should be aware of the distinction between "hard" and "soft" currencies in terms of pricing practices. Since readily convertible or "hard" currencies are most frequently used in commercial transactions, a ready market based on supply and demand pricing exists. In the case of "soft" currencies, however, governmental restrictions on trade and pricing create a double-tiered situation. Namely, an official rate of exchange is frequently sought to be enforced while outside market pricing also exists. Therefore, a much less liquid market exists in the case of soft currencies. Furthermore, a variety of factors, including handling expenses (transportation and insurance costs on what are usually smaller transactions), tend to make trading in physical currencies, especially coins, more costly than other alternatives. However, the practical convenience and need to possess physical currency usually outweighs the cost factor for individuals such as travelers. These handling expenses also account for the differences in the price of buying and selling a certain currency encountered between various establishments. In addition to the buying and selling rates quoted to tourists (so-called "over-the-counter" rates), banks also have their own "interbank" exchange rates for use when dealing with each other or with specialized foreign exchange firms. However, as noted, all rates have the characteristic of rapid and sometimes wide fluctuations.

International banks and banks having an international division are sources of another important form of foreign exchange. These departments usually do not deal in foreign banknotes. Instead, transactions occur through *telegraphic transfers*, known as *TTs*.

When a telegraphic transfer is made for purposes of buying or selling foreign exchange for spot (as opposed to future) delivery, no more than 48 hours may pass before transfer of credit from one account to the other party's account. Any delay in the TT normally subjects the party to a penalty.

Major international institutions traditionally handle large transactions for customers buying and selling foreign exchange. Commercial banks hold foreign exchange inventories in the form of working balances or have access to them at other banks through their correspondent relationships. Often, accounts are established in a variety of foreign currencies in overseas branches or with other banks. These accounts are called *nostro* or *due from* accounts.

The transfer of ownership to the funds being traded is fundamental to any foreign exchange transaction. When checks, foreign drafts, and airmail remittances are used for a transfer between U.S. dollar and foreign currencies, uncertainty regarding the value date may arise. This may be avoided by a remittance (or transfer) abroad made by the order and to the debit of the party making the payment, which is accomplished by means of a cable, wire or telex message communicated to the location where it is desired that the payment be made. The use of such messages to advise payment on receipt of funds is a routine banking operation. Protective procedures, such as the use of private codes in the messages, may be employed to prevent unauthorized transfers.

The New York offices of foreign banks play an important role in the foreign exchange business. Edge Act corporations, as well as agencies, and branches of foreign banks, are regular participants in foreign exchange markets. Furthermore, since many major foreign banks have recently established a presence in New York and in other U.S. cities, they actively trade foreign exchange, particularly their "home" currency. For example, a New York branch or affiliate of a German bank will be a specialist in trading German marks, Swiss banks generally specialize in dealing in Swiss francs, Canadian banks in Canadian dollars, and so on.

International Monetary Market

In addition to the forms of foreign exchange already discussed, trading in contracts for future delivery of currency also occurs on commodity exchanges such as the International Monetary Market (IMM), which is part of the Mercantile Exchange in Chicago. Bulk lots of foreign currency may be thought of, and traded as, any other commodity, which is why such trading occurs at the IMM. The International Monetary Market in Chicago is the most important commodity exchange dealing in foreign currencies in the U.S.; while other exchanges deal in foreign currency contracts, their markets are insignificant.

Trading in seven foreign currency futures at the IMM began on May 16, 1972. Eight currencies are presently traded. These include: the British pound, Canadian dollar, Deutsche mark, Dutch guilder, French franc, Japanese yen, Mexican peso, and Swiss franc. Trading is done by open auction on the exchange floor among registered brokers who handle customer orders.

The IMM caters to individuals as well as to smaller companies without an established bank credit line. It enables individuals, corporations, or banks to deal in foreign exchange in the same way as one deals on stock or other commodity exchanges. It therefore serves the needs of those who are often unable to obtain the services and credit lines of the larger banks trading in foreign exchange. Rather than having a single contract with each other, the buyer and seller of foreign exchange each have a separate contract with the IMM after execution of the trade. The order execution process involves use of a Clearing Member Firm (or a Futures Commission Merchant), which normally requests the purchaser to put up a margin of about 10% of the order amount before execution. The client's order is then transmitted to an IMM floor broker who actually makes the bids and offers in the trading pits. Confirmation of the order is conveyed to the originating member firm which in turn notifies its client that the order was executed. Before the expiration date of the contract, the member firm will also notify its client of payment and delivery instructions. All trading in the IMM is regulated by the Commodity Futures Trading Commission or CFTC, which is an agency of the Federal government.

The IMM has experienced rapid growth in the area of foreign currency futures due to participation by a wide variety of investors including corporate treasurers, public investors, brokers, and banks. However, anyone considering trading on the IMM should realize that important procedural trading differences exist, including time of delivery, contract size standardization, and settlement procedures. These will be further explored later on. Due to their functional differences, commodity exchanges such as the IMM are outside the banking system.

This summary review of the foreign exchange industry will be discussed in detail throughout this chapter. It is important to realize that, although each area contains its own procedural differences, one characteristic underlies all varieties of trading; that is, each area involves the exchange of the currency of one country for that of another. Depending upon the type of transaction, trading in one foreign exchange area may be preferable to another. This choice from alternative means of obtaining needed foreign exchange for immediate or future delivery is very useful in international trade, which in turn is becoming an increasingly important part of the U.S. economy.

The foreign exchange market effectively connects the monetary system of one nation with those of other nations by enabling individuals to deal in a number of different national currencies. As principal money dealers, banks are becoming increasingly aware of the importance of the international character of their services.

Market Growth

Starting in the 1960s and continuing through the 1970s, more and more banks become multinational corporations, with internationalized services provided by foreign branches, subsidiaries, and joint ventures. This trend coincided with the general development of international financial markets during that period.

The foreign exchange transactions connected with international trade and investment are usually large. As mentioned earlier, the large exchange transactions are normally handled through the trading departments of banks with international divisions and processed by means of telegraphic transfers (TT) rather than by entering into an exchange of physical banknotes. Take the example of an individual who wishes to purchase English pounds for delivery to another bank for credit of an account in England. A United States bank will have a certain inventory of foreign exchange in their account, which they will sell to that individual. If the demand for foreign currency exceeds the bank's inventory,

English pounds will be purchased in the market, either from other banks or from brokers. Thereafter, assuming the individual buyer has an account with the selling bank, his account will be debited for the amount of the currency purchased equivalent to U.S. dollars. The bank will receive instructions for delivery from the buyer, which will normally include the name and location of its bank, the name of the account holder, the name of the beneficiary and the number of the account, to prevent mistakes in transfer. Delivery occurs when the purchased currency is credited to the English account and is available in England for use by the individual or his designated beneficiary.

The level of worldwide trade has increased such transactions. For example, in 1977, imports and exports totalled approximately $2 trillion, up from approximately $350 billion in 1965. More recently, the amount of daily trading on the New York interbank foreign exchange market in 1982 was estimated to approach $20–25 billion dollars per day. The level of activity in the foreign exchange markets of the United States is attributable in part to this increased growth of international trade.

Another factor in the growth of the foreign exchange markets has been the improvements in the smooth operation of foreign exchange markets. For example, computerization and international communication networks make foreign exchange transactions virtually instantaneous. Without the ability to exchange national currencies, international commerce and investment as we know it would be greatly handicapped and reduced.

Before discussing the various types of foreign exchange transactions available in greater detail, it will be useful to identify the parties involved in foreign exchange trading, and the specialized language those parties use in trading.

Foreign Exchange Brokers

A large percentage of foreign exchange trading between banks is arranged by so-called foreign exchange "brokers" acting as intermediaries in the transactions. Brokers take bids and offers for various foreign currencies and match them up when the terms are acceptable to both sides. In 1983 there were a dozen or so foreign exchange brokerage firms in New York. These firms range in size from two to four people in a smaller firm to over two hundred and fifty people in a major firm. A broker's desk may contain up to 50 telephones with direct lines to the trading rooms of the various banks with which they deal. If a bank's foreign exchange trader needs a supply of Swiss francs, for example, he calls his broker who in turn searches out the needed quantity of Swiss francs at a certain price and concludes the deal for the bank's trader. In exchange for this service, a modest fee is charged. These fees are a small fraction of 1% of the value of the trade, varying with the currency and size of the deal. For example, a broker may conclude a $1 million transaction and earn a mere $12.50 fee. *Brokerage* is the fee a bank pays a broker for a deal.

Although brokers theoretically do not act as principals for their own account, it may happen that the currency sold to a buyer does not materialize (that is, because the seller backs out of the transaction). In such a situation, if delivery is demanded by the buyer, the broker is in effect a principal and must cover his position. Note that the broker faces a risk of loss if, before his position is covered, the rate of exchange moves in a direction which increases his costs.

Foreign Exchange Dealers

In addition to dealing with brokers there is another way to enter into foreign exchange transactions. Foreign exchange dealers represent an alternative source of foreign exchange for customers unable to deal with brokers or who have requirements not satisfied by a bank. Dealers perform an important economic function by clearing international payments. They give and receive quotes for various currencies and may discover the opportunity for profit in different markets.

A dealer will normally transact business through a variety of media, including telephone, telex, cable, or written instruction. Upon receipt of an order, the dealer in turn will "quote" a purchase or sale price, as the case may be. If the offer is accepted, a deal is made. According to whether a dealer is interested in buying or selling a particular currency, more or less competitive rates will be quoted. Naturally, a difference will exist between the buying and the selling price and represents the spread of profit, which would be immediately available were that same quantity of currency to be purchased at the same rates.

Speculation, however, is incidental to the dealer's main business of changing money. Foreign exchange dealers are usually of good financial standing and have credit lines at numerous banks. Consequently, they can normally accommodate an individual lacking the necessary credit standing with a bank or one who does not wish to deal on the IMM. In addition to these customers, dealers may also accommodate individuals with unusual currency requirements. So-called unusual currencies such as the Latin American currencies are not, as a general rule, available from banks. This is because banks wish to limit their trading activities to the strong currencies of the most industrialized countries with strong economies in order to avoid excessive risk. Despite the fact that purchase from a bank of an unusual currency for future delivery may be extremely difficult or impossible, a foreign exchange dealer may be able to accommodate such a request. A dealer may specialize in a particular currency for immediate (spot) or future (forward) trading.

When held by a foreign exchange dealer, foreign currency is not a capital asset for income tax purposes. As a consequence, any gains or losses from disposition of the currencies results in either ordinary income or loss, as is the case with sales or exchanges of any "inventory" property. The calculation of this income or loss may take into account either the cost or the lower of cost or market inventory method for the foreign currency on hand. Unlike the broker, the dealer's role in the foreign exchange industry requires that positions be taken in one or more currencies. Commercial banks active in trading foreign exchange often fill the role of dealer, however, even though their usual position is that of broker. By buying more of a particular currency than can be sold, a dealer may be in a long position. Conversely, by selling more than is held in inventory, the dealer takes a short position in that currency. Movements in the price or rate of the currency will determine profit or loss when the position is closed out, that is, when sale to a customer occurs. Foreign exchange traders in commercial banks normally have an upper limit on the extent to which they may take a position in a currency. The management of the trading department determines the permissible ceiling on such limits. A position manager records completed trades and monitors the traders' positions in compliance with authorized limits. To the extent that bank traders are establishing positions within their limits, they operate as dealers by being either "short" or "long" in a particular currency. However, once the established ceiling limit is reached, the usual bank policy is to match all further trades, that is, all sales of currency must be matched by a corresponding purchase and vice versa. When trading in this fashion, the bank trader could be characterized as a broker in the traditional sense.

Foreign Exchange Traders

Traders are the individuals who perform the actual buying and selling transactions on behalf of both brokers and dealers. In the trading room, traders are normally equipped with telephone consoles and computerized screens, which display up-to-the-minute information on prices for currencies. Following minute-to-minute movements in exchange rates enables the trader to better determine which bid and ask rates to quote.

Among traders, the senior traders have the broadest responsibility for the currency traded, and for the smooth operation of the exchange market. The rates quoted by a particular institution must be formulated to be profitable as well as competitive. Consequently, only after years of experience is the trader able to formulate quotations for banks and other customers, and to arrange for the transactions necessary to balance the daily payments and receipts resulting from maturing contracts.

Arbitrage

Just as exchange quotations may vary slightly from institution to institution, rates quoted in different geographical locations may differ as a result of variations in profitability. An individual acting as an arbitrageur will take advantage of these rate differentials. For example, the exchange rates of the banks for a particular currency may be at variance with the exchange rates quoted on the IMM in Chicago. Profit in such a situation is derived from entering the most favorable position with the two markets and arbitraging them out. Naturally it calls for a great deal of awareness and speed to take advantage of the lag in rates in one of the markets. Market forces (aided by other arbitrageurs) quickly bring rates into equilibrium, and the opportunity for fractional profit margins disappears. Of course, minute rate differentials must be sufficient to allow for costs incurred so that some actual profit results.

Arbitrage of foreign exchange occurs on spot markets and on future markets (or *forward* markets as referred to in interbank transactions).

Interest rates do not come into play when arbitraging on the spot market, but they do affect the profitability of arbitrage in futures markets. Taking advantage of the interest differentials prevailing in various countries is called *interest* or *interest rate arbitrage*. For example, it may be profitable to purchase a strong currency forward at a premium, if when converted back into U.S. dollars the actual annual yield is higher than the interest rate that one could receive by merely placing the U.S. dollars in the bank. This is only possible when the stronger of two foreign currencies calls for a premium that exceeds the differentials in interest rates otherwise gained with a domestic U.S. dollar deposit. Brokerage fee costs should also be included. By recognizing the potential for a higher annual return after the exchange of the currencies takes place upon maturity of the forward contract, the arbitrageurs—whether brokers, dealers, or traders—convert the capital into the most profitable currency.

Regardless of the foreign exchange trader with whom one does business, every counterpart to an exchange transaction must be evaluated as a credit risk. Typical buyers and sellers involved in foreign exchange transactions today include multinational corporations, travel agencies, insurance and shipping companies, airlines, banks, speculators and small investors. Particularly with the large increase in world trade already mentioned, multinational corporations account for a significant proportion of the overall trading today, reflecting an increased sophistication in the use of forward contracts to hedge against potentially adverse currency investments. Furthermore, since the issuance of FASB (Financial Accounting Standards Board) Statement No. 8 of 1975, corporate financial statements prepared according to this rule have more accurately reflected the acute effects of exchange rate fluctuations.

Recently, a new rule has replaced FASB Statement No. 8 on accounting for foreign currency transactions and foreign currency for financial statement purposes. The new standard contained in FASB Statement No. 52, which is to be implemented in financial statements issued for the calendar year 1983, calls for a changed treatment of currency holdings.

Although operations of a foreign subsidiary are denominated in local currencies, the company's overall "balance sheet" profitability and financial position must be measured in the currency of the parent (that is, the U.S.) company. As a result, potential and actual gains and losses due to fluctuations in the exchange rate will be more readily apparent.

Jargon

Before proceeding to examine the major uses of foreign exchange transactions, it may be useful to briefly define some of the expressions used in trading. Some of these terms are technical and have the same meaning as when used in other areas—such as in stock trading. Other terms, however, are merely shorthand expressions used to save time in the trading process. It is for this reason that many feel dealers speak their own language. Greater awareness and insight into the foreign exchange words and phrases listed will facilitate intelligent decision making on currency transactions.

Agio. Premium paid over and above certain prices.

Arbitrage. Buying a quantity of foreign exchange (or, for that matter, securities or other commodities) in one market and simultaneously selling it in another. This technique is utilized to profit from price differences in two different geographical locations.

Arbitrageur. An individual engaged in arbitrage, whether a broker, dealer, or trader.

Ask. Price at which sales are offered for a seller's own account and risk.

Bearish. When one anticipates that a price will decline.

Bid. Price at which purchases are sought.

Broker. An intermediary who does not trade for his own account.

Bullish. When one anticipates a price will appreciate.

Buyer's option. The purchase of foreign exchange with an option enabling the buyer to determine the date of performance within certain limits.

Cable. The spot transfer rate.

Contract rate. The rate of exchange specified in a foreign exchange contract.

Conversion. The actual exchange of the currency of one country for that of another. Conversions usually pass through banking channels.

Covering a position. The purchase or sale of foreign currency to offset possible loss or profit in the event of a change in prices.

Cross rates. The exchange rate between two foreign currencies, neither of which is the U.S. dollar.

Dealer. One who (1) buys and sells foreign exchange for his own account, (2) who holds positions for his own account, and (3) who does so for resale to others in the ordinary course of his trade or business.

Depo. Deposit.

Devaluation. Government action that changes the value of a country's currency downward in terms of other currencies.

Disagio. A discount from a price.

Discount. A rate lower than the normal spot rate.

Eurocurrency. A currency placed on deposit with a bank outside the country of issuance.

Eurodollars. U.S. dollars placed on deposit with banks outside the United States.

Fixed. When the official exchange rate of a country's currency is maintained within a specified range of fluctuation by the government (contrary to floating).

Floating. When a country's central bank does not protect either upper or lower currency fluctuation limits, the exchange rate is said to be "floating." In other words, market forces determine the currency's value. When the government interferes with free market forces, this is termed "dirty" float. If the government does not interfere, this is termed "clean" float.

Forward transactions. A transaction where the value date is more than two working days after the trade date (one day for Canada and Mexico).

Full up. When the limit on trading a particular currency or with a particular customer has been met, thus preventing the trader from dealing further.

Future exchange contract. A contract between banks or between a bank, a commodity exchange, and their customers for the purchase or sale of foreign exchange at a fixed rate with delivery at a special time. Future exchange contracts are entered to preclude risks of fluctuations in rates. They are also used for speculation.

Give. Sell.

Good date. Date when banks are open in both markets.

Hedge. Purchase or sale of foreign exchange to protect an asset or liability by fixing the rate. A hedge can be either spot or forward.

Lay off (or reverse, unwind). To offset a position by selling what has been purchased and vice versa.

Limit. The upper amount or price at which one may conclude particular transactions.

Long. A credit balance in foreign currency (or dollars) having more on account than is sold. When one who owns spot or future contracts owns more of a commodity or foreign exchange or security than one has commitments to deliver.

Mine. To buy from another.

Offer. See Ask.

Open position. A purchase or sale without an offsetting transaction.

Option. See Buyer's option or seller's option. Unlike stock options, the foreign exchange must ultimately be purchased or sold by a specified date.

Pip. Refers to fractional decimal rate quotations. See Points.

Points. Fractional quotation. Though larger than pip, often mistaken for pips during trading.

Premium. A price higher than the spot rate.

Quote. The rates at which one will buy and sell.

Rate. A numerical expression of the value of one currency in terms of another at a given point in time.

Revaluation. Government action that increases the value of a country's currency in terms of other currencies.

Rollover. A forward contract renewed or extended for delivery further in the future.

Seller's option. When the seller of the foreign exchange for future delivery can pick the delivery date within certain limits.

Settlement. Payment.

Short. When one has delivery commitments without owning the currencies. A deficit position.

Spot. A purchase or sale transaction in which the value date is two working days following the trade date (except for Canada and Mexico, which are one day).

Spread. The difference between buying and selling rates at any particular time.

Swap. A purchase and sale (or sale and purchase) of a foreign currency, usually against U.S. dollars. They can be made between two dates including spot and future dates. Swaps are a method of foreign currency borrowings through a secondary currency.

Take. Buy.

Trading date. The date when a transaction is completed.

Value date. A date on which good fund settlement is made.

Yours. To sell to another.

With this review of commonly used trading jargon behind us, we may now proceed to explore the major purposes for entering into foreign exchange transactions.

Hedging

One of the principal reasons for becoming involved in foreign exchange trading is to protect investments and to prevent additional costs as a result of exchange rate fluctuations. Covering a foreign exchange exposure through a purchase with future delivery (a *forward* transaction) is known as *hedging*. To illustrate how assets are exposed to rate fluctuation, take the example of an individual who decides to invest in Canadian bonds because of an expected higher yield. If U.S. dollars were exchanged for Canadian dollars to purchase the bonds, the actual cost of the bonds at that point in time is known. Between the time that the bonds are purchased and the time they are sold or redeemed, the exchange rate between the U.S. and Canadian dollars probably will change. As a result, when the investor converts his Canadian dollars back into U.S. dollars, he may have more or less U.S. currency than at the outset. If during this time the U.S. dollar becomes "stronger" against the Canadian dollar, fewer U.S. dollars will be received upon conversion of a certain quantity of Canadian currency. The result will be a direct reduction in the profitability of the bond yield due to exchange rates when the actual U.S. dollar return is calculated. To protect against such a possible loss, which may occur upon currency conversion when the bonds mature or are sold, the investor will hedge by entering into a foreign exchange transaction.

To do this, the individual buys (or sells) a forward contract to cover his position. By selling the Canadian currency, in the form of a forward or future contract, the rate at which the two currencies will be exchanged is fixed at a specific price. Regardless of any further increases or decreases in the exchange rates, the investor will receive a fixed amount of U.S. dollars for the Canadian dollars at the determined future date. Therefore, one eliminates the risk present whenever two currencies are involved in a transaction.

A forward exchange contract is useful when a contract calls for payment in foreign currency at some future date. For example, if under an installment sale contract 1 million German marks (DM) must be paid in one year, it would be possible to buy a one-year DM forward contract from a dealer bank or broker, to fix the cost of such contract without having to accept immediate delivery. Furthermore, aside from margin requirements, payment generally is postponed until the settlement date one year later. Therefore, for a percentage of the ultimate price, the individual is assured that no additional home currency must be paid in order to acquire the required amount of foreign exchange for payment.

Through hedging, individuals and corporations who are engaged in international trade or investment abroad are able to reduce their exposure.

Speculation

As in other investment markets, the rise or fall of the rate (or price) at which one currency may be purchased with a quantity of another creates the potential for gain or loss. Therefore, another major activity in foreign exchange markets is speculation. Typically, a speculator will simply establish a long position (that is, hold a contract or an inventory) in a particular currency in the expectation of making a profit upon resale of the currency at a higher price. Alternatively, a speculator may take a short position in a currency that he expects to decline in value against another. An open position is created in the hope of making a profit when the transaction is closed out.

As mentioned previously, commodity exchanges such as the International Monetary Market (IMM) in Chicago, cater to individuals in particular who may desire to enter the market to engage in either speculative or hedging transactions. Without the IMM, individuals would have fewer opportunities to speculate. In effect, to create a speculative position, the currency considered to be the weaker of the two is sold forward whereas the strong currency is bought or held.

The unpredictability of exchange rate movements in response to unexpected events (such as assassinations or government intervention) is significant. Consequently, speculation is risky.

The activities of speculators who enter the market also may produce disparities between the forward and spot rates of a particular currency. This may have a destabilizing effect, particularly in a situation where traders know that a government is not likely to maintain its currency at a certain level or rate any longer.

Import/Export Trade

The demands of international trade include ready access to foreign currencies and quick exchange to domestic currency to provide payment for goods and services. These needs are also satisfied by the foreign exchange market. Depending upon the currency of payment upon which the parties agree, they may or may not incur an exchange risk. For example, if a U.S. exporter requires payment in U.S. dollars, it bears no exchange risk. Instead, the foreign importer, who at a future date must pay a certain sum in U.S. dollars, bears the risk that the U.S. dollars might become more costly in terms of his home currency. Therefore, the initial decision with regard to the currency of payment will determine which party bears the risk of exchange rate fluctuations. An exporter is often compelled to invoice his shipment in a foreign currency in order to remain competitive.

Clearly, international trade would be curtailed if traders were uncertain regarding the price of goods to be received upon delivery. Uncertainty surrounding the sale of goods when two currencies are involved is removed by purchasing forward exchange contracts effectively fixing the rates between the currencies to be exchanged at a future date and thus determining the cost of goods. Forward transactions are useful in the importing and exporting trade to protect against movements in the exchange markets and to eliminate loss of assets.

Delaying payment when the foreign currency of payment is expected to decline in value is called a *lag* in payment; conversely, paying sooner to avoid paying more for foreign currency expected to increase in value is called *leading*. Importers and exporters adjust their payment schedules in anticipation of such changes. For example, if the price of the U.S. dollar is expected to drop, foreigners will delay making payments in U.S. dollars so as to be able to purchase the dollars more cheaply at a later date. Increased costs of production and overhead from the time a price is first established for goods also may affect profits when the transaction is finally consummated.

Investments

Capital investments that involve the purchase of a foreign asset require that domestic currency be changed into foreign currency when making the investment. Upon conversion back into the home currency,

FIGURE 7–1. U.S. FOREIGN TRADE (Millions of dollars; monthly data are seasonally adjusted)

Item	1980	1981	1982	1983						
				Feb.	Mar.	Apr.	May	June	July	Aug.
1 EXPORTS of domestic and foreign merchandise excluding grant-aid shipments	220,626	233,677	212,193	16,326	16,752	16,074	15,566	17,008	16,629	16,630
2 GENERAL IMPORTS including merchandise for immediate consumption plus entries into bonded warehouses	244,871	261,305	243,952	19,015	19,525	19,771	21,514	21,024	21,950	22,782
3 Trade balance	−24,245	−27,628	−31,759	−2,689	−2,774	−3,697	−5,948	−4,016	−5,321	−6,152

NOTE. The data through 1981 in this table are reported by the Bureau of Census data of a free-alongside-ship (f.a.s.) value basis—that is, value at the port of export. Beginning in 1981, foreign trade of the U.S. Virgin Islands is included in the Census basis trade data; this adjustment has been made for all data shown in the table. Beginning with 1982 data, the value of imports are on a customs valuation basis.

The Census data differ from merchandise trade data shown in table 3.10, U.S. International Transactions Summary, for reasons of coverage and timing. On the export side, the largest adjustments are: (1) the addi-tion of exports to Canada not covered in Census statistics, and (2) the exclusion of military sales (which are combined with other military transactions and reported separately in the "service account" in table 3.10, line 6). On the import side, additions are made for gold, ship purchases, imports of electricity from Canada, and other transactions; military payments are excluded and shown separately as indicated above.

SOURCE. FT900 "Summary of U.S. Export and Import Merchandise Trade" (Department of Commerce, Bureau of the Census).

intervening movements in the exchange rate will obviously affect the overall profitability of the investment. By hedging the amount of the initial capital investment through the use of a forward currency transaction, the exchange risk of placing capital in a foreign currency investment is reduced. The purchase of foreign bonds, commercial papers, corporate stocks, and other investments (such as the placement of a loan or deposit in a currency different from the home currency) is also protected by purchasing a forward contract.

Having examined the major purposes for which foreign exchange is used, let us now proceed to examine the basic types of transactions found in the market. As will be seen, each transaction has its own distinguishing procedures and characteristics. In theory, any two currencies can be traded in a foreign exchange transaction; in practice, however, most currencies are not traded against each other. Instead, one finds that the U.S. dollar is usually the anchor currency being traded in the majority of cases, due to the widespread use of the dollar around the world.

Spot Transactions

Of all transactions, the spot purchase and sale of foreign exchange is the most frequently encountered. Approximately two-thirds of all foreign exchange transactions are carried out at the spot rate. As the name implies, one may purchase foreign exchange "spot" when there is an immediate use for such funds or if the spot rate is more favorable to the buyer. This does not mean that a TT (telegraphic transfer) advice by which the actual transfer is made is sent out within 48 hours. Rather, the amount must be credited to the account on the other side within 48 hours. For example, if an individual buys $5 million U.S. dollars spot for Swiss francs on Wednesday, he must see to it that the Swiss account is credited not later than Friday. In turn, he has a credit of $5 million U.S. dollars in his U.S. account also on Friday. Thereafter, the funds are available for use by both parties on that day.

In this example, note in particular that the value date is calculated as two business days later. Therefore, foreign and domestic holidays may affect the availability of funds on a certain date. Certain currencies, such as the Mexican peso and the Canadian dollar, have value dates one business day after the trade.

Foreign exchange markets generally quote forward contract prices for most major currencies on the standard basis of 1-, 2-, 3-, 6-, 9-, or 12-month periods, even though it is possible to get a quote for an "odd" date. Normally, a bank will not enter into a forward contract beyond one year; however, in exceptional cases it may be possible to locate an 18- or even 24-month forward contract. In these exceptional cases, when initial contact with the bank is made by a seller of currency, say English pounds, for delivery two years forward delivery, the transactions will be matched for a trade. When a longer time period is sought, the bank does not itself enter into the contract due to the increased risk of rate fluctuations. Instead, it seeks a third party to match its clients' needs.

For the party seeking a long-term forward contract, the London foreign exchange market may be a possible alternative as trades in forward contracts (in major currencies) sometimes extend up to five years. Forward contracts with banks, by comparison, are limited to a rather small number of currencies. These include the Canadian dollar, English pound, French franc, Belgian franc, Dutch guilder, Italian lire, Swiss franc, German mark, the Scandinavian currencies, Japanese Yen, the U.S. dollar, and some others. Unlike spot transactions, however, all forward contracts purchased on the interbank markets are traded through the U.S. dollar. For less readily available currencies it is again possible to deal with a specialist. Banks or dealers often are able to find some solution to unusual requests.

Certain payment procedures also govern the settlement of a for-

FIGURE 7–2

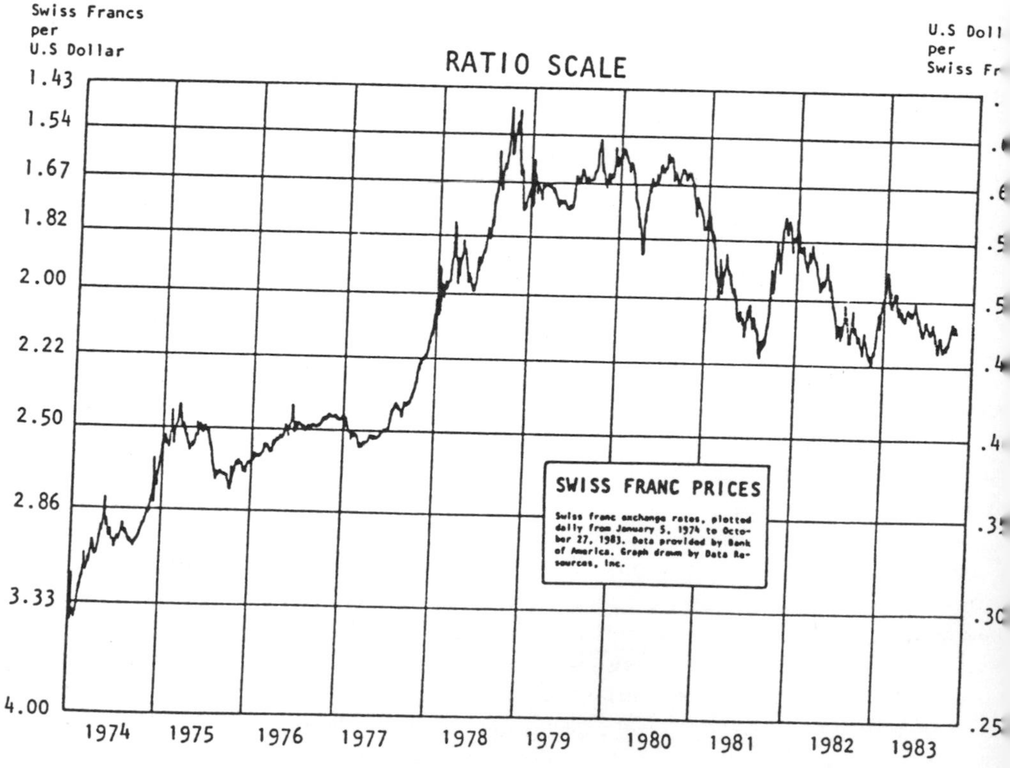
Swiss Francs
per
U.S Dollar
RATIO SCALE
U.S Doll
per
Swiss Fr
1.43
1.54
1.67
1.82
2.00
2.22
2.50
2.86
3.33
4.00
.30
.25
1974
1975
1976
1977
1978
1979
1980
1981
1982
1983
SWISS FRANC PRICES
Swiss franc exchange rates, plotted daily from January 5, 1974 to October 27, 1983. Data provided by Bank of America. Graph drawn by Data Resources, Inc.

ward contract. If purchased from a bank for delivery at a future date, the forward contract must be paid a day or two before delivery.

During the period of time before delivery, the bank does not hold a specific segregated amount of funds; rather, the bank arranges a corresponding contract with another customer who occupies the other side (that is, buyer or seller) of the transaction. When one client of the bank sells a contract, the other client buys. The strength of the banks in this area is their ability, through sheer volume of business, to satisfy both sides of the transaction.

As will be further examined when discussing exchange rate determinants, the rates for forward contracts normally differ from spot rates and reflect the future expectations and the difference in interest rates prevailing in the two countries. If the forward rate is higher than spot, the currency is trading at a *premium* (or agio). If the forward rate is lower than the spot rate, the currency is trading at a *discount* (or disagio).

Commercial banks, as well as foreign exchange dealers who hold inventories of foreign currency, also cover their exchange risks by entering forward market transactions. Whether market movements are favorable or unfavorable, the forward contract locks in a specific price for the foreign currency for a specific future date.

Options

For those who wish to hedge their position with a forward contract but are uncertain as to when payment will be required, an option contract may be purchased. For example, the payment date for goods may be based on the arrival of a shipment from abroad. Since the exact date of arrival may vary depending on shipping conditions, a forward contract with an exact delivery date may not be the best alternative.

When exact payment days are impossible to calculate, commercial banks are often asked to supply option date contracts. The option contract allows the holder to settle the contract on any day between two specified dates. The time period during which a settlement day may be chosen is usually no longer than one month. Furthermore, the option exists only with respect to date. Namely, the currency on which the option is held must in all cases be delivered by the expiration date of the contract.

There are two types of options: seller's options and buyer's options. For example, if an exporter of goods expects a foreign currency payment of £100,000 within 60 days without being sure of the exact date, he may enter into a contract to sell the £100,000 at seller's option. This means that, any time within the date of sale of the option and the following 60 days, the exporter has the right to deliver the £100,000 at the agreed-

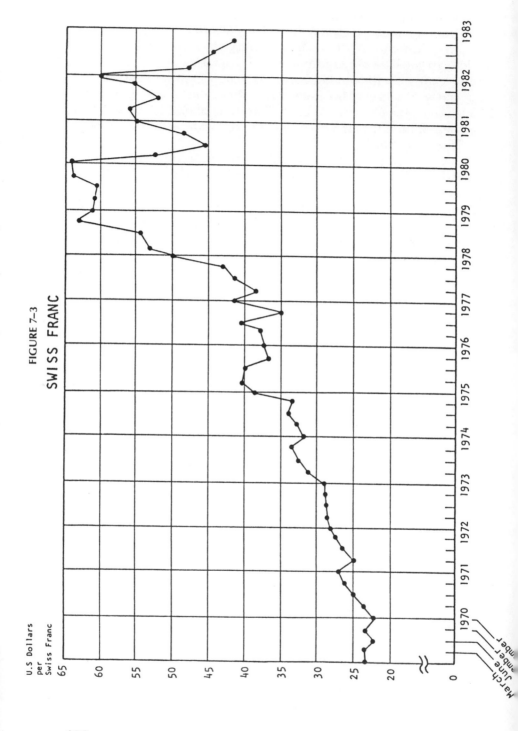

FIGURE 7-3

SWISS FRANC

U.S Dollars
per
Swiss Franc

128

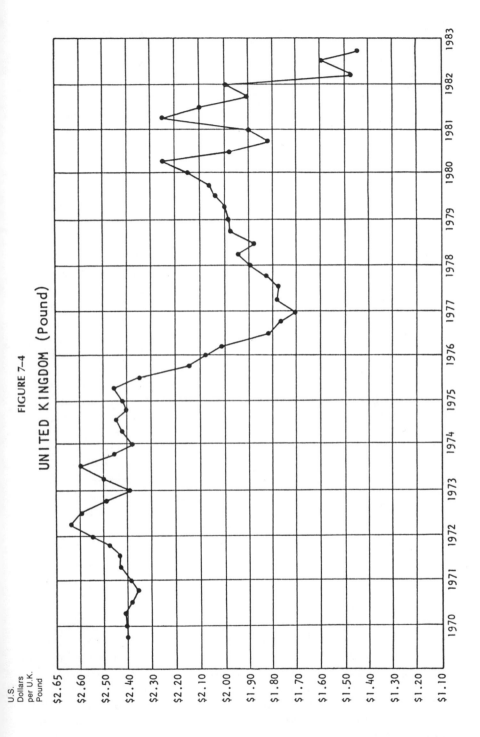

FIGURE 7-4

UNITED KINGDOM (Pound)

129

upon rate of exchange. For that privilege, the exporter pays a slight premium.

Similarly, the importer of goods may estimate that he must make a payment of £100,000 within 30 days. However, if it is possible that the shipment will arrive earlier, and if payment is due upon arrival of the goods, the importer must be ready to pay sooner than expected. He may take delivery of the money at the specified rate on any day up to the expiration of the contract. Obviously, the advantage of such an option includes the assurance of a fixed rate, regardless of fluctuations. In addition, funds will not be tied up for unnecessary lengths of time since payment is made on the date when the currency is needed.

Swaps

Another technique used to reduce or eliminate exchange risk is the foreign currency *swap*. A swap is a purchase of currency for immediate (spot) receipt with a simultaneous sale of the equivalent amount of currency for future (forward) delivery. Alternatively, a currency may be simultaneously bought and sold for two different forward dates. Usually swap dates are available in a limited number of standard maturities.

Because the trader (the bank) both pays and receives the same amount of currency at a specific rate, it incurs no exchange risk. During the period between purchase and resale of the foreign currency, the individual has use of the funds. In effect, this represents a short-term line of credit, the equivalent of short-term borrowing and lending; because it is arranged as a purchase and sale, however, little credit risk is involved. One "purchases" use of a needed currency for a period of time at a spot rate of exchange with another currency; use of the purchased currency terminates at such time as delivery (that is, the "sale," or return of that currency) must be made pursuant to the terms of the forward contract. The cost of the transaction is the difference between the two exchange rates, namely the spot/forward (or forward/forward) rates. This is known as the *swap rate*. As with other currency transactions, the swap rate may result in trading at either a premium or a discount.

It is not unusual for the swap rate to be calculated in terms of an annual percentage figure. The relationship of spot to forward rates depends on interest rates in both countries. Additional profit will be made if the return on investments made in the "swap currency" is sufficient to cover all the costs of the transaction, including foreign exchange conversion back into the home currency. If the exchange rate of the currency to be received pursuant to the forward contract has appreciated, its sale at the market rate yields an additional profit, comprised of the difference between its cost when originally bought and its price when finally sold.

Because, in addition to yielding a premium on the deal, the currency may be put to actual investment use, many dealers and banks prefer swap transactions to other types of trading. Rather than using their trading limits by entering into forward transactions and tying up funds, possibly for months, dealers especially prefer short-term transactions. Similarly, most interbank trading in foreign exchange is done on a swap basis due to the predictability and ease of calculating costs.

Although swaps are employed in interbank trading by private as well as governmental parties, the basic principles of a swap transaction apply. A principle distinction appears to be the banking channels employed to carry out the transactions. While domestic (or foreign private) banks normally trade with each other through normal banking channels—that is, through privately owned commercial banks—international trading between central banks occurs on a much larger scale and is generally carried on through trading facilities at the Federal Reserve Bank of New York.

To accommodate the needs of central banks for United States dollars, as well as to enable the Federal Reserve to acquire foreign currencies, a *swap network* has been established between the United States and 14 other nations. The Bank for International Settlements (BIS) in Basel, Switzerland, is involved with some countries in the swap network for certain currencies it holds. When desired, short-term credit lines, or *swap lines*, may be drawn upon, or to preestablished limits, by the central banks involved. The usual purpose of drawing on swap lines is to acquire the dollars or other currencies needed to finance exchange market intervention. For example, the U.S. dollars drawn under the swap network may be sold at spot on the foreign exchange markets in order to support a foreign currency by weakening the rate of exchange for the U.S. dollar.

When a central bank wishes to initiate a swap drawing, the Federal Reserve is contacted initially by phone or telex. Immediately thereafter, an exchange of cables or telexes specifying terms and conditions of the swap is made. In the case of a foreign central bank, the swap is a foreign exchange contract for the purchase or sale of U.S. dollars from or to the Federal Reserve for foreign currency, with a simultaneous purchase or sale of the U.S. dollars for delivery three months forward at a fixed rate. Rather than actually exchanging the physical currency (which may be many millions of dollars), the swap is accomplished through appropriate bookkeeping entries at both the Federal Reserve and the foreign central bank. Since both central banks are said to "create" the funds as mere bookkeeping entries, which in turn are offset by corresponding opposite transactions (that is, purchase or sale), swap drawings are claimed not to have any direct effect on the nation's commercial bank reserves or money supply. The Federal Reserve reportedly has not drawn on its swap lines as heavily in recent years as before, although foreign central banks have taken advantage of the swap network to acquire needed U.S. dollars or to dispose of surplus dollars.

The foreign exchange trading facilities of the Federal Reserve Bank of New York, as in other banks, include a modern trading room equipped with screen display units showing the latest currency rate movements. Unlike commercial banks, however, their function is to enter into foreign exchange transactions as a means of implementing the policies of the Federal Reserve Bank and the Department of the Treasury. Additionally, foreign central banks wishing to buy or sell foreign currency as well as U.S. currency may use the facilities as they would a private trader. Naturally, their large currency demands are not directly satisfied by the Federal Reserve itself. Rather, the Reserve traders act as agents for the foreign central banks by locating a commercial bank or investment banking houses large enough to handle the order to be placed. In some cases, an especially large order will have to be distributed among several banks. Minimal fees, rather than normal broker's commissions, are charged for this service. Aside from providing this service, processing the orders of foreign central banks provides essential information concerning currency movement and trading. Nevertheless, even if a central bank chooses to deal directly with a commercial bank, the information eventually reaches the Federal Reserve via reports filed by the banks.

Federal Reserve traders do not have the normal limits on currency positions imposed upon traders for commercial banks. While this facilitates the satisfaction of a correspondent bank's currency needs and provides additional flexibility when intervening in the currency markets, along with these advantages goes the increased possibility of incurring an exchange rate loss.

Interbank swap activity in general is expected to increase with the establishment of International Bank Facilities (IBFs). This is because IBFs located in the United States are able to take deposits or extend credit in Eurocurrencies to foreign residents. IBFs are discussed in detail in Chapter 6 on International Banking Entities.

Arbitrage

When, as often occurs, the swap rate does not equal the interest differential between the two countries' currencies on which it is based, a process known as interest arbitrage will take place. Arbitrage involves dealing in currencies or in financial assets so as to profit from discrepancies in the rates in different geographic markets. For example, in market A, currency a may be exchanged for currency b at the rate of 1a:2b. In market B, however, the rate may be 1a:2.5b. The arbitrageur, noting this discrepancy, will purchase currency a in market A where less b currency is required for the purchase, while selling currency a in market B for a greater gain in b currency at the end of the transaction. In effect, the original quantity of 2b is increased to 2.5b by purchasing through market A.

Naturally, such transactions must take place very quickly before the market has an opportunity to adjust the rates to each other. As other arbitrageurs take advantage of the opportunity to increase their net holdings by entering similar transactions, the combined force of the market reacting to shifts in supply and demand will bring the two market rates into line with each other. For example, if a forward rate exceeds an interest rate differential for a long enough period of time, the flow of funds toward the more favorable rate will eventually equalize the two. However, in the interim before equilibrium is reached, the opportunity for profit exists to the extent that a disparity remains after costs are covered.

Since arbitrage occurs on an international scale as well as between domestic centers, foreign exchange rates in the respective markets tend to be very close at any point in time. It may also be possible, aside from the example just given of two currencies (a and b), to find arbitrage opportunities between three or more markets. For example, if currency a can be exchanged for currency b at a rate of 1.5a:1b in market B, but in market A only 1.3a is needed to purchase 1b, a profit opportunity already exists. Assume, however, that 1b will buy 3.5c in market B, and in market C, 3.5c purchases 1.6a. In this situation, the least expensive rate for currency b will be sought to convert it into currency c at a rate of exchange that yields a higher amount of currency a when it is converted back from currency c. In the preceding example, currency b is purchased with currency a in market A at a lower rate than is possible in market B. Currency c is purchased with currency b in market B and sold in market C in order to receive a larger amount of currency a than at the onset. The result is 1.6a instead of 1.3a. A better cross-rate between currencies a and c was achieved by going through an additional market. Again, all transaction costs must be calculated when determining whether or not a profit opportunity exists. Arbitrageurs must work around the clock taking advantage of rates in various geographical locations.

In addition to discrepancies in exchange rates, arbitrage can also take advantage of differences between the interest rates offered in two nations. In doing so, investment funds will be converted from the nation offering lower interest rates to the nation with higher rates. Funds moving as a result of these activities are called *short-term capital movements*. It is prudent, when arbitraging interest rates, to hedge against an actual loss due to possible future exchange rate fluctuations under the method discussed earlier, that is, by entering into a forward transaction in order to fix the future rate of exchange for the funds invested abroad.

For example, although an investment may appreciate in value due to high interest yield, the currency of investment may depreciate to such an extent that the overall value actually declines when measured against the original currency. The practice of coupling trades between one currency and another, with the investing of the proceeds, is also known as *coverted interest arbitrage*.

Rollovers

A *rollover* may be used in a number of the transactions discussed to extend the length of time that a foreign exchange risk is covered. For example, normally a future (or forward contract) may be purchased to hedge against currency fluctuation; however, as the maturity date of that forward contract approaches, it may be necessary to extend the coverage provided by the contract. If the currency to be delivered under the terms of the forward contract is sold on spot and another forward contract is entered into, coverage against the fluctuations may be renewed without ever having been lost. This series of transactions is similar to the ones that will ultimately close out the contract holder's position, but differs by terminating in another open position. Since the rates in effect at the time of maturity of the contract may differ from those originally in effect, the cost of obtaining foreign exchange cover for the rollover time period still may have increased or decreased; nevertheless, the rollover will have provided greater opportunity to minimize that cost.

In addition to this type of transaction, the term *rollover* may also be used to describe a swap transaction where a trader buys or sells a currency for value the next business day and simultaneously sells or buys it back for value the following day.

Foreign exchange houses and banks also deal in physical foreign currencies and foreign banknotes. As a general rule, foreign exchange firms (or *houses*) in the U.S.A. maintain a larger and more varied inventory than do most banks. The inventoried amount of any specific currency fluctuates in relation to a variety of factors, including seasonal changes and political and economic developments. For example, a large supply of currencies of those countries frequently traveled to during the summer are needed during those months. As might be expected, the market for foreign banknotes is generally confined to travellers, and has only marginal effect on currency speculation.

Many banks in the United States purchase foreign currency from travellers coming to the United States. These foreign travellers usually come to a bank or a foreign exchange house to exchange their own countries' banknotes, which may not be acceptable in stores and hotels, for United States dollars. In addition, tourists returning from abroad bring back various amounts of residue foreign banknotes. The banks, in turn, not wishing to maintain too large a supply of foreign currency, usually sell them and ship them to a foreign exchange house such as Deak-Perera. This is one means of creating and maintaining an inventory of foreign banknotes, in smaller amounts for banks and in larger amounts for foreign exchange specialists.

At various times, however, it becomes necessary to augment the inventories because of increased demand for specific currencies. Banks order the currencies from foreign exchange specialists or from foreign banks. Specialists, in turn, order their money either from the country of origin or from a central banknote trading area, as exists in Switzerland. These central area dealers may buy their banknotes from dealers in other parts of the world and possibly even from banks in other countries. Naturally, one of the surest sources for meeting inventory needs is the issuing country. Swiss francs can be obtained from a Swiss bank and shipped to the United States, or English pounds obtained from an English bank. Arrangements are often made with foreign firms for shipment of needed currencies.

Sometimes, however, some countries may require government approval before such shipments can take place. Many countries limit the amount of domestic currency that can be taken out by either residents or foreigners, and others may forbid the export of their currency. Exchange controls are often enacted to shore up a faltering economy by inhibiting the "flight" of capital out of the country. Because they are responsive only to a symptom of a country's economic distress, and not the poor economic policies at its root, these controls generally have a limited and short-term effect.

Despite a country's attempt to control the outflow of its currency through exchange regulations, these obstacles are often circumscribed both by residents and nonresidents. For example, although it is forbidden to remove Russian currency from the U.S.S.R., there is a significant export of rubles to the United States and other countries mostly brought out by travellers. Furthermore, it often happens that businesspersons who are unable to obtain hard currency for their services or goods accept physical banknotes of the importing country in settlement for such indebtedness to them. They in turn transport this money out of the country, sometimes even in violation of that country's foreign exchange regulations. Conversely, a businessperson might take large sums of foreign banknotes into that country in order to pay for goods or services purchased there. Here again, there may be a violation of exchange regulations permitting only a limited amount of domestic currency to be imported.

Individuals wishing to buy and sell foreign currency require facilities in which the conversion of one country's currency into that of another may take place. The foreign exchange specialist provides access to this mechanism.

When dealing with the public, it is of the utmost importance for the dealer to know (1) the genuineness of the banknotes, (2) whether they are still in circulation in that country, (3) whether they can still be redeemed even though they may be out of circulation, and (4) the approximate value of the notes. For example, if outdated German banknotes were brought in to be exchanged for United States dollars, they would be absolutely worthless as these notes are no longer in circulation and are no longer redeemable into Deutsche marks. Although a currency collector may have some use for such notes, they are without value in everyday business transactions.

Therefore, proper training of foreign currency traders is essential to prevent the purchase of worthless banknotes. Reference books, such as *Counterfeits and Forgeries,* provide a reliable source for determining the validity and acceptability of banknotes. In addition, private services, among them the Interchange or International Currency Identification Service, provide colored photographs with descriptions of the banknotes in circulation, and may also provide fast verification of a banknote's validity.

Tellers also utilize the so-called blacklight machine for authenticating the note by indicating the quality of the paper on which it is printed. A bill printed on improper paper can be quickly compared to a bill printed on proper paper.

Hedging

Should the inventory of a specialist firm become too large, the firm can reduce its exposure to exchange rate risks by selling off a portion of the inventory either to foreign banks or to another foreign exchange specialist. Alternatively, the dealer may need a large inventory of a particular currency but want to avoid exposure to a decrease in the currency's value. In order to provide protection against such risk, the dealer may enter the futures market, selling as a hedge against any downward changes in the currency's value. Then, if the price of the currency in terms of the United States dollar falls, the loss is avoided or "hedged" by having entered the forward contract with a buyer for a fixed price for delivery at a future date. The rates for foreign currencies fluctuate daily and even hourly. As a result, it behooves a foreign exchange dealer to keep close watch on price movements in the TT (telegraphic transfer) market.

If a foreign exchange dealer merely finds himself with notes of high denominations and wishes to have smaller denomination banknotes, the larger notes are usually shipped to the country of origin to be exchanged for smaller denominations, or to area dealers who may be able to make the exchange.

In addition to exchanging foreign banknotes, the traveller, tourist, and businessperson may also present related instruments to currency specialists and banks, including travellers checks denominated in foreign currency, personal checks in foreign currency drawn on foreign banks, and personal checks in foreign currency drawn on United States banks abroad. At times, travellers checks and personal checks may bear a notice stating in which countries they are negotiable. If such notice does not stipulate negotiability in the United States or a hard currency country, then the checks should only be taken on a collection basis.

Travellers checks, which are negotiable worldwide or in hard currency countries, can be purchased against proper identification and with endorsement in front of the cashing teller. Such checks are usually purchased at more or less the same rate as the banknotes in which they are denominated. They are usually then sent to the issuing bank or country for exchange into United States dollars or for deposit into the firm's bank accounts.

Bank checks and or personal checks should be purchased only on a collection basis; that is, the dollar equivalent should be paid to the seller only after the instrument has been collected.

Checks denominated in foreign currency require a special knowledge. The teller must know whether that currency is allowed to circulate outside the country of origin. A check for currency that is not permitted to circulate outside its country may still be collected, but only by negotiation within the country's borders; consequently, no bank stamps or endorsements should be placed on such checks, which would clearly indicate that it had been negotiated abroad. For example, foreign exchange regulations in Italy forbid circulation of personal checks or bank checks (*assigno circulate*) outside the country. Consequently, if a traveller illegally carries such a check out of Italy and presents it for payment in Australia, the ultimate holder of the check will be unable to obtain settlement from the Italian bank on which it is drawn according to Italian regulations because of the Australian bank stamp placed on the back of the check. This stamp, which is routinely affixed, would show that the check had been outside Italy.

Naturally, each soft currency country has its own specific rules and regulations governing foreign payment of negotiable instruments. Foreign exchange dealers must be continually alert to developments in the countries with which they do business, keeping up-to-date with both the regulations and interpretations of their applicability to specific transactions in order to avoid serious loss and difficulty. Such regulations may be found in the Annual Report of Foreign Exchange Regulations published by the International Monetary Fund. Only a few nations are entirely free of restrictions on foreign exchange transactions. Some of these countries are Holland, West Germany, Switzerland, England, the United States, Canada, Hong Kong, among others.

Foreign Currency Futures

Currency futures generally sold through commodity exchanges represent yet another means of obtaining or disposing of foreign exchange for future delivery. Significant differences exist between trading practices used by futures markets such as the International Monetary Market in Chicago (IMM) and those employed by the foreign exchange department of a bank. As a general rule, the futures market may be characterized as more organized, and consequently more standardized, than the interbank forward market.

Since foreign exchange futures are "commodities" traded on the IMM, market efficiency and liquidity are promoted by the offering of only a limited variety of contract sizes and delivery dates. Consequently, while a bank or broker may be able to arrange a forward currency contract for any amount above a certain size and with a delivery date within a wide availability, IMM contracts are much more limited in these respects. For example, at the present time, the IMM offers eight currencies for delivery in four trading months: March, June, September, and December. In addition, each of the available foreign currency contracts must be traded in specified quantities, which may differ from currency to currency. For example, £25,000 sterling constitute one futures contract for pound sterling, whereas 125,000 Deutsche mark must be traded per contract. Naturally, the figures mentioned are subject to change by the IMM.

Other important but less significant trading differences exist between futures trading and the negotiation and execution of forward contracts. Futures transactions are entered by open auction between buyers and sellers on the exchange floor at the IMM; in the case of forward contracts, banks and brokers arrange individualized transactions by communicating with potential buyers and sellers. In addition, unlike other markets, the IMM imposes a daily price fluctuation limit on each contract traded. Finally, as far as supervisory regulation of banks engaged in foreign exchange activities is concerned, banks that deal in foreign exchange futures on behalf of third parties are regulated by the Commodity Futures Trading Commission (CFTC). Otherwise, their trading activities are subject to supervision by bank regulatory agencies, which includes comprehensive reporting requirements covering all activities. In this respect, trading in the U.S. may differ from other countries depending upon the type of regulations to which foreign banks may be subject. Due to the fact that futures contracts traded through a commodity exchange are closed out through their respective clearing houses, the risk of nondelivery or noncompliance is remote. Indeed, actual delivery of currencies is rarely sought on the IMM; although it is possible, the orientation of the market towards hedging and speculation generally results in the settling and closing out of contracts before the actual delivery date. The IMM and interbank markets do overlap somewhat in the arbitrage activities of specialized IMM members and some of the more sophisticated banks. As with arbitrage between different geographical markets, these activities tend to equalize the exchange rate discrepancies that may occur between the IMM and other markets in the USA and abroad.

Composition of the Marketplace

After reviewing the more basic types of foreign exchange transactions and their uses, we turn now to the day-to-day operations and characteristics of foreign exchange trading.

Initially, it should be understood that each foreign exchange market, as well as institutions within that market, has its own unique characteristics resulting from location, currencies handled, local exchange regulation, and market practices. These variations often produce markets that are better suited to a particular transaction than another.

Without attempting to contrast all market differences, certain general characteristics of the U.S. foreign exchange market, such as its structure and mechanics, should be explored. In the United States, the large majority of foreign exchange trading occurs in New York in interbank and brokerage activities; by contrast, Chicago is the center of foreign currency future trading occurring on commodity exchanges. Other major trading centers exist in London, Zurich, Hong Kong, Singapore, and elsewhere.

Due to the existence of many trading centers worldwide, one of the characteristics of the global foreign exchange market is its continuous trading activity. The geographical distribution of trading centers, in a variety of time zones around the world, creates a 24-hour market. In addition, several trading institutions in the U.S. and abroad have initiated round-the-clock trading, using several shifts of foreign exchange traders. While not all United States or foreign trading centers are continuously open, it now may be more or less possible, depending upon the time of day, to execute a desired currency order. As a result, in the European afternoon, when the world's largest dealing centers are open (including New York, Chicago, and Frankfurt), the market is most liquid and orders are easiest to execute. Once again due to modern communication methods, it is theoretically possible to track foreign exchange on a worldwide and continuous basis.

The rapid execution of trades within each market is crucial. When market prices are moving quickly, a dealer cannot be certain that the rate upon which his quotations are based will last longer than a few seconds. Needless to say, the longer such an open position is held, the greater the risk to the dealer of incurring losses due to exchange rate fluctuations. For this reason, prices quoted to a customer at one point in time may differ 10 minutes later. The introduction of electronic communications merely increases the pace at which these transfers must occur.

Mechanics of the Market

Speaking of foreign exchange "markets" and "trading centers" belies the fact that foreign exchange markets are not organized in the same way as a stock exchange; except for markets in currency futures, no single physical marketplace exists where buy and sell orders are centralized and executed. Instead, each trading bank, broker and dealer operates separately by means of communication links (that is, telephones and telexes). Geographic centers of trading activity do exist, however, and are often located within certain major cities. For example, New York is the center of the foreign exchange brokerage community in the United States.

A foreign exchange transaction begins with locating an individual trader who is able to handle the order at a competitive rate. Needless to say, only the most reputable foreign exchange institutions should be dealt with to avoid negligent and occasionally fraudulent transactions. Not only external trading practices, but internal controls designed to limit investor risk, should be followed by the firm. Failure to observe such seemingly innocuous practices as the placing of limits on trading, the numbering of exchange contracts to record open positions, and the failure to match long and short transactions, eventually damages not only individual investors and traders, but the credibility of the larger "marketplace" of which they are a part.

As for the actual mechanics of assuring that a foreign exchange trade has been completed, certain operations must be completed after the individual communicating with the trader agrees either to buy or sell a particular amount of currency at a specific price for some future date. Normally, the individual trader writes the necessary information regarding the transaction just completed on a prenumbered *trade ticket*, which is then sent to another individual or group of individuals with the investment firm for processing. Once completed, the trade ticket becomes part of the firm's record system.

In general, since the trader is occupied with dealing with individual clients, necessary support functions are carried out by other departments. In addition to the trading room where traders with telephone consoles and display screens are located, a typical firm will have a back-up or service department, which sends out trade contract confirmations and keeps records of trading positions and accounts, a telex room where telex orders and advices are processed, and a management group to coordinate these activities and promote the efficient and profitable operation of the firm. Clearly, each of the components of a foreign exchange organization is vital to its successful operation.

In addition to promoting the efficient carrying on of firm business, the interdependence of these various parts does little to inhibit unauthorized or even fraudulent transactions from occurring within a department. Senior management is responsible for establishing trading controls to eliminate most, if not all, risks of financial losses and for promoting policies to facilitate the smooth functioning and financial integrity of the trading department. Depending upon the degree of risk acceptable in foreign exchange operations, important decisions such as trading limits must be decided upon and enforced. Furthermore, policies for determining the creditworthiness of trading counterparties also must be established, since there is a risk that a party may not honor a contract, which would nevertheless have to be fulfilled by the bank with the matching contracting parties. As a further precaution, traders generally must attempt to offset transactions in the market as quickly as possible, in order to cover positions contract by contract; however, rapid movement in the exchange rates before the transaction can be completed occasionally makes the incurring of a loss unavoidable.

Another precaution taken by management and senior dealers is the specifying from time to time of particular trading limits for the day in relation to trading activity of the previous day in trading centers around the world. Indeed, the knowledge of experienced traders in this respect is so important to the trading department that, when a chief dealer is away, overall trading limits may often be cut.

In addition to controls for internal purposes, a foreign exchange position must be monitored daily due to the fact that, in certain countries, the government (normally through the central bank) may impose limits on the amount of local currency to be traded by local banks and by branches or affiliates of foreign banks. A variety of foreign regulations also may define who is authorized to enter the markets and impose limitations on the type of transactions that may be executed.

This does not apply to the United States and a number of other hard currency countries where foreign exchange regulations of this sort do not exist. For example, in those countries, a bank need not obtain a license or authorization from the Federal Reserve or any other governmental agency to trade in foreign exchange. Even the potential risks represented by foreign exchange exposure need not be covered by a required percentage of the bank's capital.

In general, international operations are far more difficult for bank regulatory agencies to supervise. Nevertheless, it appears that, after the 1974 failure of the German Bank Herstatt and large unauthorized speculative losses suffered by other banks, other nations with less stable economies began imposing stricter controls on foreign exchange trading. Generally, when exchange control regulations are in effect in a particular country it is important that dealers be informed of them. Should unauthorized transactions be discovered, local authorities may impose fines, revoke the firm's license to operate, and possibly prosecute the individual if he is personally subject to the foreign exchange laws of the respective foreign countries. As a general matter, those involved in international banking and foreign exchange trading are sufficiently aware of such risks to take adequate precautions, including educating their trading staff in current exchange regulations to avoid such difficulties.

Contractual Terms

Every foreign exchange trade results in a contract. Although private individuals may agree orally on the basic terms of the deal, it is standard practice to produce a written record of the transaction. Even if a simple confirmation slip is all that marks the transfer, certain information should be recorded, including the exchange rate applied or agreed upon, the quantity of foreign currency bought or sold and the dollar equivalent thereof, margin requirements (if any), the settlement date, the delivery terms, and the parties to the transaction. It is good practice for a trading firm to record accurately all this information on a daily basis for control purposes as well as for purposes of establishing details of a trade in case of future dispute over one of the terms. As discussed earlier, it is the function of the service department to detect possible errors in confirmation slips before they are mailed to the counterparty in a foreign exchange trade. Indeed, in the case of trading in currency futures, on the IMM in Chicago, a confirmation slip is the only type of documentation produced to show the completed transaction and its terms.

Of all the basic contractual terms, the exchange rate is the most important. These rates represent the price of one country's currency in terms of another's. Consequently, the actual price of all goods and services traded internationally are affected by exchange rates.

In technical terms, an *exchange rate* is a "numerical expression of the value of the currency of one country in terms of that of another country at a given time." Two methods of expressing exchange rates are currently in use; depending upon the market and currency quoted, either "European" or "United States" terms may be employed. Quotes expressed as the reciprocal of, or number of foreign currency units equal to, one U.S. dollar are known as *European terms*. In fact, this is the normal European practice, with the exception of quotes given for British pound sterling. British pound sterling always tends to be quoted as so many units (such as so many dollars and cents per pound). On the other hand, within the *United States*, normal trading practice is to quote one foreign currency unit as equalling so many dollars and cents. It is important to know which method of rate quotation is being used before beginning to trade. Extremely costly errors may result if practices are not verified in advance.

Generally, when a dealer locates a market for a particular currency and offers the customer a quotation, two figures are provided. The first number is called the *offer* (or *ask*), which is the price at which the dealer will sell the currency being quoted. The second number is known as the *bid*, or the price at which the dealer will purchase the particular currency. The difference between the two, called the *spread*, reflects the dealer's profit margin on the transaction. As a general matter, the spread between the bid and asking price is normally small unless the dealers perceive some risk concerning the future price trend of the currency. A narrow spread generally reflects the extremely competitive nature of the interbank foreign exchange network, but, aside from the competitiveness of the market, other market factors will have an impact on rate quotations.

Although the exchange rate for a particular transaction is established on the *contract* date, no money changes hands until the contract is settled on the *maturity date*. In some instances, banks require that a compensating balance be maintained to cover all or part of the amount of the transaction, so as to avoid losses that might be incurred if a party fails to perform its portion of the contract. The normal means by which foreign exchange transactions are settled involves appropriate book entries on the respective trading, brokerage, or bank accounts of the parties. *Settlement* of a foreign exchange contract is also possible by selling the contract to a third party before the settlement date, or by cancelling the contract and paying the contract holder for lost profit. Of course, these latter alternatives should be successfully completed in time to avoid performance of the terms of the original exchange contract.

While settlement dates in interbank trading are normally negotiated between the parties, settlements on the IMM are made on a daily basis through clearing agents on the IMM.

The IMM quotes the spot and the future rates *flat,* meaning that the entire quotations are both fully written out. This contrasts with future quotes from dealers, which are indicated as points *premium* or *discount* to the spot rate when only the spot rate is fully written out.

As a general matter, the spot and forward rates are determined simultaneously, reflecting the current differences in interest rates between countries and expectations of future changes. The forward price of a currency reflects the expected interest return for that currency in the market when it is ultimately sold. Therefore, calculations to determine the interest rate differentials between the two countries must be made to determine the rates of exchange at that future point in time.

Movements in the prevailing domestic interest rates will produce changes in the premium or discount paid for or charged against the forward rates of foreign currencies over their corresponding spot rates. Such movements may occur due to fluctuations in reserve requirements, the imposition of exchange controls or taxation, or other governmental intervention. Both the premium and discount rates may vary more widely than might be expected from examination of interest rate and money supply influences.

The pressures exerted by these factors on a currency may lead ultimately to the depreciation, the devaluation, the appreciation, or the revaluation of the currencies in terms of others. To illustrate the distinction between these terms, consider the following. A currency *depreciates* in value when its powers to purchase goods or services declines due to economic forces. On the other hand, *devaluation* is a governmental action taken officially to reduce the exchange rate of the domestic currency as against other currencies. A currency *appreciates* when its purchasing power increases due to economic forces. *Revaluation* most frequently is the reaction to increased purchasing power whereby authorities establish new official rates of exchange in terms of another currency.

Due to the fact that daily fluctuations in the exchange rate of a currency may create trends over a period of time, it is important for the foreign exchange dealer to be able to discern not only the actual short-term trend but its significance for future trends. For example, a slight decline in a currency's exchange rate today may not necessarily indicate a continued decline. Therefore, in order to avoid risk of loss due to rate fluctuations adverse to open positions, several economic factors and the phenomenon producing them should be examined rather than dealing in isolation, unless one is trading for the extremely short term. Naturally, unexpected events also play a role in the rate of currency, which is a reason for the great difficulty experienced when one attempts to correctly predict a future price of a specific currency.

Economic Factors

On a basic level, exchange rates vary in response to the forces of supply and demand. This elementary principle would in fact hold up in a trading situation where at a particular point in time there were more sellers than buyers. In such a case, the immediate price would tend to drop in reaction to the increased supply and lesser demand for the currency.

Most foreign exchange transactions are entered into in order either to satisfy a requirement for foreign currency resulting from an international exchange of goods and services or for speculation.

As a general matter, major changes in domestic and worldwide economic conditions have reflected a lack of economic stability and contributed to the widespread use of variable interest and foreign exchange rates. Among the numerous factors that influence exchange rates are: interest rates, political events, inflation, market psychology, future expectations, the impact of economic indicators such as gross national product (GNP), the balance of payments, the balance of trade, and short- and long-term capital movements.

An increase in interest rates, as already discussed, may provide the incentive for investors to transfer funds to the country with the higher rate of interest. This increased demand for the currency may cause the exchange rate to inflate as the currency becomes scarcer.

Political events also affect exchange rates due to the fact that news concerning government leadership, policy, and stability indicate the probability that certain economic policies or events will result. For example, news of the election of a socialist leader with plans to nationalize the major private banking and industrial sectors of the economy would promptly create a movement to transfer funds from that currency into another more stable currency (known as *capital flight*) to avoid loss of value through depreciation. The combined effect of numerous transfers or sales of currency would further lower its bid price on the market until it stabilized at some future date on a lower rate.

Because it reflects a response to anticipated, but not actual, events, this example of market reaction to political events also illustrates another factor affecting the value of a currency, that of market psychology. The reaction of the market to news of many sorts creates expectations as to the future trends in buying and selling that create price movements. If a dealer expects the currency rate to go down, then the price at which he bids for that currency is lower. Conversely, if the dealer feels that the market reaction will be favorable to some event, thus increasing the currency's rate, the bid price is quickly raised in order to increase inventory of a currency that is expected to be in high demand. Consequently, in addition merely to reacting to an event, a successful trader has an intuitive ability to predict the overall reaction of the majority of dealers and customers.

Market expectations also play a role in the quoting of a forward rate for a particular currency at a premium or discount from the spot rate. Depending upon the amount of variation between the two rates, the general market consensus as to the future price trend of a currency is readily apparent from the volume of trading and the volatility of quotes. This is not to say that predictions will prove always to be correct. Market participants, such as importers and exporters, also react to future expectations by shifting their currency sales and purchases and by "leading" or "lagging" in their payments of foreign exchange.

Inflation rates within a country affect interest and exchange rates indirectly by influencing the value of goods and services entering foreign trade. If one country is experiencing a more rapid or higher rate of inflation than another, the price of goods within each of the countries increases at different rates. This in turn may ultimately hinder the competitive position of one country's export trade. Furthermore, trends in price, cost, and income among countries are instrumental in assessing future values of their currencies. For example, the country with the higher rate of inflation may have to devalue its money in the world market. The severe effect of such a devaluation on the economy further affects the value of inventories of such currency. As a result, currency traders monitor severe inflationary developments to avoid unnecessary losses.

Governments also monitor their nation's economic developments, through the compilation of data relating to trade and currency movements and the issuance of a variety of indices. For example, the index of consumer prices indicates average prices of particular goods and services purchased by citizens. The gross national product index is another, reflecting the prices of the goods and services that comprise the national production. However, it is also important to realize that the figures released by governments should be treated with varying degrees of scepticism due to their lack of reliability. A certain percentage of the economy of a country is "underground" or not recorded. Major economic statistics of a country should be regularly examined over a period of time to be able to identify trends, and to avoid being misled by a single group or figure in the statistics. A negative trade balance may be offset by a higher positive figure for the balance of services, which might put the country in a more favorable economic position.

Balance of payment figures, which were analyzed in another chapter, affect exchange rates considerably. Exchange rates in turn influence a country's balance of payments. Negative balances indicate an outflow of the country's currency internationally. This produces a decline in the value of the currency. When such funds are transferred for short- or long-term investment, it signals that a change in the exchange rate might follow.

As a general matter, short-term movements in funds tend toward countries with stable political systems and higher interest rates. The expectations of political stability encourage favorable future currency rates, which will in turn attract short-term capital flows. Of course, any outflow of capital for investment purposes requires the domestic currency to be changed into a foreign currency. If the flow of short-term funds is sufficiently large, it will in itself affect the rate of exchange.

One of the unique characteristics of short-term capital movements is their volatility, making such transactions extremely difficult to record. As a general matter, it can be expected that there will be a flow of short-term (or long-term) capital to those stable nations offering the higher rate of interest, unless some factor, such as political risk, deters some individuals from transferring funds. The movement of short-term capital is one of the most important determinants in the exchange rate of a currency.

Theories

Observations of some of the basic economic factors just discussed have contributed to the development of major theories concerning foreign exchange rates. There is wide disagreement as to which factors bear greater responsibility for changes in exchange rates, as the following discussion will show.

In general the major theories concerning the determination of exchange rates fall into several categories, and they are discussed next.

PURCHASING POWER PARITY

The purchasing power parity theory takes as its premise the intention of individuals in two different countries to purchase a certain quantity of goods and services with a specific amount of each country's currency at a particular time, and it measures each currency's competitive success. As a result, exchange rates reflect the relative value of each currency in the international competition for those goods. For example, changes in the relative price levels within one of the countries will affect the likelihood of a purchase and eventually lead to a modification in the exchange rates. It has been said that, over the long run, this concept of purchasing power parity indicates the direction of the exchange rate as it is influenced by market fundamentals. However, over the shorter term, research has indicated this theory might not be a true determinant of future exchange rates, most probably because other important economic factors are omitted from consideration.

INTEREST RATE PARITY

Another widely accepted theory is that of interest rate parity. As observed earlier, exchange rates are significantly affected by interest rate fluctuations. It follows that exchange rate differentials will be directly influenced by interest rate differentials for short-term investments in the two currencies involved. This theory assumed a lack of major legal or political risks for investors in a particular currency.

THE BALANCE OF PAYMENT THEORY

This theory treats currency as a commodity and seeks to identify the indicators likely to affect the supply and demand of marketable "goods." For example, when it is anticipated that foreign exchange is required to pay for foreign goods, services, or investments, a corresponding decline in the domestic currency's rate of exchange is expected. A major criticism of this theory is that, notwithstanding its usefulness in explaining past market behavior, it proves cumbersome in translating its conclusions into predictions. This is due to the fact that balance of payment figures, when accurate, are merely a reflection of past events, while the exchange markets react to current and anticipated events. Furthermore, with floating foreign exchange rates, the correlation between balance of payment figures and exchange rates has weakened.

THEORY OF RATIONAL EXPECTATIONS

Under this theory, all economic indicators are used to analyze the likelihood of future rate changes, which in turn form market expectations. For example, if the currency is expected to appreciate at a particular point in time, that expectation is reflected in the current rate. If what the market expected does not materialize, the rates adjust accordingly. Overall, this theory indicates that trends are not reliably predictable due to unforeseen future occurrences.

THE MONETARY APPROACH

This theory essentially regards trends in prices and the balance of payments as the products of the current supply of currency. It supposes that the fluctuation of exchange rates results from the difference in the growth of the money supply in the economies concerned.

MONETARY EXCHANGE RATE THEORIES

In general, the monetary exchange rate theories explain the fluctuations of exchange rates in terms of the money supply. The money supply is determined both by the government's monetary policy (the *supply side*) and by the fluctuations in interest rates, prices, and economic growth (the *demand side*). In addition, a trend toward purchasing power parity between domestic and foreign prices is assumed. Fluctuations in exchange rates are attributed therefore to the effect of the monetary policies of governments and to differentials in the interest rates and levels of income and productivity found within the country. Unlike the traditional balance of payments theory (which theorizes that positive balance of payments strengthens the currency), the monetary theory sees a negative link between interest and exchange rates. Consequently, countries with continually high interest rates are found to have weak or vulnerable currencies.

PORTFOLIO BALANCE THEORIES

Individuals managing assets are guided by expected returns as well as by consideration of risks when developing portfolios. Generally, assets are spread over different forms of investments, including investments in foreign exchange portfolios. Changes made by investors often lead to rapid adjustments of prices and returns for a wide variety of financial assets, many of which are regarded as interchangeable. Unlike the more traditional exchange rate analysis, which focuses on flows of capital to meet supply and demand, shifts in existing portfolios are felt to be more significant determinants of exchange rate fluctuations.

. . .

The variety of theories concerning exchange rate determinants is indicative of the lack of a general consensus regarding which particular factor is key to predicting rate fluctuations. Nevertheless, by selecting various components of these theories, a practical approach to exchange rate determinants can be developed. Currency flucuations can be attributed to a sequence of events that are responsible for ultimately affecting the value of currency in the world market. In developing a theoretical approach to the study of exchange rates, one may include factors having a more immediate impact, such as interest rates, as well as those that may signal longer-term currency trends, such as balance of payment figures.

For example, the announcement of figures for the money supply reflects a governmental policy that affects the monetary system of a nation. If an increase in money supply is announced, the typical market reaction is an increase in interest rates. Higher interest rates in turn lead to a domestic and foreign market reaction. The domestic cost of production of goods and services will increase due to the greater cost of credit, which must be paid by companies borrowing funds. As a result of higher costs, the export price of goods and services may also rise. On the other hand, short-term capital inflows will be attracted by higher interest yields and may offset the reduction in trade and service balances. Overall, however, demands for the currency will increase at least temporarily, pushing exchange rates higher. A point will be reached when the costs of exported goods will be too high to be competitive, causing the demand for those goods to level off and, with it, domestic production. Consequently, the nation's balance of trade and services figures will decline, and, unless they are offset by a higher figure for the capital accounts, it is likely that the overall balance of payments will be affected unfavorably. These figures normally have an effect on the exchange rate of the currency despite the fact that they report past economic events because they reflect the performance of an economy overall. Moreover, if the drop in the exchange rates in reaction to these figures is significant enough, the outward movement of short-term capital will exert further pressure on exchange rates.

Thus, a continual cycle of market reaction to variable economic and monetary factors affects the exchange rate of a currency. The amount of fluctuation to be anticipated will depend upon the significance attached to events occurring within the market. In summary, therefore, a complex combination of many basic factors affects rates of exchange.

The Concept of Money

The existence of money is fundamental to the daily functioning of a society. In addition, the legal structure of a society is by necessity intertwined with the concept of money. Nevertheless, within the last half-century economists have been unable to agree upon a generally accepted definition of money. In the following discussion, we will consider money to be a form of "wealth power" or "purchasing power."

Rather than arising from any preconceived plan, the system of money developed from early barter systems. It has resulted in generally accepted exchange items that facilitate commerce and trade within and between societies. Since it is impractical to directly barter goods or services for what we want on a daily basis, an intermediary medium of exchange called money developed. For centuries, men have been accustomed to connecting the idea of money with a variety of forms of definite symbols such as animals, commodities, coins, or banknotes. Something is accepted as money only if the acceptor is confident that something of value for future exchange is being given. For this reason, a combination of the collective marketplace of buyers and sellers determines what money will be; governments that enact legislation (or issue decrees) regarding a monetary system are only responding to the economic realities formed by their constituents.

The historical mediums of exchange were gold and to a lesser extent silver. Eventually, convenient substitutes were developed. However, originally the paper substitutes that were issued were only acceptable as long as it was believed that they were backed by precious metal. Indeed, during times of major crisis, actual goods, such as cigarettes, chocolate, and the like serve as money. Consequently, such paper substitutes as currency are not money in and of themselves; rather, what is behind a substitute is the actual money. Historically, three essential characteristics have defined a class of items as money: (1) it must be divisible; (2) it must be accepted in payment of debt; (3) it must be a store of value.

Metallic currency has been in circulation for thousands of years. Under each system the unit of account generally represented a certain quantity of a particular metal. It was only after World War I that widespread use of unbacked paper currency developed. Over the years, the ever weakening link between the metallic gold standard and the basic unit of account has produced a unit of account that is increasingly abstract as a measure of wealth. The basic monetary unit of account is normally designated by local legislation, by international law, or by custom and usage. By this designation, the state attempts to regulate the unit forming the basis of its monetary system. The modern form of money is a true abstraction of economic value, used as a medium of exchange. For example, the dollar is the standard unit of value of money in the United States. However, the ownership of much modern "money" may take no physical form at all, being represented by accounting entries in bank ledgers or computers. From a legal point of view, distinctions must often be drawn between money and bank account credits.

The power of a state to determine its legally acceptable "tender" is a central feature of its historically unchallenged rights of sovereignty. This power includes the ability to issue currency, regulate the domestic money supply, impose exchange controls, abrogate gold clauses, and control decisions to devalue or revalue currency. In the United States, for example, legal tender laws serve to facilitate transactions by requiring that certain coins and banknotes be accepted as money for medium of exchange.

While a medium of exchange need not be legal tender in order to pass as money in the more general sense discussed earlier, statutory definitions are generally restrictive. An exception to this rule is the definition of money found in the Uniform Commercial Code, which states that: "Money means a medium of exchange authorized or adopted by a domestic *or foreign* government as a part of its currency." This definition rejects the narrow view of earlier court decisions that "money" is limited to legal tender, and it avoids the typical characterization of foreign currency as merely a commodity. Furthermore, Uniform Commercial Code Section 3–107(2) indicates that: "A promise or order to pay a sum stated in a foreign currency is for a sum certain in money." Thus the negotiability of instruments expressed in foreign currencies will not be defeated due to the fact that they are not expressed in terms of U.S. dollars, even if they are payable in the United States.

Note that the converse is not necessarily true. The use to which the foreign currency is put (such as a loan denominated in foreign currency versus the purchase of a forward contract) often will determine whether it is classified as a commodity as well as legal tender.

The question of the classification of foreign money obligations commonly arises in the context of legal disputes. For example, if it is alleged that a sum of money is payable as a result of a breach of contract, the specific amount and currency of payment will have to be established by reference either to the contract or to other indicators of the parties' intent, such as past practice. Ambiguities may be present, such as whether a contract reference to "dollars" means the American or Canadian variety. This issue may be further complicated in contracts distinguishing between the money of account (or the currency in which the debt is measured) and the money of payment (or the currency in which the debt is to be paid). Furthermore, any monetary claim will require an assessment of the valuation in terms of money. Fluctuations in the value of money may also require the fixing of a date by which to estimate damages.

Several approaches are available for resolving disputes concerning the valuation of monetary obligations affected by fluctuations in exchange rates. Among these theories are valorism, metallism, and nominalism. Briefly, *valorism* is a theoretical approach that bases the value and amount of the monetary obligation on the purchasing power of the units of currency. This theory is not accepted as a general rule. *Metallism* refers to a system by which all currency is defined in reference to a specific quantity of a particular metal, such as gold. This approach is obsolete in the current international monetary system. The principal of *nominalism* predominates over both metallism and valorism as a means for establishing the actual amount of payment due for either public or private monetary obligations. Simply stated, once established, the debt must be paid in the nominal amount of currency as stated in the contract or as determined by applicable law where a different money of account is involved. Thus, intervening changes in actual value are disregarded. For example, a judgment may·require the payment of 200 United States dollars in any alternate currency as, by law, amounts to 200 United States dollars, regardless of fluctuations in the actual currency's purchasing power after the award is made.

More importantly, a specific date for the rate of exchange must be established to prevent disputes arising from fluctuations in value. Decisions in the United States have tended to adopt the rate of exchange existing at the date of entry of the final decree, rather than the rate existing on the date of breach. Of course, this method of valuation may not be utilized in the courts of other nations. For example, in the case of a debt payable in England, the law permits the use of the rate of exchange prevailing when the debt became due. Unlike American courts, judgments in English courts may be denominated in foreign currency. Since a conversion of the foreign money into U.S. money is required by law, reference to officially established values is useful.

Since the nineteenth century, states have attempted to exert greater influence and control over their domestic economies by the enactment of legislation defining their monetary systems, such as by control of the issuance, form, composition, and unit of account. Some feel that the amount of power wielded by governments over the monetary system has reached the point of abuse. For example, in the United States, huge deficits created by excessive government spending, a concomitant expansion of the money supply, and a resulting inflation amount to an indirect form of taxation, reducing the wealth of all citizens with only indirect legislative approval.

If the real value of money is something that is both legislatively fixed but also, at times, subject to influences beyond governmental control, how is it to be determined? Two generally accepted value concepts—that of extrinsic worth and intrinsic worth—may provide some guidance.

The value of all things, including money, varies. The *intrinsic* value of money is measured by its domestic purchasing power, the ability to convert it into other forms of value, whether tangible or intangible. The *extrinsic* value of a currency is the measure of its exchangeability with other currencies. Significantly, money has no absolute value. For example, the relationship between the unit of currency and the prices of domestic goods and services varies as the intrinsic value of a nation's money varies; thus, prices rise as the money has less value or purchasing power, requiring more units to purchase the same items. As we have seen, this fluctuation is due to the impact of governmental and economic policies on the monetary system. This relationship may be analyzed on a greater scale when examining the extrinsic value of money. The ability to exchange the national monetary unit (such as the U.S. dollar) with monetary units of other nations fluctuates in a similar fashion, reflecting the global patterns of economic and financial trends.

Notwithstanding the pivotal role they play in the determination of a currency's value, states generally are not responsible to citizens or foreign parties for the consequences of altering the value of currency. This immunity, while presumably providing governments with flexibility in matters affecting their domestic economies, leaves individuals with little recourse in the event of a revaluation or depreciation in the value of their currency.

Evolution of an International Monetary Standard

Currencies of varying values are exchanged as a means of payment and credit for international investment, trade, and finance. However, it may be said that the U.S. dollar and to a lesser degree, the pound sterling predominate this area.

The vast number of international transactions demand a payment system that allows the relatively free movement of funds from country to country. In addition, since no single international monetary unit exists for purposes of international payments, mechanisms to allow capital movements in national currencies must be available. An international monetary system must enable the transfer of one national currency to another, even when the currency transferred is not the currency of the individual's own country. For example, the English pound was a trade currency even for those countries in which the pound was not a domestic currency. Especially before World War I, England was the international center of finance and foreign exchange. Since the English pound served as an anchor currency for worldwide trade, considerable expertise developed in London in the area of foreign exchange and finance. However, England's standing as a world financial power declined from the time England went off the gold standard in 1933.

Due to the economic depression and political turbulence of the times, several currency devaluations and changes in the gold standard occurred during the period between 1918 and 1939. It was then that the term "hard currency" came into usage. Hard currencies were currencies that, instead of being convertible into gold, were supported by reserves of convertible currencies. Typically, under a gold standard, paper money can be converted into a specific amount of gold. Thus, when currency is based on a gold standard, a correlation between gold and the nation's paper money is established in the country's monetary system. This differs from a gold bullion standard whereby only foreign central banks may exchange surplus U.S. dollars for gold (or foreign exchange may be exchanged for gold by the U.S.).

After England went off the gold standard, the value and appeal of its currency declined. Thereafter, the U.S. dollar increasingly began to gain importance worldwide. In effect, the U.S. dollar developed into a monetary reserve asset. After World War II, the U.S. dollar was generally considered "good as gold" due to the gold standard backing the value of U.S. currency. The U.S. dollar had replaced the English pound as the leading currency for international trade and exchange market intervention. However, it should be noted that, in 1933, the U.S. government outlawed the ownership of gold. United States citizens were prohibited from acquiring gold from 1933 until the laws were again changed to permit gold ownership and trading as of January 1, 1975. An official fixed value gold standard then in effect was increased from about $22 per ounce, up to $28 per ounce, and finally to $35 per ounce. Although the government tried to maintain the value at this price, economic conditions producing a negative balance of payments prevented the successful maintenance of that price level. The United States thus maintained a gold bullion standard from 1933 until 1971 when it closed the so-called "gold window."

In 1968, the United States withdrew from participation in the London "gold pool." This was an association of countries that included the United States, Belgium, England, France, Holland, Italy and Luxemburg and that agreed to supply the pool with enough gold so that individuals could purchase gold at a stated price of about $35 per ounce. Although the U.S. had a vast majority participation in the obligation to supply gold, only foreigners were permitted to make purchases from the pool. Needless to say, the huge drain on the gold stock of the United States at an extremely undervalued price finally forced withdrawal from the "gold pool" arrangement.

One of the central reasons for American participation in this arrangement for so long was related to the extremely low supplies of gold held by foreign countries in the post-World War II period. This situation made it impossible to get redemption in gold for foreign currencies accumulated by the U.S. The gold pool arrangement, however, enabled foreign governments to come to the U.S. Treasury and exchange U.S. dollar claims and holdings for gold at $35 per ounce. In addition, the U.S. government could go to foreign countries and exchange accumulated foreign currency for gold at the same $35-per-ounce rate. Thus, this system subsidized the faltering European economies during a period of instability, and it was extended to a point that was finally detrimental to the U.S. economy.

The link to a fixed gold value was also the weakness of the Bretton Woods System, which until 1971 called for maintenance of a fixed rate of exchange for the U.S. dollar in terms of gold. As described elsewhere in this volume, during the establishment of the International Monetary Fund (IMF) at Bretton Woods, member countries agreed to maintain the value of their currencies within a certain permissible range of fluctuation in terms of either a specified amount of gold (or U.S. dollars in the case of other nations). However, the United States agreed with the IMF to maintain the gold convertibility of its currency and assured a fixed buying and selling price of $38 per ounce.

The economic pressures referred to earlier led to increasing U.S. dollar reserves held by foreign central banks, who could then demand to exchange them for the undervalued United States gold. On August 15, 1971, the gold window, which allowed U.S. dollars to be converted into gold, was closed. Thereafter, the U.S. dollar became a nonbacked currency. In addition to suspending the dollar's convertibility into gold in 1971, the United States also devalued the dollar by approximately 8%. Thereafter, the members of the IMF met to establish a new par value and permissible limits of fluctuation from parity. As a result of this meeting, the Smithsonian Agreement also established with the European Economic Community (EEC) an independent parity arrangement. Today, the European Monetary System is comprised of eight member countries: Belgium, Denmark, France, Germany, Holland, Ireland, Italy, and Luxemburg. The values of these currencies must presently be maintained within 2.25% in either direction of the established parity in terms of the other currencies for a total acceptable fluctuation of 4.5%, with the exception of Italy which is permitted to fluctuate within a 6% limit. The functions and development of the current European monetary systems are discussed in Chapter 12.

Special Drawing Rights

In addition to the implementation of the special monetary agreements arranged between nations, the IMF created special drawing rights (SDRs) in reaction to the need for a reserve asset created by the removal of gold as backing for currencies. Generally speaking, the SDR is composed of a "basket" (or average value) of selected principal convertible currencies. The currencies of which the SDR is composed are adjusted from time to time. For example, a new change in composition of the SDR came into effect January 1, 1981. Currently, the SDR is comprised of a certain percentage of value of the U.S. dollar, the Deutsche mark, the French franc, the Japanese yen, and the Pound sterling. The IMF serves as a clearing house for SDRs, which are created by international monetary agreements. They may be exchanged for those currencies comprising the "basket" if the necessary IMF conditions are satisfied. Although in this sense, SDRs serve as a reserve asset for national central banks, the usefulness of the SDR system has been questioned, generally due to the fact that SDRs are not able to be directly used for settlement of international monetary obligations according to IMF provisions. The use of the IMF SDR is restricted to transactions between the IMF and certain other entities including member countries. The concept of the SDR basket of currencies, however, is employed in certain international financial transactions as a method of stabilizing or reducing the effects of currency value fluctuation by employing an "average" of the value of several currencies.

Evolution of the Current Monetary System

Despite the Smithsonian Agreement and the attempt to establish a workable parity system, most major countries had abandoned official rate schemes with the collapse of the agreement in 1973. With the exception of certain major European currencies, exchange rates were allowed to "float" against those of other nations. The abandonment of any attempt at maintenance of an official exchange rate marked the end of the stability previously found between the currencies of most major industrial nations. This has resulted in a continuous and often wide fluctuation in international rates of exchange—fluctuations that are exacerbated if national monetary authorities are unwilling or unable to intervene in foreign exchange markets on behalf of their currency.

A currency that is allowed to "float" without market intervention or other influence from its government is said to be on a *clean float*. With this type of system, the direction in which the rate may move is very uncertain due to its complete dependence on economic forces.

Most modern systems use a *dirty float*, which means that varying degrees of support are given to the nation's currency to prevent undesirable fluctuations, particularly when speculation may have the effect of depreciating the currency's value. The government, usually through its central bank, buys and sells foreign currencies to affect the value of its national currency. Several variations on the float systems may accommodate the particular demands of a currency under certain economic conditions. For example, a downward fluctuating exchange system may be adopted to limit the rate of depreciation in value under conditions of rapid domestic inflation. Alternatively, a system may continually depreciate its currency in reaction to continuous and sustained inflation, as happened in Brazil.

To counteract the trend toward extreme rate fluctuations, most countries, to a greater or lesser extent, intervene to influence their currency's value. For example, the Federal Reserve Bank of the United States periodically engages in market intervention practices to influence dollar-dependent foreign markets. Floating systems receive only perfunctory supervision by the International Monetary Fund. Considering the important economic effects that the rate of exchange may have upon a nation's financial well-being, the predominant use of a dirty float system by world governments is understandable.

In contrast to the nations that implement floating systems are those seeking to restrict the fluctuation of their currency's exchange rate. These systems include the fixed parity and pegged systems.

Under a *fixed parity arrangement*, the currency exchange rate is held within certain limits, which are themselves adjusted only when conditions require, as when policy objectives change and require a new parity to implement these policies. The artificial restraint thus limits the currency to a fixed parity, and movements in the rate are limited to a preestablished percentage. For example, the European Economic Community (EEC) bears a resemblance to a fixed rate parity system. Governmental support and intervention are necessary for the successful maintenance of a fixed parity. Therefore, the success of such a system will depend upon the ability and financial resources of a nation to control its exchange rate over a length of time.

Other nations, many of which are less developed countries (LDCs), peg the value of their currency to the value of a readily convertible foreign currency such as the U.S. dollar, the British pound, and others. Due to inflationary and economic changes within these LDCs, the currency pegs, or fixed values, may be frequently changed. Although many countries peg the value of their currency to the U.S. dollar, a few other currencies are also used. Nevertheless, currency buying and selling rates are maintained in terms of the current value of the pegged currency. Not only foreign currency but other valuables may serve as the basis of valuation. For example, the value of the currency may be defined in terms of the SDR or of a group of other currencies. In the climate of today's volatile economy, a floating system has a considerable advantage over a fixed system of exchange by providing the flexibility to adjust to rapidly changing economic factors.

Despite the emphasis in the preceding discussion on a government's ability to influence its currency's exchange rate through support and intervention, the international market finally determines the rates. The efforts of governments to fix exchange rates over any length of time have failed so frequently that the goal of stable exchange rates appears to be unrealistic in today's economy.

Nevertheless, governments retain a significant ability to influence the value of their currency. The fiscal and monetary policies of a nation have a great impact upon the value of the country's currency. Through control of important economic factors, such as the growth of the money supply and rate of interest, monetary authorities can either "stimulate" or "dampen" economic activity, producing changes in domestic prices that may ultimately influence balance of payment figures. Of course, other factors also contribute to the exchange rate of a currency, and so money supply figures are merely one of several important determinants of future exchange rates. Nevertheless, it is certain that fiscal and monetary policy has become a major determinant in the overall position and stability of a nation's currency.

In many instances, it is the policy of governments to intervene in foreign exchange markets through their central banks. This practice has been especially prevalent since 1973 when major currencies began floating. Even though no longer required to maintain a par value, many governments continued to support their nation's currency value in the market. Thus, a large degree of collaboration exists between the central banks engaged in market intervention and their governments. In fact, very few, if any, central banks operate independently of other sectors of government. For example, the Federal Reserve Bank of New York has acted as agent for the U.S. Treasury by buying U.S. dollars in the foreign exchange markets to maintain the price of the dollar.

The price to a government of intervention in the currency market is dear. Although the motive behind intervention is to secure the value of the currency at a certain level, usually what occurs is a costly depletion in government reserves. Thus, depending upon a nation's resources and intervention skills, its attempt to control currency value may prove to be as detrimental as the result in an unfettered market.

Foreign Exchange Controls

Attempts to keep the value of a currency stabilized frequently take the form of exchange controls. Basically, these controls are comprised of numerous governmental regulations aimed at controlling the movement of the nation's currency and rationing foreign exchange with prescribed limits. In this respect, foreign exchange controls are examples of monetary policy having an effect on a nation's economy. Nearly every country has exercised controls of one sort or another over international currency transactions. Furthermore, these controls have been directly imposed by most governments. They are implemented by a branch of the government or by one of its agencies or through the central bank.

In comparison with other nations, the United States is among the least restrictive in its control over foreign exchange transactions. In general, U.S. regulations are currently limited to requirements to report foreign exchange activities to the Department of the Treasury. In addition, banks report information concerning their foreign exchange positions to supervisory agencies. For example, the Department of the Treasury recently delegated responsibility to the SEC for assuring compliance with the Currency and Foreign Transactions Reporting Act of 1970 by securities brokers and dealers. As a result, the SEC adopted Rule 17a–8 effective January 4, 1982, which requires brokers and dealers to file reports and keep necessary records on currency transactions. The rule requires brokers and dealers to make a report on domestic currency transactions of more than $10,000, as well as on the import and export of currency and monetary instruments with values of $5,000 or more. This is just one example of the type of reports that must be filed in the United States concerning currency transactions.

Depending upon the importance attributed to the policy of exchange control, regulations of varying complexity and severity will be issued. Frequently, exchange controls are imposed as an emergency measure to protect a nation's currency supply. However, the basic function of such controls is to limit the ownership and use of specified currencies by those subject to such regulations. Extraterritorial applications of exchange control regulations over individuals and property is often claimed, although governments frequently meet with a variety of legal obstacles in such attempts. Exchange controls may also be imposed on a domestic level.

Although the terms "exchange control" and "exchange restriction" are often used interchangeably, a distinction should be kept in mind. Restrictions tend to be a more defined group of control measures that actually prohibit or significantly interfere with international payment transactions. Nevertheless, exchange control measures may themselves be very comprehensive. For example, a government may require all purchases and sales of foreign exchange to be made through an official agency such as its central bank. In that instance, all transactions requiring payments to or from the country would be required to pass through government channels. Individuals would not be free to send payments directly, such as by wire transfer, without meeting the necessary requirements. Often, these requirements include obtaining a license or transfer permit to make or receive payments. Thus, if goods are exported from the United States to a country with stringent exchange regulations, payment for such goods would be forthcoming only when compliance with control regulations has been completed.

In reality, such a system grants the government a monopoly over all foreign exchange transactions, with the ability unilaterally to interfere or suspend such transactions. An additional risk to the parties of such transactions is that regulations may be significantly changed at any time, thus interfering with expected payments. No type of governmental assurance of transfer can be completely relied upon in all instances. For example, it is possible that a "guarantee of transfer" may be revoked at a future date if circumstances change, regardless of the wording of the "guarantee." Needless to say, substantial losses may be incurred when dealing with such countries. Delays may often be encountered, as well as controls that do not permit payment for goods to be obtained except under narrowly defined circumstances.

The effect of controls on foreign trade further frustrates the economic recovery of the country imposing controls. For this reason, such control measures are notoriously counterproductive in the long run. Furthermore, since the controlled currency system is heavily dependent upon governmental support, and is thus artificial, real economic forces may frustrate the aims of the controlled system. Speculators may readily ascertain that the currency value of such a nation is no longer able to be artificially maintained and will be able, through market activity, to bring about the inevitable drop in value by selling out the currency. Thus, due to the severe impact of exchange control regulations on the trade of a nation, only those countries with significant balance of payment problems will impose controls that significantly interfere with the flow of international trade payments.

EXCHANGE CONTROL PRACTICES

The exchange controls that authorities may use to impede payment mechanisms take many forms. Since the underlying purpose is to control currency movements, the possible regulations are numerous. For example, the inflow and outflow of capital for investment purposes may be restricted for both residents and nonresidents. Another frequent control includes the requirement that all foreign exchange (such as U.S. dollars) entering the foreign country be converted into the national currency at artificially low fixed rates. Frequently, the rates allowed may vary according to the underlying transaction for which the currency is being used, which leads to multiple exchange rates. For example, the rate of exchange at which U.S. dollars may be converted depending upon their use can be much lower than the market rate offered outside the controlled country. In effect, this increases the actual cost of the goods being purchased in terms of U.S. dollars in the preceding example. This creates a multiple exchange rate system that gives effective control over to special governmental agencies. Multiple exchange rates in variably invite additional speculations and activities adverse to the nation.

Instead of offering lower rates of exchange, governments may impose exchange taxes, or *tolls*, on the purchase of foreign exchange, which vary with the use of which the currency will be put. A similar revenue-raising method is the licensing or permit requirement. Unspecified requirements and subjective criteria will frequently be encountered when such licensing requirements exist. For example, lengthy delays may result if the policy is to discourage particular types of transactions.

Although various difficulties are encountered when attempting to comply with foreign exchange regulations, perhaps the most serious situation, apart from outright confiscation, is the blocking of accounts. As the name implies, payments to which an individual is entitled may be credited to an account with a prohibition against freely drawing funds from the account. The circumstances under which it may be permitted to withdraw blocked funds may be so restrictive, in fact, as to require sophisticated planning. Foreign exchange specialists (such as Deak-Perera) are engaged in the business of handling situations calling for specialized knowledge of currency regulations.

All these considerations comprise an important aspect of international investment and trade known as *political* and *currency risk*. Uncertainty surrounding future governmental actions that may affect investments is often significant enough to deter individuals from taking on the risk involved. It should be noted that this same risk is present whenever deposits of funds are made in foreign banks abroad; that is, they may at a future date become subject to foreign exchange regulations making withdrawals of the funds difficult or impossible. Similarly, branches or affiliates of foreign banks must be aware of applicable exchange limitations when operating within countries with currency controls.

Whenever contracts calling for international payments are entered into, the presence and impact of foreign exchange regulations should be carefully analyzed to avoid unforseen loss. Numerous cases involving foreign exchange regulations have arisen, thus adding to the development of international monetary law. As a general matter of customary international law, nations have historically been free to implement foreign exchange controls subject to only a few limitations, such as those prohibiting discriminatory treatment and confiscation of property without just compensation. As previously mentioned, even severe exchange restrictions, such as those establishing blocked accounts, generally will not be found to be confiscatory if use of the funds is merely limited and not permanently prohibited.

Many nations seeking to lessen the impact of their foreign exchange regulations on trade have entered into various arrangements, such as bilateral trade agreements, switch transactions, and clearing agreements. These various agreements establish trading quotas between the respective countries and allocate a certain sum to be available for payment of specified goods. Normally, the transfer of funds between countries is made through bookkeeping entries at central banks. In particular, countries with nonconvertible currencies, such as Comecon countries (the Eastern European Communist Countries), typically utilize such agreements. Since money still serves as the unit of account in establishing prices for goods sold under such systems, they are not characterized as strictly barter-type arrangements. Nevertheless, they often serve as a solution for payment difficulties created by foreign exchange regulations.

In response to restrictive local foreign exchange regulations, international trade continues by adapting to the marketplace. Private barter trade and counter-trade arrangements are increasingly found worldwide. By utilizing a variety of trade and financing techniques within the regulated market, sellers can reach otherwise restricted markets.

In conclusion, it can be said that the international monetary system, as well as the foreign exchange industry, has evolved to meet the needs of an expanding international marketplace.

Bibliography

Battan, Dallas. "Foreign Exchange Markets: The Dollar in 1980." *FRB of St. Louis* (April 1981).

Blin, John, Greenbaum, Stuart, and Donald Jacobs. *Flexible Exchange Rates and International Business.* British-North American Comm., 1981.

Bretton Woods Agreement Act. 22 U.S.C. §§286 et. seq. 1964.

Chappatte, P. "Free Movement of Capital in Europe." *International Financial Law Rev.* (May 1982), p. 35.

Christov, R. "Contractual Pricing and Foreign Currencies." *I.C.L.F.*, 2, No. 6(August 1981), p. 323.

Gold, Joseph. "International Monetary Law in an Age of Floating Currencies." Reprinted from *Proceedings of the 73rd Annual Meeting of the American Society of International Law.* April 1979.

Goodman, L. S. "How to Trade in Currency Options." *Euromoney* (January 1983), pp. 73–74.

Grey, H. Peter. *International Trade: Investments and Payments.* Boston, Massachusetts: Houghton Mifflin Co., 1979.

Hudson, Nigel R. *Money and Exchange Dealing in International Banking.* New York: John Wiley and Sons, Inc., 1979.

Johnson, Harry and Alexander Swoboda, eds. *Madrid Conference on Optimum Currency Areas, 1970.* Cambridge, Massachusetts: Harvard University Press, 1973.

Kredietbank. *Weekly Bulletin,* 22(May 29, 1981).

Kubarych, Roger M. *Foreign Exchange Markets in the United States.* FRBNY, 1978.

Mandich, D. R., ed. *Foreign Exchange Techniques and Controls.* Washington, D.C.: American Bankers Association, International Banking Division, 1976.

Mann, Fritz A. *The Legal Aspect of Money*, 3rd ed. Oxford University Press, 1971.

McKinnon, Ronald. *Money in International Exchange: The Convertible Currency System*. New York: Oxford University Press, 1979.

Meznerics, Ivan. *International Payments: With Special Regard to Monetary Systems*. Alphen aan den Rijn, The Netherlands: Sijthoff and Noordhoff, 1979.

"Money and Finance." *The Economist*, 277(November 29, 1980), pp. 1–24.

Oppenheim, Peter. *International Banking*, 3rd rev. ed. Washington, D.C.: American Bankers Association, 1979.

Ruck, A. "Understanding Foreign Exchange Trading." *Euromoney* (April 1981), pp. 117–18.

Shuster, Milan R. *The Public International Law of Money*. Oxford: Clarendon Press, 1973.

Silard, S. "Money and Foreign Exchange." In *International Encyclopedia of Comparative Law: State & Economy*, Vol. XVII. J.C.B. Mohr (Paul Siebeck) Tubigen, W. Germany and Moaton, The Hague, Paris.

"The Swap Network and Bank Reserves." *Fedpoints 19*, FRBNY, 1982.

8

Eurodollar Lending

In both the domestic and international area, among the most profitable of the many services offered by a bank is its loan department. Profits are generated by loans supervised by competent credit management. In addition, when the international division possesses sufficient expertise, the bank has the potential for additional sources of revenue. These include: currency trading on foreign exchange markets, management fees produced by syndication of loans, and other business generated as a result of recognition of the international lender's status.

The syndication of international loans has developed as one of the more significant methods of providing credit on a large scale while spreading the risk among several lenders. Therefore, this chapter is divided into an overview of the Eurodollar market and an analysis of the major aspects and functions of a syndicated loan. Although opportunities for increased business exist, international loans require risk assessment and credit structuring not made in the domestic loan process.

In the international, as well as domestic, lending markets, any loan agreement will contain the minimum required statements that: (1) the bank agrees to lend a specific amount of money if certain conditions are satisfied and (2) the borrower agrees to repay the principal amount with a certain percentage of interest on certain dates. As one observer has commented: "All the rest—most of the documents—is included to protect lenders against certain risks or to spell out what will happen if those risks occur."

Significant variations between domestic and international loan agreements reflect the distinctive risk and market conditions under which each is marketed. Consequently, commercial as well as legal considerations dictate the form and content of the agreements. For this reason, an understanding of markets, such as the rapidly evolving Eurodollar market, is essential to an adequate assessment of the risks involved in an international loan agreement.

Eurodollar Market

Eurodollars may be defined as United States dollars on deposit in banks located outside the country of issue. Similarly, Eurocurrencies would consist of foreign currency denominated deposits held at banks located outside the issuing country. These definitions illustrate the distinctive extraterritorial nature of these "currencies." It is important to realize that these Eurocurrency deposits are merely bookkeeping entries. In other words, the location of the physical currency is the country of issuance despite the fact that the deposits are shown to be outside the jurisdiction of the issuing country. No cash actually changes hands. Instead, transactions are recorded on the books of banks located outside the jurisdictional—and regulatory—control of the issuing country.

The Eurodollar market serves as an international money market used by commercial banks and institutions around the world. The Eurocurrency market is comprised of those banks located outside the country in whose currency the deposits are denominated. This would include foreign branches of domestic banks as well as foreign banks. As mentioned, the total Eurocurrency market is composed of all foreign currency denominated accounts which, besides the Eurodollar, is mainly composed of Euroyen, Euroguilders, Eurodeutschemarks, and Euroswissfrancs. The "market" for such Eurocurrencies is centered in London. Nevertheless, substantial markets also exist in Hong Kong, Luxembourg, Singapore, the Cayman Islands, and the Bahamas. These centers can compete effectively with banks located in the issuing countries (that is, country of the currency). For example, Eurodollar deposits are a substitute for U.S. dollar deposits at banks located in the United States. However, only a few United States banks are involved in these markets due to the level of expertise and capital commitment required. Although there is presently a shift in the number of loans in major markets, most syndicated loans for Eurocurrencies are arranged in London due to the high level of expertise found there, even if ultimately the loans are booked elsewhere for tax or other reasons. In addition, the large majority of Eurocurrency loans are denominated in Eurodollars.

The Eurodollar deposits may vary in several respects; the basic format, however, is the same. A foreign bank or a foreign branch of a United States bank (including International Banking Facilities, or IBFs) will take a short-term dollar deposit of usually three to six months. Thereafter, it will either be converted to a local currency or lent out at rates higher than those being paid on the deposit. In either case, the acquisition of the money will be on a "covered" basis. That is, a forward sale at a fixed rate will be arranged at the time the deposit is purchased or converted to local currency so that exchange risks due to fluctuation in the currency value are eliminated. The various types of instruments available on the Eurodollar market will be discussed in a later section.

Market Development

Events occurring in the late 1950s and early 1960s prompted the development of a Eurodollar market. The political climate during that period was such that there was rising concern on the part of the U.S.S.R. regarding the security and free accessibility of its U.S. dollar deposits. Rather than risk possible confiscation or blocking of their accounts, the U.S. dollar denominated deposits were placed in banks located in London. In that way, the accounts were beyond the jurisdictional reach of the United States by being booked outside its territory. This method was used since the U.S.S.R. did not wish to convert its U.S. dollar holdings to weaker and less reliable currencies. Thus, the creation of U.S. dollar denominated accounts outside of the United States at that time offered a more politically secure arrangement for the funds.

Further spurring the development of the Eurodollar market was the enactment of laws and regulations designed to improve the United States balance of payments by reducing outflow of capital for foreign investment. For example, the Interest Equalization Tax of 1964 and the Foreign Direct Investment Regulations prevented U.S. capital markets from funding domestic or foreign capital needs for operations outside the United States. It was during this period that the growth of the Eurodollar market accelerated. In addition, the number of foreign branches of U.S. banks established during this time increased significantly, due in large part to the fact that the transactions of these branches were not subject to regulations applicable to domestic institutions.

Therefore, dollars were drawn away from American banks to higher-yielding foreign accounts. The absence of regulatory controls, interest rate limitations, and reserve requirements imposed on domestic deposits, allowed offshore banks to offer a higher interest rate on deposits while realizing a greater rate of return than on domestic deposits.

The reserves of oil-exporting OPEC countries increased dramatically from $8.5 billion in 1972 to $73.6 billion in 1980 due to increases in oil prices during that time. The growth in petrodollar surpluses led OPEC countries to place significant sums in short-term Eurocurrency deposits. As a result, petrodollars were at one time the largest source of funds for the Eurocurrency market.

Nevertheless, the main motivations for placing U.S. dollars in the Eurodollar market are lower costs of regulation as well as higher returns on funds. This is reflected in the fact that, from 1966 to 1973, growth in the Euromarket was much greater than during the years after the 1973 oil price increase. Therefore, deposits of OPEC oil fund surpluses in the Euromarket can be said to represent a redistribution in the ownership of wealth and Eurodeposits.

During the market's formative years, fixed time deposit accounts lured investors to place their funds in the Eurodollar market. Time deposits remain the dominant form of Eurodollar investment, in maturities ranging from overnight to several years, with the majority of deposits taken from three to six months.

Investment Alternatives

In addition to time deposits offered at fixed rates and comprising the bulk of interbank liabilities, several other alternatives are available for the Eurodollar investor. The major investment vehicle is the *negotiable certificates of deposit* (CD). This serves as a receipt for a U.S. dollar denominated deposit held at a bank located outside the territory of the United States. There are also variations of the CD designed for certain sectors of the market. For example, so-called TAP CDs and TRANCHE CDs are issued for different types of investors. When CDs were issued to "tap" the Eurodollar market for funds in denominations of from $250,000 to $5,000,00 they acquired the name *TAP CDs*. In contrast, *TRANCHE CDs* are aimed at smaller investors, as they are issued in aggregate amounts broken down into several $10,000 certificates, each having the same interest rates, issue dates, payment dates, and maturities. This allows access to the Eurodollar market by the group of investors holding certificates that aggregate to meet minimum investment requirements.

Finally, other frequently used instruments include floating rate Eurodollar CDs and floating rate notes. Both of these negotiable bearer instruments adjust to fluctuations in market interest rates. Both the lender and the borrower would effectively limit their interest rate risk due to the interest readjustment feature. The specific terms regarding interest earned, effective time periods, and methods of readjustment would vary according to the institution and market conditions. However, these rates are often determined with reference to the London Interbank Operating Rate (LIBOR). LIBOR represents the rate at which major Eurocurrency banks are willing to place Eurodollar deposits with each other.

Interbank Trading

Frequently, Eurodollar transactions consist of a series of interbank deposits whereby banks holding deposits of U.S. dollars redeposit the funds with another bank, which in turn makes a loan to its customer. This interbank market developed as the size of the Eurodollar market grew. It happened that the demand for loans did not always match the volume of Eurodollar deposits of a particular institution. Therefore, to make use of "excess" deposits and receive interest on them to offset expenses, the practice of interbank redepositing began. Today, interbank trading is an important component of the Eurocurrency market. In fact, the volume of deposits being offered and sold between banks has added a new aspect to a bank's foreign exchange activities. Trading on future exchanges in Eurodollar CDs is also possible. Furthermore, arbitrage transactions between deposits in U.S. banks and banks in the Eurodollar market keep interest rates in line with forces of worldwide supply and demand. Nevertheless, interest rates offered on Eurodollar deposits are normally higher than those available for domestic deposits. In sum, two distinct Eurodollar markets exist: the interbank market and the market between Eurodollar banks and nonbanking entities.

Market Activities

The Eurodollar market specializes in accepting short-term deposits and in making short-term loans. These funds are used to satisfy liquidity requirements of banks and financial firms, as well as being used for trade financing and interest arbitrage. If access to a longer-term market is desired, the smaller Eurobond market offers an alternative. With the growth of the market, various "rollover" devices developed for both CD deposits and loans. As with CDs, the rolling-over of a Eurodollar loan achieves the same effect as entering a loan with a longer term; applicable interest rates are periodically adjusted by the terms of the loan agreement, however, to reflect fluctuations in the current market rate. Changes in short-term deposit rates, ordinarily based upon LIBOR (or the London Interbank Operating Rate), account for such fluctuations.

In a Eurodollar loan context, the lender will acquire a deposit, normally at an interest rate fixed on the LIBOR in effect two days from the date of acquisition. The amount of the deposit and its duration will match the amount of the loan and the period for which it will be outstanding. A loan agreement typically reflects this practice by setting the loan interest in relation to the LIBOR rate two days from the beginning of the loan period.

Growth of the Market

Numerous factors combine as incentives for the maintenance and growth of the Eurodollar market. Among these factors is the competitive structure of the Eurodollar market where spreads between lending rates and borrowing rates are narrower than those found in other markets. In addition, since the deposits are generally held outside the regulatory jurisdiction of the United States, no reserve requirements pursuant to Regulation D or interest rate restriction imposed by Regulation Q of the Federal Reserve Board are imposed by U.S. banking authorities if the applicable criteria are met. The major factor enabling Eurocurrency banks to claim exemption from normal reserve and interest rate limitations is the ability of the holder of deposits in "foreign" branches to demand payment only *outside* of the United States, regardless of special circumstances. Conversely, if payment of foreign branch deposits is guaranteed by domestic institutions, such deposits would be subject to Regulations D and Q. Thus, the rapid growth of the Eurodollar market in the last two decades can be traced to the effort to move funds outside the regulatory limitations of the United States authorities.

Amendments to Regulations D and Q still maintain significant exemptions. The absence of these regulatory factors, while adding a potential risk for the investor, at the same time lowers the deposit-holders' costs in maintaining deposits. This in turn allows the setting of higher interest rates on deposits and lower rates on loans, permitting effective competition with domestic lending centers. However, one of the effects of the recently enacted Monetary Control Act of 1980 was to modify the Federal Reserve's powers governing regulations such as those concerning reserve requirements. Thereafter, to prevent Eurocurrency funds from entering domestic markets, a reserve requirement was imposed on foreign office lending to residents of the United States.

Because of the large percentage of Eurodollars coming from American money markets, interest rates on Eurodollars are sensitive to fluctuations in short-term rates offered in the United States. Rapid transfer of short-term funds between markets occurs in response to rate changes. On the other hand, interest rates for Eurocurrencies other than Eurodollars are linked to rates offered in European or Asian markets.

Due to the fact that the Eurodollar market depends heavily upon market confidence and favorable interest rate positions in comparison to other markets, sizable shifts in funds may have significant effects on the market. For example, a sudden loss of depositor confidence may produce widespread withdrawal of funds, possibly creating a financial crisis. Such was the case in the failure of the Bankhaus Herstatt in 1974 (to be further discussed). Conversely, an increased demand for Eurodollars is created when credit becomes available at rates lower than those offered in domestic markets.

In addition to interest rate regulations and market security, tax considerations also enter as factors responsibly for the growth of Eurocurrency markets. For example, local tax authorities, desiring to promote the growth of Eurocurrency markets on local territory as a means of stimulating the local economy, have provided favorable tax treatment for sales booked in their jurisdiction. Frequently, they are reluctant to impose regulatory measures, even at the insistence of the United States, since to do so would simply drive business to another more favorable jurisdiction.

A combination of factors have been responsible for the maintenance and growth of the Eurodollar market. Let us now examine some of the risks inherent in the Eurodollar market.

Assessing Risk

The decision to lend is based upon the bank's assessment of the risk that the funds lent will not be repaid with the interest and at the time agreed upon. Assessment of risk affects not only the decision to lend, but also the structure of the loan and the interest rate to be charged as compensation for what is, in fact, a calculated gamble. While some of the risks to be found in Eurodollar transactions are amenable to negotiation and apportionment between borrower and lender, some general types of risk must be borne in mind by both parties when initially deciding to enter the market. Three major areas of assessment include currency risk, country risk, and credit risk. Among these, currency risk and country risk are factors unique to the international nature of the loan to be considered.

CURRENCY RISK

Currency risk encompasses two major forms of risk exposure: risk of fluctuation in currency value and risk of interference with repayment from local exchange control restrictions.

The transfer of funds across international borders requires conversion from one national currency into that of another, whether the transfer be the original transmission of loan funds, periodic advances of funds, or debt repayment. As explained in the chapter on foreign exchange, the exchange rates at which currency conversions are made constantly fluctuate. It is therefore possible that throughout the duration of the loan, as fund transfers become necessary, the desired currency will either be unavailable or prohibitive in cost. Obviously, this subjects the parties to a potentially serious risk of exposure to unpredictably greater funding costs than originally bargained for. The borrower, who will be making payments perhaps years from the signing of the loan agreement, is not the only party to face this problem. The lender also faces this risk when making periodic advances of funds, called *drawdowns*, as well as when receiving repayment of funds whose value may differ greatly from the time of lending.

Normally, the funds advanced will be denominated in the loan agreement as the national currency of the lender. Repayment of principal and interest will be similarly fixed. The lender's specification of currency of payout and return reflects an assessment of the relative stability of that currency against other available currencies. In light of the fluctuating nature of currencies on world markets, the lender by choice seeks to place the risk of disadvantageous fluctuations in currency price and availability on the borrower. It should be mentioned that exposure to changes in exchange rates may be hedged against by entering into a forward contract for the amount of the currency at risk. This limits exchange rate exposure by locking in the price at which a particular currency may be either sold or purchased, depending upon the type of contract.

In addition, the Eurocurrency market itself serves as a factor in assessing currency risk. As discussed earlier, Eurocurrencies are deposits of the currency in a country other than that of the bank holding the deposit. These deposits exist due to the variations in exchange rates between countries and reflect the depositors' desire to profit—albeit in fractions of a percentage point—from the discrepancy.

The "market" for such deposit accounts reflects profits to be made from the ability to marshal funds of a particular currency at a rate fractionally less than the current exchange rate. Because of the escalating volume and individual worth of international loans, the fractional advantage of a Eurocurrency loan thus produces significant extra profits for lenders due to the reduced costs of acquiring needed funds. Finally, fixing interest on the loan in terms of current Eurocurrency rates (LIBOR) assures that a falling market (in which Eurodollars are worth less than at the time of the loan) will not adversely affect repayment value.

Another consideration in currency risk is the free availability of currencies that may be subject to foreign exchange restrictions in the borrower's country. Eurodollar transactions have the potential for encountering government action in the form of interference in the flow of currency by the government's foreign central bank or official agency. This risk of interference with the movement or return of currency used to make interest or principal payments is associated with any international transaction. Thus, a clear assessment of the domestic and international political climate surrounding the transaction is required. Such interferences with accessibility of funds and international commerce frequently will have little to do with economic gain, as was strikingly demonstrated at the time of the Iranian hostage crisis in late 1979. The freezing of Iranian assets by the Carter Administration effectively prevented the repatriation of those assets to Iran. Another example is the recent nationalization of Mexican banks with imposition of conversion and transfer controls on foreign currency accounts.

While provision for repayment of funds in an alternate currency more readily available may be specified in a clause of the loan agreement, it is prudent to seek permission for the export of currency from local exchange control authorities in the event that default requires execution against the property of the borrower held on foreign territory. It should be mentioned, however, that, regardless of the wording of such transfer guarantees or agreements, it is within the range of possibility that foreign governments will abnegate such guarantees by decree or change in regulation.

COUNTRY RISK

Political, economic, and jurisprudential conditions in the borrower's country will have obvious and far-ranging impacts on the decision to lend. This aspect of the loan decision may illustrate the limits of pure legal or economic analysis as experience and judgment are heavily called upon in assessing and limiting this risk. As will be later illustrated, certain risk factors may be anticipated in the loan agreement and guarded against. Nevertheless, adequate and realistic evaluation of political and economic events can mean the difference between a profitable loan transaction and a default situation.

In regard to defaults, one should realize that, in the event of a breach of the agreement, legal remedies will vary from state to state. Moreover, these legal remedies may be either inconsistent or in conflict with each other and thus should be provided for in Eurodollar transactions. Otherwise, disputes may arise as to the proper legal principles to be applied in the event of disagreement between the parties. Perhaps of more importance, the sophistication and integrity of local tribunals and judicial systems, upon which the parties will rely to enforce their agreement, must also be considered.

Eurodollar transactions are particularly vulnerable to jurisdictional disputes. Since, in effect, Eurodollars are "foreign currency" in every country, no one country can be relied upon for support in the event of a deposit holding bank's failure. Unlike banking systems such as that of the United States, the Eurodollar market does not have an official "lender of last resort," such as the Federal Reserve Bank to which it may turn in the event of an emergency.

In effect, the failure of a Eurocurrency deposit-holding institution means a loss of funds since no insurance or lender of last resort is available to cover Eurodollar holdings. Thus, the relative soundness of foreign banks as compared to banks in the United States becomes an important factor in Eurodollar lending. The sources of domestic regulatory costs, such as reserve requirements, interest rate limitations, and deposit insurance, also provide significant protection to investors from bank failure or negligence and the consequential loss of deposits.

To illustrate the potential risk involved with this factor, consider the failure of Bankhaus Herstatt in 1974. Significant involvement in Eurodollar trading led to huge losses that left the bank insolvent. German banking authorities closed the bank when it was discovered it was no longer able to meet sizable Eurodollar repayment obligations. Due to the time differences between Germany and other countries, such as the United States, transfers of currency involved in foreign exchange transactions reached Bankhaus Herstatt just prior to its collapse without having the converted transfers returned to banks in the United States. Total losses were suffered by the transferring institutions. Needless to say, the effect upon the Eurodollar market was severe. Due to the fact that Eurodollar deposits are often redeposited in the interbank market, an immense chain reaction resulted in multiple losses of hundreds of millions of dollars among several institutions.

The aftermath of the Herstatt crisis was a restructuring of the Eurocurrency market by major participants, which effectively shifted the bulk of future Eurodollar business to larger, more established institutions. For quite a few years following the collapse of Herstatt, smaller institutions paid premiums for access to Eurocurrency deposits if they gained access at all. This even further increased the volatility of the market in reaction to world events. Under certain conditions, the Bank for International Settlements is now functioning as an emergency lender to the Eurocurrency market as well as serving as an agent for central banks in the market. In addition, it seems that, with Switzerland, central bankers of the "Group of Ten" countries agreed in 1974 to offer assistance to foreign branches of banks under their supervision should an international financial crisis develop, thus serving as the functional equivalent of lenders of last resort for the Euromarket.

CREDIT DECISIONS

Greater costs are incurred in acquiring information with which to assess risks in dealing with foreign banks, particularly those new to international markets. Credit officers must deal with a greater lack of credit information when making an international investment decision as compared to similar investment in a domestic context. In addition to the usual evaluative aspects, which will be outlined here, some factors unique to the international credit decision will now be mentioned.

For example, the lending officer must evaluate:

- character and business reputation of the borrower;
- business history and financial policies of the institution;
- balance sheet, in particular, cash flow and earnings impact of the loan request; and
- source of repayment funds and anticipated developments in the future prospects of the borrower.

Despite the knowledge of which factors to assess, however, significant differences between domestic and foreign business and accounting practices frequently pose difficulties when a straightforward credit analysis based on domestic principles is attempted.

For example, alien legal concepts, translation problems, and unfamiliar business practices leave much to be desired when attempting to develop a consistent system of international loan analysis. Accounting practices and reliability of data differ drastically from what can be expected when dealing with a domestic borrower. Furthermore, it is extremely probable that differences in currency exchange rates over the time period being analyzed prevent a clear picture of the borrower's past and present situation. Effects of currency fluctuations on the balance sheet figures illustrate the problem encountered. In sum, therefore, these three risk factors—currency risk, country risk, and credit risk—present special circumstances to be evaluated, which lead to greater costs when evaluating foreign investments.

It is emphasized that these problems, as noted, require assessment and evaluation from a commercial as well as legal perspective. While they may be addressed within the legal document embodying the parties' agreement, they reppresent factors affecting the profitability of the transaction and its potential for success as well as being technical allocations of risk.

Until recently, American banks participated in Eurodollar markets solely through their overseas branches and subsidiaries, which previously were totally exempt from reserve requirements of Regulation D and interest rate limitations of Regulation Q. Thus, these overseas entities could acquire deposits without the overhead costs of their domestic parents. Dissatisfaction with the competitive disadvantage to domestic institutions created by this policy was coupled with skepticism regarding the extent to which an additional "new" unregulated source of dollars would actually undermine the Federal Reserve's attempts to provide monetary stability. This led to a relaxation of banking restrictions and the creation in 1982 of International Banking Facilities (IBFs), which function as "offshore money centers" for international lending. (IBFs are discussed in greater detail in another section.)

Nevertheless, still only a few United States banks could be characterized as active in the Eurodollar market due to the level of expertise and funds needed to enter and remain the market.

Syndication

Loan requirements for international finance are often so substantial that no institution could or would want to undertake the entire credit commitment. This economic reality has led to the development of the syndicated loan, whereby several banks join together to share the rights and responsibilities connected with the extension of a substantial loan. Therefore, syndication involves a number of lending banks, which when acting in concert are effectively able to extend the size limit of loans that could be made individually on the Eurodollar market. The banks are also able to spread their risks amongst themselves. Each lender's obligation is generally separate.

Syndication of the lending commitment among several participating banks adds flexibility to the making of Eurocurrency loans, a development that benefits both borrowers and lenders. Many of the technical functions of credit evaluation and servicing are provided by a *lead bank* who typically is an experienced international lender. The function of a lead bank will be further discussed. As a result of this procedure, access to the international lending market has been provided to relatively unsophisticated banks whose limited resources would otherwise prevent their being direct lenders. The resulting larger "pool" of loan funds permits borrowers to arrange loans of a size that would be beyond the capabilities of individual institutions, due to limitations such as those found in U.S. banking regulations. For example, the limit on the amount of credit that may be extended to one borrower by a bank is currently 10% of the bank's capital and surplus. However, as of 1983, proposals to increase this limit are under consideration.

The needs of borrowers, such as multinational corporations and governments, called for a larger source of available funds. Furthermore, an opportunity for syndicate banks to enter profitable transactions was also perceived when the idea of syndication first developed. Though not without uncertainties and pitfalls, the rapid growth of the segment of the loan market attests to the enthusiasm with which it has been received. Recent growth in the field of medium-term syndicated Eurocurrency loans in Europe, as well as in the United States, reflects a sustained demand for this development of international lending. Finally, the establishment of consortium banks owned by a group of major international banks further facilitates the negotiation of very large credits. This market serves the credit needs of large borrowers such as multinational corporations, governments, and money market institutions.

The syndication process requires the involvement of several participant-lenders from the outset and entails several steps aimed at meeting the requirements of individual lenders, as well as those of the borrower. These include: formation of the loan package, marketing to other participants, and administration of the loan. The responsibility for accommodating the demands of this divergent group falls on the lead, or *manager*, bank.

At the outset, the lead bank's, or manager's, responsibility is to negotiate with the borrower and determine the most efficient and profitable means of selling the loan. This is accomplished through credit analysis and a full assessment of the risk factors. Thereafter, interest in the package terms is solicited from other prospective participating banks who may ultimately join with the manager to extend credit. Participations may be offered on the general market, in much the same way that securities might be offered. However, due to this similarity the manager runs a risk of subjecting the offering to rigorous disclosure requirements under securities laws. Nevertheless, a wider and more diverse group of participating banks is obtained. This potential area of liability will be further discussed in the section relating to the offering memorandum used in a typical syndicated loan agreement. Let it be mentioned, however, that if it is found that the offering of loan participations constitutes an offering of a "security," significant disclosure requirements will have to be complied with. Alternatively, a more selective offering may be made in which a limited number of institutions are invited to participate. Although this procedure may qualify as a "private offering" for exemption under the securities laws, there is a possibility that the loan may not acquire a sufficient number of participants.

Typically, one of three distinct means is available for the manager to market the loan. Briefly, these include:

1. the best-efforts,
2. the firm-commitment, and
3. the preadvanced type of syndicate.

A *best-efforts syndication* contemplates a completed set of terms and conditions that will be offered on the market by the manager and, if not accepted by lenders, withdrawn with no further commitment to the borrower. On the other hand, the *firm-commitment* syndicate presupposes a commitment to lend by the manager, who, if unsuccessful in marketing the loan to others, will assume the unmarketed portions on its own books. Managers normally will not agree to underwrite a syndicated loan. As a result, borrowers typically agree on the best-efforts method. Finally, a *preadvanced* syndicate provides for a firm commitment by the manager to lend at specified terms, with the right to participate the loan out at a later date. Variations of these three main methods of marketing the loan also exist and vary with the agreement of the parties.

Each of these variations allows for flexibility in the means of structuring the participation so as to appeal to the risk-conscious lender. On the one hand, with a *direct* loan, each of the participants is given a set of notes evidencing the indebtedness of the borrower. This method is utilized in cases where a well established, highly creditworthy borrower or collateral is involved. On the other hand, when the borrower is not so substantially recommended but has had the foresight to utilize a well established manager, use of *indirect* participation may be called for. In that instance, the loan is funded directly through the manager's assets, with participants receiving certificates evidencing indebtedness owed to them by the manager. The difference in parties ultimately liable on the loan is the distinguishing legal consequence of choosing direct or indirect loans. For example, in a direct participation, the borrower remains liable to each participant on the individual notes. With the indirect format, each participant has recourse only against the manager for default on its certificates, while solely the manager has rights against the borrower. In any event, there are numerous ways to grant participations that will affect the legal position of the parties.

After agreeing on terms with the borrower, securing a mandate letter to proceed, and enlisting participants for the syndication, such as through preparation of the information memorandum, the role of the manager (or of a separately retained agent) becomes largely administrative. An agency clause or separate agency agreement is used to appoint an agent separate from the lead bank. In addition to receiving and transmitting notices of drawdowns, the manager (or its agent) will be responsible for calculating the applicable interest for each period and for overseeing the transfer of funds. In general, it is the lender's responsibility to monitor compliance with the provisions of the loan. It will also serve as the conduit for periodic distribution of financial statements and other documents and communications required by the parties. Thus, after initially representing the borrower, the manager becomes responsible to the participating banks. The extent of potential liability to the loan participants will later be discussed in the context of syndicate management.

As this general overview of the syndication process indicates, the manager's position is fraught with potential conflicts of interest and difficulties. In fact in recent years the formerly enviable position of manager or lead bank has lost some of its attractiveness due to the potential risk of liability. To illustrate this potential for conflicts of interest, the borrower will rely on the manager's expertise in structuring and promoting the syndication on terms favorable to it. On the other hand, the participants may tend to rely on the manager's judgment and information for the fullest disclosure of material information about the borrower and its country's financial and political condition. Furthermore, as the loan progresses, participants will rely on the managers to exercise diligence in supervising the borrower's ability to repay principal and interest. Therefore, the potential for problems requires that the manager at all times seeks to foster an atmosphere of good faith and disclosure when conflicts do arise, so that the parties may adequately protect their own interests.

Let us now turn to additional consideration of matters covered in a typical loan syndication transaction by considering the major items contained in standard documentation.

Documentation

Loan documentation has a dual purpose in the context of a syndication. First, in describing and promoting the participation, it acts as an inducement to investment, which increasingly becomes tacitly incorporated in the final agreement between the parties. This marketing function is performed by the *placement memorandum,* which describes the financial background of the borrower and the nature of the loan requested. Second, the documentation performs evidentiary and apportioning functions by describing the commitments, responsibilities, and remuneration of the parties while at the same time assigning to each its portion of risk.

This role is filled by the traditional loan agreement and, where called for, supporting guarantees and notes. While terms of loan documentation vary from loan to loan, it is possible to generalize about the format typically used. This will be the focus of the remaining portion of the chapter. It is important to realize that, depending upon the type of loan required, a specialized document will be prepared. For purposes of illustrating the functions of various provisions contained in syndication documentation, a hypothetical loan syndication transaction will be analyzed. Let us say that the Central Bank of Gazpacho seeks to raise $100 million to finance economic development projects in the agricultural-industrial sector of the province's economy. The placement memorandum contains information identifying the borrower. For example, the brorrower may be identified as the province's central banking institution. Reference to anticipated use of funds will also be contained. In our example, funds will be used for loans to be made directly to approved agricultural product-processors through the bank's branch office. Modernization of agricultural methods, expansion of land and existing industrial facilities, and improvement of transportation and communications services are part of the province's ambitious economic recovery program. Thus, the loan proposal is part of an ambitious economic recovery program aimed at revitalizing a declining domestic economy to restore foreign investor and creditor confidence. These circumstances typify those of many developing nations in search of foreign funds. Although a lack of domestic political and economic stability might undermine the confidence of foreign investors in providing capital for projects that might later be confiscated or destroyed, the country's natural resources and industrial potential may warrant sufficient optimism for other, more protected forms of investment.

NEGOTIATION AND MANDATE LETTER

The first step in the process of developing a final agreement to form the loan syndicate is negotiation between the manager and the borrower. Terms of the credit and price are discussed and can be the most difficult yet crucial aspects of the syndication process. However, once terms are agreed upon, the manager will next prepare to sell the credit to the market. Therefore, a *mandate letter* will be obtained from the borrower, which authorizes the manager to arrange and market the credit on its behalf. The mandate letter summarizes the principal terms of the loan. The next step in the management of the loan transaction for the manager is supervision or preparation of the information or placement memorandum.

PLACEMENT MEMORANDUM

The *placement memorandum* provides information concerning the general terms of the loan and the economic and financial backgrounds of the borrower and its guarantors, if any. The labeling of the document as a "memorandum" rather than as a "prospectus" reflects the trade's attempt to distinguish the offering of the loan from that of a "security," which, as mentioned earlier, might subject it to stringent registration and disclosure requirements. Analysis of securities laws possibly applicable to the transaction is called for particularly in situations where note instruments are issued evidencing the debt. As a general matter, therefore, the manager and/or preparer of the memorandum must be aware of the securities legislation in the jurisdiction where the document is being prepared or circulated for issuance or distribution. For example, the Securities Act of 1933 and the Securities Exchange Act of

1934 of the United States, as well as the Companies Act of 1948 and the Prevention of Fraud (Investments) Act of 1958 of Great Britain, may affect loans involving U.S. and British jurisdictions. In addition, the extent of responsibility regarding accuracy of the memorandum contents must also be ascertained prior to public distribution. Since the information memorandum plays such an important role in the participants' decision whether or not to join the syndication, the accurary of statements and the avoidance of information or omissions that could be construed as misleading or deceptive is the responsibility of the manager.

The action against the syndicate manager of the Colocotronis loans, the European-American Banking Corporation (EAB) illustrates the potential liability that participants may seek to impose upon managers pursuant to securities laws.

Briefly, the facts were as follows. Colocotronis loan participations were sold to plaintiffs—American participating banks—who alleged that this constituted a sale of securities within the meaning of United States (and state) securities laws. Furthermore, they claimed that the syndicate manager had a duty to diligently and carefully inform itself and to advise the plaintiffs of all material facts relating to the loans. The plaintiffs claimed that EAB was allegedly guilty of making untrue statements of material facts and of omission to state material facts with the result that they were induced to acquire participations in the then defaulted loan.

As noted, the memorandum prepared by the manager is frequently based on information supplied by the borrower. The information provided is often of the most general nature and, because presented for promotional purposes, may contain information unverified by the manager. In an attempt to limit its liability for these representations, the manager will often seek to disclaim responsibility for the facts and claims presented. Similarly, participants will be encouraged to perform their own independent credit investigation. Statements of warranty stating that such independent investigations were in fact made may also be sought. Nevertheless, the effectiveness of such safeguards against liability varies and depends to a large degree upon the extent of diligence and culpability found on the part of the manager. For this reason, it is prudent practice to secure independent outside legal counsel, as well as aiming for accurate and complete disclosure in the placement memorandum.

As more lenders enter the market, banks must increasingly rely on the manager's judgment and reputation in assessing credit risk due to the time and resources required for a sophisticated credit analysis. One observer has noted that the result of this reliance on another lender's credit assessment, in the absence of widely established market standards for syndicated loan composition and structure, has resulted in two standards for issuing credit. Namely, a generalized standard is applied to domestic loans whereas a less verifiable standard is utilized for international loans. The combination of a lack of judicial or legislative intervention, along with a rapidly expanding market representing a variety of legal systems, has contributed to and at times promoted this condition. Therefore, it is difficult to generalize regarding the "market practice" of disclosure. The permissable degree of reliance on promoter representations tends to vary with locale as well as with an individual promoter. Nevertheless, it is crucial for the manager of loan syndications to be aware of the pitfalls encountered in the routine preparation of memorandum.

LOAN AGREEMENT

An examination of the various provisions of a syndicated loan agreement brings us full circle to the opening remarks of this chapter: Beyond the essential agreements to lend and to repay, with interest, funds of a certain variety and amount, a loan document consists of descriptions of certain contingencies representing risk to one or all parties and of provisions included to reduce those risks. The specificity with which these designations and provisions are declared is dependent upon many factors, not the least of which is the local market custom. For example, while one region may prefer highly specific instructions regarding the procedures to be employed by the agent in the event that LIBOR is unavailable to compute the current interest or drawdown, another regional market may find this cumbersome or even restrictive of common good business sense and thus seek to avoid such specificity. A careful draftsman will thus appreciate the market customs of the parties in order to anticipate the degree of flexibility that may be incorporated into the loan documents.

A summary of documents prepared for our hypothetical loan to the Bank of Gazpacho follows. It may be noticed that several measures are specifically aimed to preserving the lender's, rather than borrower's, interests, thus reflecting the relative bargaining position of the parties in one particular case.

Definitions

This section defines important terms utilized in the agreement sometimes including definition by reference to other portions of the agreement where those terms are defined. Although a seemingly innocuous portion of the document, key limitations on loan commitments, lending procedures and participation in the loan are made. For example, the obligation to lend becomes enforceable only upon the *effective date* of the agreement (the date of the closing) and ceases to be enforceable upon a *termination date*.

COMMITMENT TO LEND AND BORROW

A description of the lending and borrowing procedure is included. For example, a *commitment period* limits the obligation to lend to a period from the effective date of the agreement until two years from the date of the closing. In addition, the commitment to lend is several, rather than joint, among the lending banks. In other words, each bank is solely responsible for the lending of its share of the total commitment. Therefore, if one of the syndicate lenders defaults on its commitment, the remaining lenders do not assume the added burden. It should be noted, however, that on certain loans such as project loans, a default may so jeopardize the success of the enterprise that one bank's failure to lend may be grounds for termination of the obligation to lend on the part of the nondefaulting banks.

Under the terms of the Gazpacho agreement, the borrower is not actively committed to borrow. Instead, it is purchasing a right analogous to an option to borrow, which may be exercised at any time during the commitment period through the device of a drawdown. This procedure calls for:

- this borrower to give notice to the agent designated by the banks at least seven days in advance of the date it wishes to make the drawdown (which date also starts the accruing of interest);
- the aggregate amount required from the banks (which is then divided among them in proportion to each bank's total commitment and includes all participating banks); and
- the New York account to which the funds should be credited.

The giving of this notice irrevocably commits the borrower to borrow the stated amount ratably from each bank. There are ten specific time periods between the effective date and the termination date for the making of drawdowns.

The agent, in turn, is required to give each bank five days' notice of the drawdown date and amount. A time of day is also designated when each bank shall make these funds available to the agent for transmission to the borrower's account.

REPAYMENT

Repayment of principal is scheduled in equal installments commencing on the fifth anniversary of the closing date. Prepayment is provided for, but it is limited to a minimum amount and requires prior notice to the banks. All repayments are made ratably to the several banks in proportion to their loan commitment then outstanding. Should one bank receive a larger payment than it is entitled to, the others are granted a right of contribution against it.

Note that both the drawdown and repayment procedures are designed to limit exposure of lending banks' funds, and they serve as a protection against volatile shifts in lending costs.

INTEREST

Interest on outstanding funds is due in semiannual installments, beginning six months from the date of the closing. Interest is computed by the agent through use of a formula based on the current LIBOR, which essentially provides for a margin of bank profit of from ¾ % to ⅞ % over the current cost of acquiring the funds. LIBOR is frequently calculated using the average of rates offered by selected reference banks. Once it has computed the applicable interest, the agent so notifies both the borrower and the lenders. The interest provision of any Eurodollar loan is subject to negotiation and may vary.

In the event that a LIBOR rate is unavailable or inadequately covers the bank's costs of funding their commitments, perhaps due to unavailability of Eurodollars, notice of this fact is required to be given to the borrower and guarantor. Thereafter, negotiations ("in good faith") to supply a "substituted" basis for the interest rate will begin. Subject to the approval of the banks, this substituted basis is used only for the limited period of LIBOR instability.

In the event no agreement is reached, the individual banks are free to select a substituted basis that reflects costs of procuring the required funds plus margin. After notification, the borrower then has the option to either approve the substituted basis or to prepay the loan in full. Its commitment to borrow remains irrevocable.

The agent is given the authority to determine whether circumstances giving rise to the unstable LIBOR rate have ended, and whether use of the substituted basis should terminate.

NOTES

The borrower's indebtedness is evidenced by interim notes delivered to the agent for the amount of each drawdown. These are exchanged at the termination date for definitive notes to be held by the individual banks pending repayment.

FEES

Among the more attractive aspects of loan syndications, from the point of view of the major banks that organize them, are the fees to be earned in arranging them. The Gazpacho agreement provides for three types of fees:

- *Commitment fees*—A fee is paid for the portion of the total loan commitment that remains undisbursed (undrawn) from the effective date of the agreement. The fee is computed at the rate of ½% per annum on the daily average of undisbursed funds, and it is payable in semiannual installments. This compensates the lender for funds committed to the borrower that may not be otherwise used.
- *Management fee*—Soon after the effective date, a fee is paid to the manager banks for their services in arranging and supervising the syndication. The amount is decided by prior arrangement and is based on the total amount of the loan.
- *Agency fee*—A yearly fee is paid to the agent of the banks for services rendered in the administration of the ongoing lending and repayment of funds.

PAYMENTS AND TAXES

Specifics regarding method of payment by the borrower are included. For example, the time of payment as well as the currency, account, and bank are indicated.

Payments are specifically exempted from taxation or levy in this borrower's country. The borrower agrees to make additional payment to any bank of whatever amount necessary to insure the bank's receipt of the amount it would otherwise have received but for the imposition of additional fee or tax requirements. Note that this in effect creates a separate legal status for the lenders due to the tax exemption granted this particular transaction. Also, assurance of obtaining the total repayment amount is thus achieved.

The borrower further agrees to indemnify the banks for losses due to subsequent changes in reserve requirements in the banks' home jurisdiction, which would otherwise cut into the availability of bank funds, thereby reducing its profit. This is of particular advantage to lenders, as the imposition of a reserve requirement or increase in current requirements on Eurodollar accounts would inhibit the availability of lending funds. Any increase in cost to the banks in acquiring additional funds to meet their loan commitments is thus covered by such a provision. Alternative currency clauses provide for repayment in another currency if certain criteria are met.

CONDITIONS PRECEDENT

In the agreement described are conditions that prevent the bank's lending obligations from becoming effective until all conditions have been fulfilled. These conditions fall into two categories: those to be performed before the initial drawdown, and those affecting each subsequent draw-down. Among the former are delivery of a guarantee for the borrower's obligation, opinions by local and foreign authorities as to the corporate and constitutional power of the governmental bodies involved to enter into the agreement, and acquiescence by local representatives to act as agent for the borrower and guarantor for purposes of service of process. In the latter category are the standard condition of no-default, no changes in material circumstances, and the delivery to the agent of the interim note described in a preceding section.

REPRESENTATIONS AND WARRANTIES

In this section the borrower makes representations as to its legal and corporate authority to enter into the agreement: for example, that the borrower is duly organized, has full power and authority, an absence of defaults, no liabilities, and the necessary government approvals. It also warrants its capacity to fulfill the obligations undertaken by it and assures that no recording or filing requirements are a condition prece-dent to legal validity of the documents. Supplemental representations are made with respect to the tax-exempt status of the loan proceeds. This has the effect of indemnifying the banks from losses occasioned by changes in the country's tax law.

WAIVER OF SOVEREIGN IMMUNITY

It is of special importance in a loan involving a foreign state (or state branch or agency) as borrower or guarantor to obtain a statement dis-claiming any right to the protections afforded by the sovereign immu-nity doctrine. Otherwise, the property of the borrower or guarantor be shielded from attachment in the event of default. A further safeguard is the characterization of the loan as a "commercial" rather than "gov-ernment" transaction so as to prevent the transaction from being con-sidered outside the jurisdiction of domestic courts as could happen under the restrictive theory of sovereign immunity.

It should be mentioned that in the United States, the restrictive theory of sovereign immunity is embodied in the recently enacted For-eign Sovereign Immunities Act of 1976. Foreign governments, branches, or agencies are not granted immunity in disputes involving commercial rather than governmental activities. Furthermore, irrevocable waivers can be agreed upon and may be extended to cover property of a foreign state as well. Naturally, application of the sovereign immunity statute to particular loans will vary according to the factual differences encoun-tered in the extension of a loan for specific uses. It is interesting to note that, until recently, British courts applied the doctrine of absolute sovereign immunity to all legal proceedings involving a foreign sovereign. In addition, waivers could be withdrawn at any time prior to commencement of legal proceedings. Needless to say, waivers offered lenders a worthless assurance of repayment by foreign sovereign borrowers as they were granted absolute immunity. However, this doctrine was modified recently in the case of Trendtex Trading Corporation Ltd. v. Central Bank of Nigeria, Court of Appeal 1977. As a result, the British Courts will approach a standard closer to that of the restrictive theory of sovereign immunity. In any event, it is of the utmost importance to obtain a full legal analysis of the potential effects of applicable sovereign immunity statutes whenever a sovereign borrower is involved, particularly in view of the increasing number of governmental defaults.

COVENANTS

The most significant covenant made in any loan agreement is that of the borrower to repay the loan to the lender. Additional covenants as a rule represent the lender's attempt to limit the borrower's business activities, which may jeopardize its investment. Typical covenants have utility whether the loan is made in a domestic or international context. For example, the loan agreement may contain a covenant restricting use of the loan funds to a specific purpose.

Of central importance in the international loan context are covenants restricting encumbrances on the borrower's assets so as to protect the priority of the lender's security interests. A *pari passu* covenant would specify that the bank's right to be repaid is not subordinated to the rights of any of the borrower's other unsecured creditors. *Pari passu* covenants relate to unsecured indebtedness and are therefore usually accompanied by "negative pledges," which cover secured indebtedness. Furthermore negative pledge covenants protect the lender's position in the event of default while indirectly serving to inhibit the assumption of excessive debt by the borrower. Usually, the negative pledge prohibits mortages, charges, pledges, and liens as well as any other encumbrances on the borrower's assets.

The problem of balancing adequate protection for the lender against the borrower's legitimate credit needs has largely been responsible for the great variety of negative pledges. Financial covenants may also be included such as those whereby the borrower agrees to supply periodic financial statements to the lender. A clause regarding preservation of assets may be necessary in addition to financial covenants even though both are aimed at preserving the funds or assets eventually to be used for repayment. Since they normally prohibit specific actions, which may jeopardize the lender's rights in the borrower's assets (that is, the borrower shall not sell, transfer, lease, or otherwise dispose of any assets), they permit a breach of the loan agreement to be more easily detected.

ACCELERATION OF MATURITY

The events constituting default of the agreement by the borrower or guarantor are described in this section of the agreement. The standard events triggering default include failure of payment, warranties, or representations, insolvency of the borrower or governmental confiscation of its assets, and changes in circumstances giving rise to insecurity on the part of the banks. This allows a significant leeway for the lending banks to withdraw from their commitment without liability. Defaults result in termination of loan commitments and acceleration of repayment obligations. Therefore, default clauses are among the agreement's most carefully drafted provisions.

In the Gazpacho agreement, the agent is to notify the borrower of a termination of the bank's obligation to lend in the event of a default. All fees payable under the terms of the agreement become immediately due, together with funds actually lent with accrued interest. In the agreement, the borrower explicitly waives presentment and demand for payment along with the right to protest or receive notice of any kind after default.

RELATIONS AMONG BANKS

This section describes the rights and obligations of the lending banks. This includes the distribution of payments made and liability for expenses. In the Gazpacho agreement, payments made by the borrower are to be applied to costs, interest, and principal, in that order, regardless of any order subsequently indicated by the borrower. Distribution is to be made to all banks in proportion to their loan commitment. Any bank receiving total or partial payment sooner than they are entitled to is obligated to share any excess with the other banks in accordance with distribution of payment terms. An exception is made for funds due and received from the borrower in connection with transactions unrelated to the loan participation.

The duties and powers of the agent are described. It is usual practice for the agent to escape liability for those actions taken that are based on the opinion of legal counsel. Clarification of the actions to be taken, as well as specific triggering events, is quite important for lenders as well as the agent. The removal of discretion on the agent's part, especially in situations calling for notification of a default, protect the lender from risk of greater loss and the agent from liability for failure to act. A useful provision to include defines the circumstances under which an agent is to act when the lending banks call for conflicting action. That is, the agreement may provide that an agent is to take instructions from the majority of the banks, usually defined on the percentage of funds lent. In addition, agents frequently seek to limit their liability by providing that its duties are of an administrative and mechanical nature. The legal effectiveness of such provisions in a particular jurisdiction should be verified. Finally, it should be mentioned that rights of indemnification for expenses incurred for authorized legal acts are normally included. However, if not stated, rights of indemnification are generally implied in cases of dispute. Finally, it should be mentioned that problems may be encountered if the agent should happen to default. For example, the syndicate will still be liable for the loan to the borrower if the agent becomes insolvent before distribution of funds to the borrower. However, once the borrower gives the agent funds for repayment, he is discharged from the repayment obligation even if the agent misdirects the funds or defaults. Regarding reliance on information provided in the offering memorandum, an important stipulation puts the obligation of independent investigation and evaluation of the borrower's credit-worthiness on the participant banks. A separate warranty may be required to evidence the fact that such independent investigations took place. As previously mentioned, this provision attempts to relieve both manager and agent of potential liability for misrepresentation, such as when a borrower's financial condition is explained to "unsophisticated" lenders. Regardless of such warranties, it can be expected that courts will judge their effectiveness with consideration of the expertise of the party making the warranty.

COSTS AND INDEMNIFICATION

As is generally the case, this section places liability for costs of pre-agreement negotiations on the borrower. In addition, expenses of the agent and managers in executing and supervising the loan, as well as legal fees, are also allocated to the borrower. In the event that the borrower prepaid the principal amount, it is assigned the costs of loss of margin incurred in the liquidation of bank deposits held to fulfill the loan commitment. Finally, the borrower agreed to indemnify the agent, banks, and manager against costs resulting from legal proceedings connected with the loan.

MISCELLANEOUS

As a final point in our discussion of provisions typically included in a loan agreement, several miscellaneous provisions are included. For example, a choice of law and submission to jurisdiction clause indicates that the applicable law government the participation is that of New York. Furthermore, submission to the jurisdiction of the courts of the United States and of New York State is agreed upon. Significantly, enforcement of decrees of the courts of the United States in the country of the borrower is specifically provided for, as well as in any other jurisdiction in which properties, assets, or revenues may be situated.

Another point covers assignments. The borrower agrees that it may not assign its rights or obligations under the agreement without the consent of the banks. The lenders, however, may assign, sell, or grant participations in the loan without any restraint unless the transaction occurs prior to the end of the commitment period.

Conclusion

The syndication of international loans has developed in response to ever increasing credit demands of large borrowers. The Eurocurrency market is a main source of funding for international banks and institutions. With sufficient expertise, the extension of Eurocurrency loans offers the opportunity for increased revenues and business. However, some of the dangers present in such transactions must be appreciated and carefully analyzed. The special provisions found in international loan documentation reflect the market's response to these added elements of risk. These provisions should adequately anticipate problems that may develop. Nevertheless, they are no substitute for prudent credit decisions. This fact is increasingly being illustrated by the recent total defaults of many significant borrowers.

Bibliography

Bee, Robert N. "Syndication." In *Offshore Lending by U.S. Commercial Banks.* Washington, D.C.: Bankers' Association for Foreign Trade and Robert Morris Associates, 1975.

Calhoun, A. D., Jr. "Eurodollar Loan Agreements: An Introduction and Discussion of Some Special Problems." *J. Comm. Bank Lending,* 60(September 1977), pp. 23–27.

Cates, A. "Role of Managers and Agents." *Int'l Fin. L. Rev.* (June 1982), p. 21.

Goodfriend, M. "Eurodollars." *Economic Rev.* (1981).

Lichtenstein, Cynthia C. "U.S. Banks and the Eurocurrency Markets: The Regulatory Structure." *Banking L. J.,* 99, No. 6(1982), pp. 484–511.

Little, Jane. *Eurodollars: The Money-Market Gypsies.* New York: Harper and Row Publishers, Inc., 1975.

Luckett, Dudley. *Money and Banking,* 2nd ed. New York: McGraw-Hill, 1980.

Mitchell and Wall. "Eurodollar Market: Loans and Bonds." In *International Financial Law—Lending Capital Transfers and Institutions.* 1980.

Oppenheim, Peter. *International Banking,* 3rd rev. ed. Washington, D.C.: American Bankers Association, 1979.

Wood, Philip. *Law and Practice of International Finance.* London: Sweet & Maxwell, 1980.

Youard, R. G. A. "Lender Know Thyself." *Euromoney* (September 1981), p. 34.

9

Bank Examination and Supervision

An important component of the banking industry is the pervasive regulation and supervision by the governmental authorities to which it is subject. Initially, it is useful to distinguish between the regulation and supervision of banks. While *regulations* consists of the official issuance of rules and regulations governing banks, *supervision* encompasses the actual monitoring and examination of the activities of individual banks so as to assure that they are operating in accordance with applicable laws and regulations. In addition, bank supervision covers both external (or market-related) and internal (or operational) aspects of a bank.

Purpose of Bank Examination

Bank examination refers to the process by which the internal operations of individual banks are monitored and so serves as the primary method by which the industry is supervised. This chapter presents an overview of the agencies responsible for bank examination in the United States, and of their procedures. Using the American system as a representative model, the general focus will be on banks engaged in international activities, namely commercial banks, and will avoid a review of the supervision accorded such institutions as savings and loan associations, investment banks and credit unions. In addition, it should be mentioned that overseas activities of U.S. commercial banks are also generally monitored in accordance with the procedures to be discussed.

Finally, while supervisory agencies and procedures differ from nation to nation, their influence on the business decisions and operations of individual banks is a common factor, and forms the underlying theme of this discussion.

Bank examination serves the purpose not only of monitoring the functioning of individual institutions but of evaluating the stability of the industry as a whole. This dual function developed in response to the unstable conditions prevalent throughout the 1930s in the American banking industry, attributed in large part to a lack of sufficient regulation and supervision of bank operations. Responsibility for bank regulation and supervision is allocated by law and custom among both state and federal agencies. The rules and regulations promulgated by these banking authorities address nearly every function of bank establishment and operation. Therefore, let us briefly review the various agencies and authorities responsible for the regulation and supervision of banks.

Examining Agencies

The *Office of the Comptroller of the Currency* (OCC) is part of the United States Department of the Treasury. This agency is responsible for the chartering and supervision of all national banks. To be a national bank, a bank's charter must have been granted by the federal government. The frequency of examination of a national bank to assure its sound operation in compliance with legal requirements is determined by statute and agency policy. Because agency funding comes from assessments charged to national banks, the Office is financially autonomous from Congress. Specially trained examiners perform the actual examination in accordance with agency guidelines and procedures.

The *Federal Reserve System* (FRS) is another agency with broad supervisory authority. Comprised of a Board of Governors and a network of district Federal Reserve Banks and branches, the FRS functions as the central bank of the United States. As such, it is responsible for the development of U.S. monetary policy and the supervision of the banking entities that are its members. The FRS performs these functions through its control over the money supply and the issuance of regulations to which member banks are subject. It is an independent agency both structurally and financially. The FRS performs many important functions, which will be discussed later, among which is the examination of member banks.

The *Federal Deposit Insurance Corporation* (FDIC) is an independent government corporation established to insure deposits held in its member commercial and savings banks. Currently, the maximum amount insured per depositor and per account is $100,000. This insurance provides protection against possible losses resulting primarily from bank failure. The FDIC has the authority to examine all of its members, and, due to the fact that virtually all commercial banks are members of the FDIC, it serves as the overall examiner of the greatest proportion of commercial banks in the United States. This also results in overlapping agency responsibilities, as we shall see. Even though the FDIC is a government agency, it is totally supported by the insurance premiums assessed against a bank, which are based upon the amount of deposits held by the institution. These premiums pay both operating expenses and claims by deposit-holders; however, if the funds available to pay for depositors' losses prove to be inadequate, the FDIC can borrow additional amounts from the U.S. Treasury. In addition to insurance protection, a failing institution may be assisted by the FDIC through the extension of loans, the purchase of assets or placement of deposits in the institution. If need be, a merger with a "stronger" bank may be arranged or, when necessary, a receiver will be appointed for liquidation.

State banking departments and commissions function concurrently with the federal agencies already discussed and have the authority to regulate and examine the state banks they charter. The regulations imposed on state-chartered institutions vary from state to state. For example, many, but not all, states impose an *asset maintenance* rule requiring a foreign bank operating a branch or agency within the jurisdiction to hold assets in excess of at least 8% of local liabilities. In addition to being examined by local state banking departments for compliance with state requirements, state-chartered banks remain subject to examination by the federal agencies (with the exception of the Office of the Comptroller of the Currency) of which they are members. Finally, certain aspects of state regulation affect all banks, including national banks and others not subject to state examination. For example, national banks may be subject to certain limitations imposed by the states in which they organize (that is, branching limitations).

The *Securities and Exchange Commission* (SEC) is a federal agency charged with the responsibility to regulate participants in the securities market of the United States. The SEC is also responsible for regulating and monitoring the securities activities of bank holding companies (BHCs) and their affiliates (as well as of banks having over 500 shareholders). The banking activities of a BHC are supervised by the Federal Reserve, of course, and banks in general are not directly subject to SEC supervision. Banks are not permitted to act as dealers of publicly traded stock, but rules and regulations substantially similar to those of the SEC that govern other securities related activities are promulgated and enforced by the respective bank regulatory agencies. This supervisory authority, though a related activity, is independent of the bank examination powers, which are the focus of this chapter.

Each of these agencies issues specific regulations with which their respective member banks must comply. While each operates within its own guidelines, it also must function in conjunction with others. Because all examining agencies have certain goals and standards in common, the Federal Financial Institutions Examination Council Act of 1978 established a Council known as the *Federal Financial Institutions Examination Council* (FFIEC) to develop more uniform reporting standards and examination guidelines to be used by all federal supervisory agencies. The FFIEC members include: the Comptroller of the Currency, the Chairman of the Board of Directors of the FDIC, the Chairman of the Board of Governors of the Federal Reserve System, the Chairman of the Federal Home Loan Bank Board, and the Chairman of the National Credit Union Administration Board. The Federal Reserve Board and other agencies have in fact altered their supervisory operations to comply with the guidelines developed by the FFIEC. Thus the frequent inconsistencies in standards and procedures between agencies having concurrent examining authority may gradually be eliminated. A certain degree of revision of individual agency guidelines continues to occur in response to evolving supervisory needs.

Allocation of Examination Responsibility

All commercial banks are supervised by either the Office of the Comptroller of the Currency, the Federal Reserve System, the Federal Deposit Insurance Corporation, or the respective state banking departments of which they are members. Many banks, however, may be subject to a greater number of examinations due to the fact that they are affiliated with more than one agency; as a result, there may be a certain amount of overlap in supervisory authority. Nevertheless, it frequently occurs that the agencies themselves agree to allocate or divide certain responsibilities.

This is especially useful since certain types of banks are required to be members of a particular agency. For example, national banks, chartered by the federal government through the Office of the Comptroller of the Currency, are required to be members of the Federal Reserve System and to obtain FDIC insurance. The Comptroller is responsible for assuring that national banks are complying with applicable laws including those governing bank organization, expansion or consolidation, and general operations. The examination powers of the OCC include the assessment of the quality of a bank's management, as well as of its loan and investment portfolios. The Federal Reserve Board and the FDIC normally leave the supervision and examination of national banks to the Comptroller of the Currency despite the fact that all three agencies have concurrent examination authority.

Unlike national banks, which are required to join the FRS, state-chartered banks do not have a mandatory requirement of membership in the Federal Reserve System, but they may become members on a voluntary basis. FRS membership conveys certain advantages to both national and state banks. For example, members are permitted access to the Federal Reserve's safekeeping facilities and its discount window, which may be used to accommodate both temporary and seasonal borrowing needs. The FRS performs other important functions, such as providing services to the member banks, the determining of the interest rate (discount rate) to be charged members borrowing at the Reserve's discount window, and the serving as a clearing house for their check collections. Furthermore, the FRS has numerous enforcement responsibilities such as occasionally regulating members' foreign exchange activities, compliance with Truth in Lending Act requirements, and monitoring reports on extensions of credit for the purchase of stock.

Certain institutions receive particular attention from the FRS, among them bank holding companies, Edge Act and Agreement Corporations, and state member banks. In the case of state-chartered member banks, examination may be made in conjunction with state banking authorities. Together with the OCC, the FRS is responsible for a greater number of institutions involved in the international market than all other regulatory agencies.

All members of the FRS are required to obtain deposit insurance by joining the FDIC; consequently, all national banks, as FRS members, have FDIC insurance. On the other hand, while not required to do so, a state-chartered nonmember bank will frequently apply for FDIC membership as a means of enhancing its commercial marketability. By statute, the FDIC is granted authority to examine all member banks. As a practice matter, however, the FDIC normally is selective in its examination efforts, concentrating on insured state banks that are not members of the FRS. As mentioned earlier, state banks are also supervised by state banking departments of each state. If a state-chartered bank is insured by the FDIC, the FDIC also has the right, but not the obligation, to examine that institution. Depending upon the FDIC's perception of the quality and reliability of local state banking departments, the FDIC often will elect to avoid a duplication of effort by leaving the examination of some state banks to their state banking departments. For example, the state banking department of New York State has a reputation for competence and reliability; as a result, FDIC and Federal Reserve examiners usually do not join the New York State banking department examiners. In the majority of states, however, the FDIC and/or the FRS will accompany the local state banking department teams. With the passage of the International Banking Act, now foreign bank branches also may become FDIC-insured upon application, examination, and approval. Thus, we have seen that, despite the overlap of supervisory responsibilities between the agencies, certain institutions and activities are more closely monitored by one agency than another that may also have supervisory authority.

Agency Enforcement Powers

Certain powers have been granted to supervisory agencies to assure compliance with regulations and examination requirements. The fact that the agencies have such powers available to them facilitates the enforcement of their duties. The Comptroller's Office may impose a variety of enforcement measures, ranging from civil money penalties to the most severe measure, that of revoking a bank's charter and appointing an FDIC receiver. Charter revocation may occur, for example, when a bank refuses to permit access for examination or declines to give needed information to examiners. The OCC also may issue a cease and desist order against the offending institutions and suspend or remove responsible officers and directors for illegal activities. In addition, an institution's insurance may be terminated or the results of the bank examination report may be published. The Board of Governors of the FRS has enforcement powers similar to those of the OCC, including the ability to levy civil money penalties, remove a state bank from FRS membership, suspend or remove officers and/or directors of a bank for violations, and issue cease and desist orders. Despite the availability of these formal enforcement powers, it is likely that the agencies first will exhaust more informal channels such as telephone calls, visits, and letters to the institution's management.

Supervision of Foreign Banking Institutions

The International Banking Act of 1978 (IBA) authorizes federal agencies to supervise foreign banking institutions doing business in the United States. It lays the groundwork for a uniform national regulatory system for foreign bank branches, agencies, and representative offices located in the United States. Prior to enactment of this legislation, Federal charters were rarely obtained by foreign institutions, due both to restrictions on "membership" in the federal agencies already described, and to the business and regulatory advantages over domestic banks that often could be achieved. The relatively insignificant presence of foreign banking institutions in American markets prior to the 1960s further inhibited any efforts to impose federal supervision.

In the absence of a federal regulatory presence, supervision of foreign banking institutions was left to the respective state authorities under which the institutions' activities were chartered. The resulting lack of uniform rules and examination procedures, while acceptable on a local market level, became increasingly damaging to domestic banks as foreign banks' share of the national market expanded. By taking advantage of local rules and nuances in examination formats, a foreign bank could achieve cost savings not possible for a domestic competitor bank subject to more stringent FDIC rules. Furthermore, since foreign banks were not subject to the prohibitions against interstate branching imposed by the McFadden Act and the Federal Reserve Act, these advantages could be extended across state boundaries. Other federal prohibitions applicable to American banks also had provided advantages to foreign competitors, including the prohibitions on owning and investing in commercial enterprises, and on underwriting, selling, or distributing securities.

The International Banking Act seeks to eliminate the regulatory advantages favoring foreign banking institutions at the expense of domestic banks. The federal regulatory structure chosen by Congress for the IBA had two broad objectives. First, it introduced the policy of uniform treatment to the banking sector as a means for treating foreign banking operations as the competitive equals of their domestic counterparts. Second, it established measures for the federal supervision of such operations.

In order to achieve these objectives, the International Banking Act introduced several major changes in federal banking policy, including:

1. An option for federal licensing of foreign branches and agencies as well as for subsidiaries.
2. Mandatory deposit insurance for foreign branches engaged in retail banking.
3. Imposition of reserve requirements on foreign branches and agencies.
4. Limitation on the further expansion of multistate deposit taking activities. (Multistate operations existing prior to enactment of the IBA are grandfathered.)
5. Extension of the nonbanking prohibition of the Bank Holding Company Act to foreign banks operating branches, agencies, and commercial lending companies.
6. Appointment of the Federal Reserve to act as the residual examining agency in order to insure federal regulation of existing multistate activities of foreign banks.
7. Removal of restrictions preventing foreign banks from establishing Edge Corporations or acquiring a majority interest therein. Similarly, the IBA eliminates the requirement that all directors of Edge Corporations be American citizens.

Although the IBA seeks to advance the objective of national treatment and parity for domestic and foreign banks, it falls short of complete competitive equality. Congress expressed concern for certain fundamental differences in the structure and function of foreign and domestic banks, such as the tendency of some nations to permit banks to engage in various types of nonbanking activities normally prohibited to domestic banks by the United States Congress. Believing that an across-the-board application of federal laws restricting nonbanking activities would unfairly discriminate against foreign banks currently in operation, Congress limited the reach of those restrictions by including "grandfathering" provisions in the Act, as was done for the existing multistate operations. These IBA provisions permit companies that were active in nonbanking activities as of September 17, 1978 and foreign bank branches operating before July 27, 1978 to grandfather these activities. However, in order to continue nonbanking activities after 1985, certain statutory requirements must be met. Interstate banking opportunities are now curtailed by Section 5 of the IBA, which prohibits the establishment of deposit-taking offices in more than one "home" state unless the law of the other state so permits and the mandatory activity-limiting agreement is entered into with the Federal Reserve Board. The bank may continue operation in those states where its activities are grandfathered.

Congress made an additional distinction between foreign and domestic banks. All foreign bank operations, including state-chartered entities, are under at least minimal federal supervision and control, unlike state nonmember banks, which are not subject to FRB regulations. Besides being subject to mandatory federal reporting requirements, foreign banks (including state-licensed branches and agencies) are required in certain instances to comply with the reserve requirements applicable to Federal Reserve member banks.

As a general matter, therefore, the IBA has the effect of bringing foreign banking organizations under the authority of federal supervisory agencies, such as the FDIC and the Federal Reserve Board, in addition to the state banking departments.

Examination Procedures

Now that we have examined the general purpose of bank supervision and the agencies responsible for examining particular banking institutions, let us turn to an overview of the actual examination process. An effective examination can provide the basis for determining the soundness and quality of a bank's management, directors, and operations while assisting the agency (as well as bank management) in locating possible areas of weakness to be corrected. Each of the agencies has a staff of trained examiners who are responsible for verifying that a bank's operations are in compliance with agency guidelines and regulations.

However, all banks subject to the agency's jurisdiction are required by law to comply with established information requests. Naturally, the true effectiveness of bank examination lies in the skill and experience of the examiners implementing agency guidelines and regulations. Compilation of the information gathered from on-site examinations, along with the data contained in the reports of condition required to be filed with the agencies, forms the major enforcement tool of bank supervision agencies.

A bank examination is not designed to take the form of a bank audit, which, by comparison, is designed to uncover fraudulent transactions and record errors of every type. Instead, an analysis of certain data is made by examiners under the assumption that the information provided, including bank records, is reliable. Of course, this assumption may permit certain existing fraudulent activity to continue undetected for some time, even where an independent outside auditing firm has prepared certain financial statements for inclusion in the bank's records. Nevertheless, due to the extensive responsibilities involved in properly examining a bank under current practices, this risk is considered low enough to not warrant the technical review of all bank transactions required in the case of a bank audit performed by independent CPAs.

An internal audit may be timed, in fact, to coincide with a pending examination. When the bank arranges for its yearly directors' audit with a CPA firm, that firm may, in turn, coordinate its audit with the examination of either national or state supervisory authorities. Generally, the audit and the examination are conducted at different times to avoid conflict and overlapping. Once the CPA audit is completed, a copy of the statement, findings, and recommendations is submitted to the Board of Directors rather than to the management of the bank. In addition, a copy is made available to government examiners. Rather than undertaking another bank audit, supervisory agencies thus are free to concentrate their examination efforts on a review of official bank practices and policies to ascertain the underlying soundness of the institution. The following sections will identify examination procedures and the areas of bank operation upon which examiners focus.

Regarding the frequency of bank examination, a consistent monitoring program is the goal. National banks used to be examined a minimum of three times every two years to the OCC; however, the National Bank Act now allows for the examination of national banks to occur as often as necessary, without imposing a minimum examination schedule. More frequent examination would be called for where bank problems are discovered and are being monitored for rectification. The Federal Reserve attempts to examine its member banks on an annual basis. Depending upon the performance record of a particular institution, the extent and timing of its examinations may also be altered. Other examining agencies set their own examination schedules, which may be coordinated when objectives overlap. Typically these examinations will occur every 12 to 18 months.

One of the major elements of bank examination is surprise; advance warning to the institution that it is about to be examined is the exception rather than the rule. Instead, examiners arrive unannounced to take control of bank operations for examination. As a practical matter, they arrive at the entrance of the bank prior to opening time. In addition, if the bank is small or medium-sized, they first take the keys to the safes (or require them to be opened in their presence) in order to make a physical count of the monies and securities inventoried there. Once the count is completed, access to the safe is made available to the staff of the bank. Of course, while this procedure is underway, a sufficient amount of cash is given to the tellers for the normal conduct of business. The purpose behind taking control of the securities and money is to ascertain whether shortages exist or whether assets are being misused. Naturally, the size of the institution determines whether an actual counting is possible; obviously, this method cannot be utilized for larger banks with several branches. Large banks have their own internal examining teams whose inspectors report directly to the Board of Directors and not to the general management. Nevertheless, whenever the very largest banks are examined, three hundred examiners may appear at the bank one morning to start an examination. Due to the extreme size of these institutions, however, even that number of examiners may be insufficient for a thorough examination.

Before arriving at the bank, examiners prepare by studying the report of the previous examination. Previous reports reveal problems and shortcomings found during the prior examination and assist the examiner by indicating those areas warranting special attention. Therefore, bank examination procedures will then be adapted to meet the needs of particular institutions. Many uniform policies and procedures are followed by the OCC, the FRS, and the FDIC in their examinations. The Federal Financial Institutions Examination Council will accelerate the trend toward uniformity.

As a general matter, the examination strategy is developed using guidelines established by agency manuals, and it takes into account information sought by standard agency reports. The examiner in charge will determine the extent to which the basic areas of bank operations will be examined. After deciding upon general examination objectives, the actual analysis of various key areas of bank operations will begin. For example, each department is examined individually, including the commercial, consumer, international, trust, and electronic data processing departments. A review is made of the quality of assets (particularly loans), adequacy of capital, liquidity of assets, quality of management, overall compliance with rules and regulations, projected earning potential, and adequacy of internal audit and control procedures. Each category is assigned a rating number based on assessment of proper functioning. Information obtained from this review is ultimately compiled into the examiners' report for evaluation and recommendation.

The Focus of Examination

The classification of assets, particularly loans and investments, is a vital part of the examination process, and serves as a major indicator of the bank's condition. Compliance with the numerous rules and regulations governing the lending activities of banks is verified, including conformity with lending limits and restrictions on the types of loans to be written. When classifying assets, their financial "viability" is of primary significance. During the preparation for the examination, the examiners will analyze the so-called adverse classification of loans of the previous examination to determine whether these credits and loans have been corrected. If a lack of compliance with certain standards is discovered during the examination, a loan may be "classified," and categorized as either substandard, doubtful, or a loss, depending upon the likelihood that it will be necessary to "write off" a portion or all of the value of the asset on the books of the bank. In addition, a classified item may be listed in the report with special mention. An example of a bad loan likely to be so classified upon examination is one made to an insider in excess of permissible limits for a risky investment that is under-collateralized. Adverse classification of an asset effectively serves notice on investors, depositors, and management that the item should be discounted as a measure of the institution's financial strength.

An inadequate loan file also may trigger an adverse classification. For example, when a mortgage has been granted on a home, the file should show that the current premium for adequate fire insurance has been paid in order to prevent a loss of collateral in case of a fire or other disaster. A recent financial statement of the borrower (that is, no more than one year old) is also necessary to prevent classification of the loan as substandard. In addition, the bank files must reflect the fact that real estate taxes are paid up to date; if this fact is not shown in the loan file, it is considered deficient and the mortgage may receive a substandard classification. A record of delinquent interest payments also gives a warning signal to examiners and may possibly necessitate a charge-off of the loan. The charge-off of a loan means that enough reserves must be set aside to protect deposits in the event the borrower defaults. Examiners analyze the real estate holdings of the bank acquired due to foreclosures of mortgages. They check whether the real estate is suitable for sale at a future date, which should not exceed one year, as well as if efforts are being made to dispose of such holdings. Lending activities are examined from the point of view of concentration of the loan portfolio in certain categories (that is, auto loans, student loans, mortgages); if overly concentrated in one field, the examiners may suggest a more even distribution.

The examiners should verify that applicable lending limits are not exceeded. The amount that can be lent by state and national banks to any one borrower or entity in which the borrower has a substantial interest is limited by law. The former lending limit for national banks of 10% of unimpaired capital and surplus has been increased to 15%. Several exemptions permit banks to go over the 15% lending limit to a certain extent.

Under the general lending limit rules, no funds in excess of applicable lending limits may be lent to any one borrower, to "related parties" (including family members), or to institutions in which the borrower has a substantial interest. The lending limit percentage is computed on the capital and capital resources of the bank, which include capital, surplus, reserves and undivided profits. If a particular borrower requires funds in excess of a bank's lending limits, the loan may be syndicated; that is, two or more banks acting together will provide the loan funds and divide their participation in the arrangement in compliance with their respective lending limits. (See Chapter 8, "Eurodollar Lending.") If the bank is involved in international lending, the special risks present in such portfolios must also be assessed, particularly country and currency risk problems. In particular, the foreign exchange risk is a major aspect in evaluation of outstanding international loans.

Numerous other assets are analyzed by the examiner in making a thorough evaluation of the bank's condition, and these assets will be examined to determine the value at which they are carried. The value of real estate should reflect its depreciated value; for example, the bank building may have been written down to a fraction of the original value of the building. The fact that a building originally worth, say, $1 million has depreciated in value, as a result of wear and tear, to $100,000, will have an obvious impact on an appraisal of the bank's solvency.

The bond portfolio of the bank is another important aspect of bank examination. Every bank invests in bonds to varying degrees and their classification, quality, and maturity date will be examined. A bank is supposed to hold only readily marketable bonds of high rating, which may be issued by certain corporations as well as by government or municipal agencies. The purchase of corporate bonds is subject to the lending limits of the bank as well as to certain conditions, however. Although banks are not permitted to purchase stock, convertible corporate bonds may be held provided the bank paid no more than a token premium on the bond for the convertibility. Of course, the value of convertible bonds may greatly increase after purchase due to their convertibility. Consequently, although the bank may not convert these bonds into shares, it is permitted to sell those bonds on the market, thereby realizing a profit.

While a bank is not permitted to own and trade stocks, it may hold stock as collateral for loans. Technically, these shares are merely held on deposit with the bank to secure their owner's obligation, and they are not owned by the bank. Generally, the bank must ascertain that the borrower has good title to the stock prior to accepting them as collateral. Furthermore, in order to facilitate sale in the event of a default, they are usually delivered with a signed transfer slip or endorsed blank authorizing the holder of the shares (that is, the bank) to transfer title. For this same reason, shares registered in the street names maintained by stock brokerage houses and banks are also preferred.

Another permissible form of loan collateral is the certificate of deposit. After the CD is secure with the bank, a percentage of the funds may be borrowed against it. Since any interest or principal that remains unpaid will be deducted from the CD, the loan extended should not equal 100% of its face value. When a CD is pledged to secure a loan, the bank will hold the money as security in the event that the loan is not repaid by the expiration date of the CD. A higher rate of interest generally is charged on the loan than is paid on the CD. Collateral in the form of either CDs or bonds thus offers the bank assurance of payment.

When collateral is not furnished, bank examiners must look for some other form of guarantee on the loan and evaluate it for its credit worth. Borrowers without sufficient collateral to qualify for a loan may offer the bank a guarantor or a coendorser in order to qualify. If the bank wishes to consider this proposal, the credit history and financial standing of the guarantor must also be examined. In addition, it is vital for the bank to properly advise the guarantor of any delinquency or failure of the borrower to make payment; otherwise, the guarantor may be relieved of his obligation if default occurs.

Compared to other countries, the method of evaluating bond portfolios in the United States is rather unusual in permitting the bank to carry the bonds in its portfolio at their original acquisition price rather than at their current market price. Consequently, a portfolio's "book" value may not reflect its true worth, and it may be over- or under-valued. For example, banks purchasing New York City bonds, which subsequently dropped 50% in market price, were permitted to show this position at the original acquisition price rather than written down to their true value. This is a weakness in the banking system of the United States. In fact, if banks were required to write down asset value to reflect current market prices of certain bonds, some banks would have to close down. Nevertheless, this system is justified by the theory that banks normally acquire bonds with the intention of holding them until maturity rather than for speculation or short-term investment. Because the face value of the bonds is the amount received, this value is used when valuing the portfolio for examination purposes.

Municipal bonds are often a favored portfolio item because their tax-exempt status reduces the bank's tax exposure. In addition, bank supervisory authorities encourage banks to help local municipalities by purchasing bond issues. Government and municipal bonds can be used by banks to secure government and municipal deposits, and the government may insist on the securing of its deposits with government bonds. Similarly, municipalities normally insist on securing their deposits with either government or municipal bonds. Once again, distribution of exposure is important since even municipalities can get into financial difficulties. Therefore, the examiners will look for a prudent limit to the bank's exposure in municipal bonds. The maturity dates of bonds held in a portfolio may also be examined to verify that they do not fall due at one time but are spread over several years.

A thorough examination will not only focus on the assets of the bank, but it will measure and evaluate its capital reserve and subordinated debt as well. By *capital*, we mean the capital contributions paid in by shareholders in return for their stock. If the paid-in capital exceeds the assigned par value, a surplus is created. On the other hand, *reserve* is what the bank accumulates from earnings. Subordinated debt refers to its bonds or other obligations of its own which the bank may have sold to outsiders. When these bonds have a maturity in excess of twelve years, they are considered for this purpose as part of the primary capital of the bank.

Contingent liabilities of the bank are generally not recorded on the books of the bank; nevertheless, they must be scrutinized to determine the means by which they are secured and the adequacy of the collateral. For example, a letter of credit is generally not recorded as a liability of the bank. However, when a bank issues a letter of credit on behalf of a customer, the examiners check the credit rating of the customer, the quality of collateral, if any, and the financial statement of the customer.

As a general rule, current liabilities should be matched by current assets. If the current asset to current liability ratio is higher than one to one, this will more than satisfy the requirement. Furthermore, banks should neither be over-loaned nor under-loaned. This is reflected in the bank's liquidity ratio, which measures the proportion of deposits to loans. Although there is no minimum requirement set by law, bank examiners may criticize an institution for taking undue risks in its lending practices. The bank's ability to meet depositor needs and bank demands is analyzed in light of the institution's rating and asset size. Conversely, an inadequate loan level may lead to criticism for not adequately performing the banking functions for which it was licensed. Therefore, an adequate balance must be maintained between the deposit-holding and loan functions.

If a bank should happen to have excess or surplus funds, the most advantageous thing for the bank to do is lend these surplus funds to other banks. These are called *federal funds*. The federal fund market is primarily an interbank market in which deposit balances held at federal reserve banks are loaned for short periods. For example, when a member bank finds it has more funds available than are needed to meet its own reserve requirements, it may lend federal funds at an agreed-upon rate to a bank in need of those funds to meet its own reserve requirements. Though normally referred to as "purchases and sales of federal funds," these transactions are loans, generally made on a day-to-day basis.

The analysis of liquidity also extends to the bank's payables and receivables. Payables are demand deposits, which can be withdrawn at any time. Receivables are the demand loans, recallable at the bank's discretion.

Trends in deposit and lending activity are indicative of the bank's ability to compete in the banking market and, indirectly, of the quality of the management's business judgment. Consequently, the examination will focus on whether the volume of demand and time deposits expanded or contracted and whether interest paid on deposits and received on loans increased or decreased. One area of particular interest is the amount of long-term credit (that is, mortgages) extended by the bank. If over-lending by the bank results in an insufficient supply of time deposits to meet possible demands from depositors, it may be in a serious situation. To avoid this, the bank will be directed to limit its long-term mortgages to only a certain percentage of its time deposits (or "interest-bearing deposits"). Finally, economic factors such as inflation will be considered in valuing longer-term loans. The inflation rate signifies the extent to which there is a devaluation of the actual purchasing power of the repayment funds. Consequently, this devaluation factor should be included in the final calculation of the actual profit (or loss) of bank mortgage activities. Indeed, "book" profits and actual profits may be quite dissimilar, just as, in recent years, interest paid on the funds of depositors has only rarely kept pace with inflation.

It is generally expected that a bank's net earnings should approximate 1% of the bank's total footing. Total footing includes all the deposits and the capital of the bank. Thus, a bank with a total footing of $100 million should have a net profit of $1 million. Profitability varies widely, of course, with the majority of banks earning less than 1% of the total footing, while some may earn as much as 2% or more. If the net earnings are found to equal only 1/10% of the total footing, the examiners will report that the bank has poor management. An improvement in management is then called for when the report is made to the Board of Directors. If no improvement occurs, the examiners will try to take steps to bring improvement about.

When the bank's deposits are being assessed, particular attention is given to volatile and very active accounts. Take, for instance, a bank that has a correspondent bank relationship. The correspondent bank accounts that are set up to service these relationships tend to be very active. It is good bank procedure to reconcile these accounts frequently, at least once a month. Examiners verify whether or not such reconciliation has taken place; if it has not, this reflects poorly on the administration of the bank. Furthermore, if large discrepancies are found when the examiners themselves reconcile these accounts, a notation is also made of that fact in the examiner's report. Smaller banks often ask their correspondent banks for assistance and participation when lending larger amounts, in order to avoid criticism for concentration of loans.

Another feature of bank administration that is closely examined is whether the bank promptly pays its accounts payable. Payment delays often reflect poorly on the proper administration of the collection department of the bank.

These specific examples serve to illustrate the type of information gathered by bank examiners during the course of the examination. We have seen that the classification of assets (particularly loans) is a vital factor in the determination of a bank's soundness, as is the adequacy of the bank's liquidity and capital resources. Of course, specifications for the adequacy of capital vary among regulatory agency guidelines. The daily operations of a particular bank, such as its loan and deposit activities, reflect the strength or weakness of management policies. Such general considerations influence the examiners' final determination as to whether or not a bank should be considered as a problem bank perhaps as much as the ratings assigned individual bank department functions.

Examination Results

After the results of the examiner's report are compiled, the information is exchanged with other supervisory agencies. Thus, if a bank is found not to be functioning well, or if there are inefficiencies or shortcomings, the report is "red-flagged" and other agencies may begin planning appropriate action. The FDIC in particular has an interest in such reports due to its own important financial responsibility. Examiners are also supposed to discuss the results of their findings with bank managers and the Board of Directors, although certain findings relating to violations of banking laws and regulations are kept confidential for enforcement purposes.

The examination reports consist of two parts. One portion is officially prepared for the board of the bank; another internal report is prepared for the examining authorities. Other than for circulation among related agencies, the examination reports of the Comptroller, the Federal Reserve, the FDIC, and the state banking departments are not in the public domain, and they are available only to members of the Board of Directors and to the officers designated by the Board of Directors. The report, marked confidential, cannot leave the premises of the bank. Exempt from disclosure under the Freedom of Information Act, bank examination reports are available only to bank supervisory agencies.

Bibliography

Bank Holding Company Act of 1956 as amended 12 U.S.C. §1841 et seq. 1980.

Bank Merger Act, 12 U.S.C. §1828. 1982.

Change in Bank Control Act of 1978, 12 U.S.C. §1817, 1982.

Committee on Banking, Finance and Urban Affairs. "The Operations of U.S. Banks in the International Capital Markets." 96th Congress, 1st Session. December 1979.

Comptroller of the Currency. Administrator of National Banks. *Comptroller's Manual for National Banks.* Washington, D.C.: U.S. Comptroller of the Currency, published annually.

Federal Financial Institutions Examination Council. *Annual Report.*

Foreign Bank Operations and Acquisitions in the United States. Hearing before the Subcommittee on Financial Institutions Supervision, Regulation and Insurance of the Committee on Banking, Finance and Urban Affairs. House of Representatives, 96th Congress, 2nd Session. Parts I and II.

Glasser, L., ed. *Evolving Reporting and Disclosure Requirements for Banks and Bank Holding Companies.* New York: Law Journal Press, 1976.

Luckett, Dudley. *Money and Banking,* 2nd ed. New York: McGraw-Hill, 1980.

McFadden Act, 12 U.S.C. §36. 1970.

Office of the Comptroller of the Currency. "Federal Supervision of State and National Banks: A Study by the Comptroller General of the United States." Washington, D.C.: U.S. Comptroller of the Currency, 1977.

"Regulation of Foreign Banks in the United States: A Symposium." *U. Ill. L. Forum* (1980), pp. 1–25.

Robertson, Ross. *The Comptroller and Bank Supervision.* Washington, D.C.: Office of the Comptroller of the Currency, 1968.

U.S. Board of Governors of the Federal Reserve System. *The Federal Reserve System: Purposes and Functions*. Washington, D.C.: 1979.

Whitley, S., Schlichting, W., Rice, T., and J. Cooper. *Banking Law*. New York: Matthew Bender, 1982.

10

Bank Holding Companies

A discussion of bank holding companies (BHCs) is as much a discussion of organization—and the regulation of organization—as it is one of banking or economic theory. BHCs are specially defined entities through which most of the activities described elsewhere in this volume are performed. BHCs combine centralized overall management with limited liability and functional autonomy for each division. In recent years, the expansion in the variety of bank-related activities has spurred the proliferation of these entities, so much so that most of the larger U.S. banks are now held by bank holding companies.

Because BHCs are entirely artificial in nature, existing as mere creations of the law, an understanding of their statutory underpinnings is particularly important. The establishment, operation, activities, and expansion of bank holding companies are governed by federal statutes and regulations. These include the Bank Holding Company Act of 1956, as amended (the BHCA), both the Securities Exchange Act of 1933 and the Securities and Exchange Act of 1934, and by regulations of the Federal Reserve Board. The International Banking Act of 1978 also has considerable impact on the activities of foreign BHCs. Federal preemption of control over BHCs notwithstanding, the BHC Act specifically reserves to the states the right to legislate the operation of BHCs. Thus, a state may prohibit, within its borders, activities allowed by the federal BHC Act.

The Bank Holding Company Act establishes the standards for the formation and operation of bank holding companies. The actual responsibility for the day-to-day supervision of BHCs has been placed with the Federal Reserve. The Board may require reports and make examination of each BHC in order to assure compliance with the BHC Act. In particular, BHCs and subsidiaries often must obtain the approval of the Federal Reserve Board prior to undertaking specified activities, and they must submit to its examination and report filing requirements. Although standards differ from those governing the activities of banks, the laws and regulations issued thereunder are nonetheless comprehensive. It should be mentioned, however, that foreign BHCs may in some instance have different provisions apply to certain activities.

The aim of the Bank Holding Company Act is to assure that BHCs are engaging only in activities of a financial nature in a manner consistent with sound practices, while preventing monpolistic concentrations of resources among a few BHCs. Banks are permitted to engage in activities that might not have otherwise been allowed due to the BHC Act. Although prior to the 1970 Amendments to the Bank Holding Company Act, only companies holding one bank, as defined by the Act, were subject to such regulation, the 1970 Amendments eliminated the prior distinction that had been made and subjected all BHCs to its provisions. BHCs and their subsidiaries are subject to supervision by the Federal Reserve, the FDIC, the Comptroller of the Currency, and the SEC among others. The BHC Act requires banks that are BHCs or subsidiaries of BHCs to be insured by the FDIC.

The provisions of the BHC Act have been amplified from time to time by regulations of the Federal Reserve Board. Regulation Y is a particularly significant example serving to clarify and interpret the Bank Holding Company Act's application to specific activities of BHCs. It contains guidelines as to which activities are considered acceptable for a particular BHC and clarifies the application of statutory standards to BHC operation. Regulation K (International Banking Operations) acts in a similar fashion to govern the interstate banking operations of foreign BHCs and defines exemptions from the nonbanking prohibitions contained in the Bank Holding Company Act. These regulations are constantly updated and amended to reflect changes in the policy of the Federal Reserve Board.

BHCs also fall within the regulatory supervision of the Securities and Exchange Commission (SEC) if applicable statutory criteria are satisfied. As a result, a company classified as a bank holding company is subject to the registration and reporting requirements contained in the Securities Exchange Act of 1933 and the Securities and Exchange Act of 1934. Thus, issuance of securities by BHCs, as well as subsequent securities-related transactions, will be subject to SEC scrutiny rather than that of strictly bank regulating agencies. Naturally, certain circumstances may offer the BHC exemption from certain SEC requirements. Nevertheless, these exemptions form part of the securities laws to which BHCs are subject.

Definition of Bank Holding Company

The first section of the Bank Holding Company Act (BHC Act) provides that, within the limited exception of certain company holdings, a *bank holding company* is any company that has control over any bank or over another BHC. Certain short-term exemptions from BHC status exist, however, and include the acquisition of shares under certain circumstances such as underwriting, proxy solicitation, and shares acquired for debts previously contracted. Each of the key elements of this definition—"company. . . control . . . bank (or BHC)—is itself subject to special definition.

A *company* may be a corporation, partnership, business trust, association, and certain other trusts that are subject to specific conditions. Natural persons controlling one or more banks do not qualify as a company and may not be classified as a BHC. Corporations of which a majority of shares are owned by any state or by the United States are excluded from the term "company."

The subsidiary of the company must be a "bank"; however, not all banking institutions are included in the special definition provided by the BHCA. For example, Edge Act or Agreement Corporations organized under Section 25(a) or Section 25 of the Federal Reserve Act are not "banks" under BHCA; similarly, other institutions that do not do business in the United States, except as an incident to their activities outside the United States, are excluded. In addition, the qualifying institution must accept demand deposits *and* be engaged in the business of making commercial loans. The Board indicates that the institution engaged in a regular commercial loan business, rather than entering into occasional loan transactions, is considered to be engaged in the business of commercial lending.

Due to the passage of the International Banking Act, foreign bank holding companies that were previously exempt from the BHC Act provisions are now subject to certain requirements, which will be examined later in more detail. As a general matter, however, the International Banking Act of 1978 (IBA) now requires that, if a foreign bank or a company owning such foreign bank does business in the U.S. through a branch, agency, or commercial lending company, it is subject to the provisions of the Bank Holding Company Act to the same extent as a BHC. However, it may be possible for a foreign organization to satisfy certain exemption requirements, in which case the foreign organization will escape the extraterritorial effect of the BHCA on its activities. The most significant impact of the IBA on foreign BHCs is the increased control over interstate operations and nonbanking activities and investments.

The most troublesome of the three elements needed to constitute a bank holding company is that of control. For purposes of the BHC Act, *control* is present under any of the following circumstances:

1. The company directly or indirectly owns, controls, or has power to vote 25% or more of any class of voting securities of the bank or company.
2. The company controls in any manner the election of a majority of the directors or trustees of the bank or company.
3. The Federal Reserve Board determines (after notice and opportunity for a hearing) that the company directly or indirectly exercises a controlling influence over the management or policies of the bank or company.

A company that directly or indirectly owns, controls, or has power to vote less than 5% of any class of voting securities of a bank or company is presumed not to have control over that bank or company. This presumption exempts companies having insufficient control over a bank's affairs from supervision as a BHC. If neither of the latter two listed conditions of control is present, the limit on ownership of voting stock must be less than 25% to avoid classification as a BHC.

In addition to these statutory provisions, other criteria, such as that found in Regulation Y, aid in the determination of the control requirement. As a general matter, no distinction is drawn between "direct" and "indirect" forms of control exercised over a bank or another BHC. For example, *direct control* is conclusively presumed when, as already noted, the company owns, controls, or has power to vote 25% or more of any class of voting securities of the bank or company. On the other hand, *indirect control*, such as that exercised through a wholly owned subsidiary of the company, will cause shares held by the company's subsidiary to be "attributed to," or treated as if directly owned or controlled by, the company.

A subsidiary relationship is defined by the Bank Holding Company Act by the same standards of control used to characterize a BHC. Consequently, bank stock held by the subsidiary will be attributed to its parent when the parent has:

1. direct or indirect ownership, control, or power to vote at least 25% of the voting shares of the subsidiary;
2. control over the election of a majority of the subsidiary's directors;
3. direct or indirect controlling influence with respect to the management or policies of the subsidiary, as determined by the Federal Reserve Board after notice and an opportunity for a hearing.

Thus, the Federal Reserve Board looks beyond the company, and it includes bank stock held by its subsidiaries in examining the company's control over a bank or other BHC. Excluded from this definition is the subsidiary of an Edge Act Corporation, so long as its activities are restricted to those permitted an Edge Corporation.

Indirect control over a bank or another BHC need not be exercised through a subsidiary; it may also be exercised through a company's trustee holding or directly or indirectly controlling shares for the benefit of the company, its shareholders, members, or employees. Indirect control is also established when shares have been transferred subject to the direct or indirect control of a transferee that is indebted to the transferor or that has one or more officers, directors, trustees, or beneficiaries in common with or subject to the control of the transferor. This form of indirect control over the transferred shares of the bank or BHC may be disproved only by a determination of the Federal Reserve Board after an opportunity for a hearing, that the transferor is not capable of controlling the transferee.

The control tests indicate that the Federal Reserve Board may determine whether a company exercises a controlling influence over the management or policies of a bank or company. In order to more routinely make this determination, the Board established presumptions of control in Regulation Y. These are divided into one conclusive and five rebuttable presumptions of control.

If the Board determines that the transferability of 25% or more of any class of voting securities is conditioned in any manner upon the transfer of 25% or more of any class of voting securities of another company, holders of either group of securities so affected will constitute a "company" for purposes of the BHC Act unless one of the issuers meets the requirements for subsidiary status. This determination by the Board constitutes a conclusive presumption of control.

Regulation Y contains five detailed situations representing rebuttable presumptions of control, any of which may lead to the finding that control is being exercised over a bank or another BHC. The first two link ownership of more than 5% of any class of voting securities with additional elements that indicate the possibility of control or influence over the policy making and activities of the bank or other BHC, either by the existence of an employer/employee relationship or influence over the voting securities. The third and fourth presumptions cover agreements or understandings whereby the operation of the bank or company is influenced or restricted in some fashion. Certain agreements are exempt from this consideration, such as bona fide loan transactions. The final rebuttable presumption provides that direct or indirect ownership of securities immediately convertible at the holder's option into voting securities constitutes ownership or control of voting securities.

In sum, both direct control and certain forms of indirect control over a bank (or other BHC) are sufficient to satisfy the requirement of control for purposes of defining a BHC. Application of the control requirement is far from a simple matter, and it must be analyzed carefully in light of the various standards and presumptions used to interpret that aspect of the bank holding company definition. As we have seen earlier, a company that has control over a bank or over any other bank holding company will be considered a bank holding company and thus become subject to the laws and regulations governing BHCs.

The basic purpose of the BHCA is to regulate BHCs, and not the banks that they own or control. Although BHCs have been in existence for many years, they were free of supervision and control until the passage of the BHC Act of 1956. The primary objectives of the BHC Act are: (1) the control of BHC expansion, in order to avoid the creation of monopoly or restraint of trade in the banking industry and (2) the expansion of BHCs into nonbanking activities that are sufficiently related to banking to maintain the requirement of separation between banking and commerce established by the Glass-Steagall Act. The supervisory provisions of the BHC Act follow from these goals.

With the exception of certain "grandfathered" BHCs, the Douglas Amendment to the Bank Holding Company Act [Section 3(d)] generally prohibits bank holding companies and their subsidiaries from owning banks in more than one state, regardless of whether the bank is acquired by purchase, merger, or consolidation. Thus, BHCs are subject to the principle of the McFadden Act, which prohibits interstate branching by members of the Federal Reserve. The only instance in which the Federal Reserve Board may approve the acquisition of an out-of-state bank or its assets is when the acquisition is expressly and specifically authorized by the statute laws of the state in which the acquired bank is located; within state boundaries, state law governing branching becomes the standard for application of the McFadden Act. This prohibition also applies to foreign bank holding companies as a result of the enactment of the International Banking Act of 1978. In effect, these prohibitions impose a geographic limitation upon the interstate banking operations of holding companies. It is important to recall, however, that the BHC Act defines "bank" to include institutions that either accept demand deposits or make commercial loans. Therefore, nonbanking subsidiaries of BHCs may freely operate across state boundaries.

The jurisdiction of the BHC Act extends to banking and permissible nonbanking activities within the U.S.; as a result, its provisions do not cover the overseas operations of both domestic and foreign BHCs. This vacuum is filled by Regulation K, which describes the permissible overseas activities and investments of member banks, BHCs, and Edge and Agreement Corporations. Neither Congress nor the Federal Reserve Board, however, has attempted to restrict a foreign bank's overseas operations or investments to conform them to U.S. domestic banking requirements. Due to the difficulties of extraterritorial enforcement, and the potential for conflict with customary international law, foreign non-banking activities and investments of foreign banking organizations are generally exempt from U.S. nonbanking prohibitions.

Section 4 of the BHC Act enumerates the activities in which a BHC may engage. Unless exempted by a provision of the BHC Act, a BHC's activities are limited to:

- banking;
- managing or controlling banks and authorized nonbank subsidiaries;
- furnishing or performing services for subsidiaries; and
- engaging in activities determined by the Board to be closely related to banking.

Therefore, the BHC Act generally prohibits a holding company from engaging in nonbanking-related activities, including through the ownership or control of shares of a nonbank company. As previously noted, the intent of these provisions is to assure a proper separation between activities related to banking and those of commerce. In addition, the provision permitting BHCs to engage in banking activities is directed only to BHCs that are themselves banks, and it does not include nonbank BHCs. Nonbank BHCs may, however, engage in these activities through a bank whose shares it holds or controls.

This concept of separation between banking and commerce has been amplified by the Federal Reserve Board through the issuance of Regulation Y. This regulation contains a list of activities for BHCs that the Board has determined to be sufficiently "closely related to banking," as well as a list of nonacceptable activities. The failure of several large U.S. banks has tended to restrict the development of a wider range of permissible activities. Nevertheless, it is thought that allowing BHCs to enter certain banking-related areas will increase competition and improve financial services to customers.

The following list is an overview of permissible BHC activities. Regulation Y should be examined for specific requirements that must be met when engaging in any one of the following activities:

1. making or acquiring loans and other extensions of credit;
2. operations as an industrial bank, Morris Plan Bank, or industrial loan company (see limitations);
3. servicing loans and other extensions of credit;
4. performing trust activities;
5. acting as investment or financial advisor;
6. leasing real and personal property;
7. making equity and debt investments in corporations or community welfare projects;
8. providing bookkeeping and data processing services;

9. acting as insurance agent or broker in limited circumstances;
10. acting as underwriter for certain insurance directly related to BHC extensions of credit;
11. providing courier services of limited nature;
12. providing management consulting advice to nonaffiliated banks;
13. issuing money orders, travelers checks, savings bonds.

These are, naturally, subject to change by amendment of the Board.
Activities not considered closely related to banking include:

1. insurance premium funding;
2. underwriting;
3. real estate brokerage;
4. land development;
5. real estate syndication;
6. management consulting;
7. property management;
8. operation of a savings and loan association.

Finally, to these activities should be added certain "grandfathered" provisions listed in the BHC Act as amended. Depending upon whether the activities engaged in would be considered incidental or banking, the prior approval of the Federal Reserve Board may or may not be required. For example, prior approval must be obtained when initially forming a BHC. Prior approval must also be obtained before a BHC acquires control over more than 5% of any class of voting shares of a bank. Other requirements of this nature are contained in the BHC Act, and they apply generally to BHC formations and expansion activities.

The Bank Holding Company Act provides certain exemptions from the general prohibition on engaging in nonbanking activities. Among these are included the following:

1. any company that, as of January 4, 1977, was both a BHC and a defined labor, agricultural, or horticultural organization;
2. any qualifying holding company covered in 1970 that was more than 85% family-owned, as defined, though the company must still register as a BHC, file reports, and comply with BHC Act provisions regarding expansion; or
3. with respect to any other BHC, the prohibitions do not apply to ownership or control of shares of any company engaged in a limited number of specified activities enumerated in the BHC Act.

A fourth exemption, and perhaps one of the most utilized, covers a situation in which one company acquires not more than 5% of the outstanding voting shares of another. Recall the earlier discussion regarding the presumption of no control if less than 5% share ownership is held. The so-called 5% *rule* enables BHCs to acquire an interest in the voting shares of any company up to the permissible limit. In addition, shares of the kinds and amounts eligible for investment by national banking associations are also exempt. Among the investments eligible for national banks is ownership of shares of: Edge and Agreement Corporations, safe deposit companies, Federal National Mortgage Association, small business investment companies, bank service corporations, state housing corporations, foreign banks, and others. Furthermore, the amounts of such investments may be limited. Numerous other types of share ownership are also exempt, provided statutory criteria are satisfied; however, since a general overview of BHC Act provisions is the aim of this discussion, a detailed analysis will not be undertaken.

Prior to the enactment of the International Banking Act of 1978 (IBA), foreign BHCs enjoyed more exemptions from the prohibitions of nonbanking share ownership than their domestic counterparts. Indeed, throughout the discussion that follows, it should be remembered that prohibited nonbanking activities engaged in by a foreign bank or its affiliate prior to the enactment of the IBA are "grandfathered" and can be continued. In general, these grandfather clauses are aimed at preventing the financial disruption and inequity which would have resulted had divestiture been immediately required, as was the case upon passage of the 1970 BHCA amendments.

The aim of the IBA is to assure a competitive equality between foreign and domestic banks and BHCs operating under certain forms in the U.S. It charges the Federal Reserve with responsibility for the development of this national policy for the regulation of foreign banks.

Prior to passage of the IBA, foreign banks did not fall within the BHC Act definition of "bank," thus leaving them free to operate banking and nonbanking entities in more than one state. Currently, as a result of the IBA, foreign banks, branches, and agencies are required to select a "home state" for their U.S. banking operations. In addition, foreign banks and companies are generally subject to the statutory provisions of the BHC Act. Foreign BHC operations in the U.S. are subject to essentially similar requirements, including the fundamental requirement of separation between banking related and commercial activities.

Because most foreign bank operations in the U.S. are conducted through branches and agencies, the application to them of the BHC Act's nonbanking prohibitions has significantly improved the competitive standing of domestic BHCs. This grandfather status terminates, however, if a foreign bank or affiliate acquires a U.S. bank. BHC Act prohibitions on nonbanking activities now also apply to:

1. a foreign bank with a U.S. branch bank, agency, or commercial lending company;

2. a foreign company controlling both a foreign bank and a domestic commercial lending company; and
3. any company of which a foreign bank or controlling company, mentioned in entries 1 and 2 is a subsidiary.

In light of the great freedom to engage in nonbanking enterprises that was enjoyed by foreign banks with non-BHC U.S. branches and agencies, passage of the IBA represents a significant change. Furthermore, the foreign bank or BHC now faces the same geographic expansion restrictions as confronted by its domestic competitors. Finally, foreign banks with federal branches or agencies in the U.S. now must maintain a capital equivalency deposit with a bank that is a member of the Federal Reserve. Thus, the IBA has brought foreign banks within the scope of U.S. monetary controls.

Many of the activities of a BHC involve participation in transactions that mostly occur outside the United States, and special accommodations are made for the foreign activities of the BHC. Federal Reserve Board regulations and the BHC Act specially provide for domestic BHCs, which shares in foreign companies doing only a specifically limited business within the United States. Regulations Y and K also attempt to avoid any impacts upon foreign activities of BHCs operating within the U.S. In general, a BHC organized under the laws of a foreign country, which is principally engaged in the banking business outside the United States, is exempt from the prohibitions against acquisition of nonbanking interests. Regulation K, for example, describes the circumstances in which a U.S. banking organization will be permitted to invest in foreign companies doing domestic business in the United States. Significantly, the regulation requires that the U.S. activities of the foreign company must be incidental to its international or foreign business. Furthermore, the location, nature, and control of the foreign company must also be limited in order for the BHC's investment to be permissible.

The International Banking Operations Amendment to Regulation K became effective on October 2, 1980. They apply to foreign banks and foreign banking organizations with respect to limitations on interstate banking under Section 5 of the IBA, and to foreign banks and foreign bank holding companies with respect to exemptions from the nonbanking prohibitions of the BHC Act and IBA.

Both foreign banks and companies that control U.S. banks are BHCs and are thus subject, with one exception, to the nonbanking limitations on nonbanking activities enumerated by the BHCA. Two exemptions also are available to such organizations:

1. Discretion is granted to permit a foreign company to engage in any activity or investment approved by the Board.

2. A foreign institution principally engaged in the banking business outside the U.S. may hold shares of foreign nonbanking companies that engage in business in the U.S.

The latter exemption is, of course, a limitation imposed by customary international law, and central to its application is the definition of "principally engaged." The test for making this determination, once measured in terms of the volume of assets and revenues, has been revised. A company qualifies for the exemption if more than half the organization's worldwide business, exclusive of its U.S. banking business, derives from banking activities occurring outside the U.S.

Alternatively, the first exemption, as noted, permits an application for a specific determination of eligibility to be made to the Board. Under this exemption, foreign banking organizations may:

- engage in any kind of activities outside the U.S.;
- engage in activities incidental to activities outside the U.S.;
- own or control voting shares of any company not engaged in any activity in the U.S., other than those incidental to its international or foreign business;
- have certain ownership of voting shares in a fiduciary capacity;
- engage in activities in the U.S. that consist of banking or financial operations of the types permitted by regulation, or allowed under an order as provided for in BHC Act Section 4(c)(8); these activities require the prior approval of the Board.

Specific interpretations and possible amendments to Regulation K should be consulted for the exact requirements involved when engaging in activities.

The expansion of BHC holdings and interests in other ventures is also regulated as a means of preventing the development of monopolistic market combinations and concentrations of assets. As discussed earlier, one important limitation on BHC expansion is geographic, through extension of the interstate branching prohibitions of the McFadden Act to BHCs by the BHCA Douglas Amendment. Note one exception: If a BHC already owns or controls a majority of voting shares of a bank, additional shares may be acquired without the usual approval required from the Federal Reserve Board.

When expansion of a BHC results in a change in the control or ownership of BHC interests, whether through merger or acquisition, one or more of several applicable statutes may come into play, including the BHC Act, the Bank Merger Act, and the Change in Bank Control Act. In general, any change in BHC control must be approved in accordance with BHC Act standards. Furthermore, prior approval of the Board must be obtained prior to any expansion or acquisition of banking interests, unless the transaction is one specifically exempt from the approval requirements. If the resulting bank will be a state member bank, approval of the merger proposal under the Bank Merger Act is needed. When a merger is contemplated, the anticompetitive effects of the merger must be weighed against the convenience and needs of the public. Similarly, the acquisition of an existing BHC or bank is governed by the BHC Act or the Change in Bank Control Act of 1978 if the acquisition of control (that is, ownership of power to vote 25% or more of any class of voting stock) is not otherwise governed by the Bank Merger Act. As with the Bank Merger Act, the BHC Act legal standard contains consideration of anticompetitive effects of the transaction. In the case of purchase and assumption of a failed bank by another bank, the Federal Deposit Insurance Act may also apply.

In addition to these statutes briefly mentioned, the majority of states also have statutes regulating the acquisition of bank control that may also be operative. Therefore, consideration of several possible sources of regulation must be undertaken prior to expanding or changing control of BHC operations.

Conclusion

In conclusion, bank holding companies are entities regulated by the Federal Reserve Board to engage in certain banking-related activities. If the requirements for classification as a bank holding company are met, the BHC is subject to the provisions of the Bank Holding Company Act as well as Regulation Y of the Federal Reserve Board. After enactment of the International Banking Act of 1978, foreign banks and companies were also subject to those regulatory provisions (with certain exceptions) in order to achieve a more competitive equality between foreign and domestic BHCs.

Bibliography

Bank Holding Company Act of 1956 as amended, 12 U.S.C. §1841 et seq. 1980.

Blaine, C. G. *Federal Regulation of Bank Holding Companies.* BNA, 1973.

12 C.F.R. Part 211 as amended (effective June 14, 1979) (Regulation K).

12 C.F.R. Part 225 as amended (effective December 1, 1971) (Regulation Y).

Foreign Bank Operations and Acquisitions in the United States: Hearings before the Subcommittee on Financial Institutions Supervision, Regulation and Insurance of the Committee on Banking, Finance and Urban Affairs. House of Representatives, 96th Congress, 2nd Session. Part II. Serial No. 96. 77(1981).

Goldberg, Lawrence and Lawrence White, eds. *The Deregulation of the Banking and Securities Industries.* Lexington, Massachusetts: Lexington Books, 1979.

Heller, Pauline. *Handbook of Federal Bank Holding Company Law.* New York: Law Journal Press, 1976.

Mortimer, Harold. *Bank Counsel.* New York: Practising Law Institute, 1981.

Securities Act of 1933, 15 U.S.C. §§77a-77aa. 1982.

Securities Exchange Act of 1934, 15 U.S.C. §§78a-78kk. 1981.

Taubeneck, T. D. "Now All U.S. Banks Can Be Merchants." *Euromoney* (April 1983), p. 129.

White, James J. *Teaching Materials on Banking Law.* St. Paul, Minnesota: West Publishing Company, 1976.

Whitley, S., Schlichting, W., Rice, T., and J. Cooper. *Banking Law.* New York: Matthew Bender, 1982.

11

Swiss Banking

Introduction

The mention of the subject of Swiss banking evokes a common reaction of misunderstanding, rooted in mystique built up over the last half century. Due to the prominence of Switzerland as an international banking center, a clarification of the characteristic functions of the Swiss banking is essential for international businesspersons and lawyers and also serves as a useful model for the study of international banking. Indeed, Switzerland's banking system ranks with the United States system as among the world's most sophisticated in its merging of public and private regulation. Considering that Switzerland is a nation of only approximately 6.5 million individuals, it is astonishing that the Swiss banking system occupies the important place that it does in the world banking community. It is for this reason that Switzerland was chosen from among several leading international banking centers to illustrate how one nation's banking system may differ greatly from the next.

Much of the myth surrounding Swiss banking has been generated by the strict bank secrecy found in Switzerland's custom and law, a feature which is now by no means unique to that country. This tradition of confidentiality often tends to overshadow the diversity of services and depth of technical expertise which are the true hallmarks of the Swiss system. These factors are responsible for Switzerland's preeminence as both a monetary conduit and depository. This chapter will examine the Swiss banking system and students should take particular note of the contrasts between it and the banking system of the United States.

COMPONENTS OF THE SWISS SYSTEM

Traditionally, the central banking institution of Switzerland, the Swiss National Bank (*Schweizerische National bank—Banque Nationale Suisse*) has divided the Swiss Banking industry into the following categories:

1. the national or "big" banks,
2. the cantonal banks,
3. the credit cooperatives or *Raiffeisen* banks,
4. the private banks,
5. the miscellaneous Swiss-held banks,
6. foreign-held banks in Switzerland,
7. the mortgage bond banks of *Pfandbriefzentralen*, and
8. the investment trusts or mutual funds.

This classification tends to be arbitrary since the categories overlap. These banks fill virtually every banking need within the Swiss system. In addition, the giro systems, which operate as payment transfer systems through either the postal service or the Swiss National Bank, supplements the traditional banking systems.

NATIONAL OR BIG BANKS

The national—or "big"—banks, as they are called, are merely Switzerland's large multinational banks, offering every conceivable banking service to the public, even though the primary thrust of their business is in the commercial banking sector. These banks formed during the early industrialization of Europe as collective associations of private banks. At present, the big banks are still heavily involved in commercial and trade financing, both nationally and internationally. Unlike U.S. banks, which are prohibited from doing so by the Glass-Steagal Act, the big banks of Switzerland are involved in the trading of securities, with this area accounting for a growing part of their overall profits. Big banks are also becoming increasingly involved in the commodities and forward exchange markets, handling both spot and forward contracts.

The big banks of Switzerland trade on securities and commodities exchanges both on their own account and on the accounts of their individual clients. In the latter respect, the banks act as brokers for their clients, thereby giving the client a full range of investment services under one roof. The various types of accounts available to the client at the big banks, and in a somewhat less visible manner at the private banks, are discussed later in the chapter.

As of this writing, primarily five banks in Switzerland qualify as big banks. Of these five, the three largest are among the largest banks in the world and enjoy excellent reputations in the international arena.

The "big three" banks, as they are called, are the Union Bank of Switzerland (*Schweizerische Bankgesellschaft*), the Swiss Bank Corporation (*Schweizerischer Bankverein*), and the Swiss Credit Bank (*Schweizerische Kreditanstalt*). All national banks are publicly held and required under Swiss law to publish periodic balance sheets and liquidity statements. It should be noted, however, that they are not required to publish profit and loss statements.

CANTONAL BANKS

The cantonal banks, though in some instances very large, are primarily responsible for domestic and particularly cantonal banking. The original purpose for founding cantonal banks was to stabilize credit and money conditions as well as to encourage savings within the canton. In fact, this is still the aim of many cantonal banks today.

Each of Switzerland's 26 cantons (including the six half-cantons) has at least one state created cantonal bank and three of the larger cantons (including Berne, Geneva, and Vaud) have two. This brings the total number of cantonal banks to 29. These banks are given either state capital or state deposit guarantees. Being entities of the state, cantonal banks are required by law to make public certain types of information that other banks can avoid disclosing. This does not, however, release them from the constraints imposed by the Swiss bank secrecy laws.

The lending rates of the cantonal banks are slightly lower than the rates of the big banks, and, as a result, they control a large percentage of the domestic mortgage market. All cantonal banks are members of the Association of Cantonal Banks, which they formed as a link between themselves and the Swiss federal government. This organization also acts as an internal regulatory association.

CREDIT COOPERATIVES

The credit cooperatives, or *Raiffeisen* banks, are localized banking institutions established to provide credit to depositors so that they may better the local community. These cooperatives are grouped into associations that act as administrative centers and liaisons with the federal banking authorities. The U.S. equivalent of the *Raiffeisen* banks would be credit unions; unlike *Raiffeisen* banks, however, credit unions are not primarily involved in rural financing.

Loan associations in the *Raiffeisen* system have a central bank for clearing called *Die Zentralbank des Schweizer Verbandes der Raif-*

feisen. This umbrella organization provides the somewhat small and numerous *Raiffeisen* banks with an organizational center and allows them, through centralized cooperation, to take advantage of situations that otherwise would be outside their normal individual range. As a result of this greater organizational ability and more extensive reach, credit cooperatives, in recent years, have begun to expand beyond limited agricultural financing and entered into small-scale commercial financing as well. The current growth in the *Raiffeisen* sector is rapid, although it should be remembered that these banks were originally meant to function only in rural areas.

PRIVATE BANKS

In contrast to the relatively accessible credit cooperatives are the relatively discrete private banks. More than any other type of bank in Switzerland, these banks have contributed to the mystique associated with Swiss banking. Private banks represent the oldest form of banking in Switzerland, and they are the basis from which all other types of banking in Switzerland, particularly the big banks, have developed.

Private banks cater to a wealthy clientele, and, as a result, they are selective and quite secretive. Many of the world's oldest and greatest fortunes rest within the private banks in Zurich, Geneva, and Basel. The amounts of these deposits can only be estimated, as the private banks are not required by law to publish a balance sheet, though they still must file a periodic statement with the Swiss National Bank. These banks are either closely held or organized in some form of partnership; as a result, the liability of the directors or partners to the client is direct. The personal liability of the bankers, coupled with the increasing popularity of big banks, has caused the number of private banks to decline over the last few decades. In addition, Swiss private banks frequently go out of business upon the death of the owner since Swiss law requires unincorporated business firms to carry the name of one of the unlimited partners. Despite this decline, however, private banks remain tremendously important to the world's economy, particularly in light of their vast amounts of undisclosed holdings and their ability to offer, to those who wish to have it, a truly discrete and personalized banking environment. It should be mentioned that private banks are also subject to the Federal Banking Law including requirements of independent auditing. In addition, many private banks are members of the Swiss Private Bankers' Association.

MORTGAGE BOND BANKS

The mortgage bond banks, or *Pfandbriefzentralen*, are set up to issue long-term mortgage bonds with varying maturities to finance mortgage activities. Many other banks use these banks to convert short-term mortgage debt into long-term mortgage debt. At present, Switzerland remains the most heavily mortgaged nation in the world in terms of *per capita* mortgage debt, and the *Pfandbriefzentralen*, along with the country's low inflation rate, have contributed a great deal toward this.

FOREIGN-OWNED BANKS

After World War II Switzerland experienced a sudden growth in the number of foreign-owned banks and foreign branches. In addition, foreigners purchased interests in established Swiss banks. This activity accelerated in the years between 1950 and the early 1970s. Potential regulatory difficulties were perceived by the Swiss National Bank, which works closely with Swiss banks to achieve stability in monetary policy. Voluntary credit restraint was more difficult to obtain from foreign entities. As a result, a permit system for the establishment of banks by foreigners was introduced by the Federal Council. In addition, special requirements were established as a condition for granting a license to foreign-controlled banks.

GIRO SYSTEM

The various other financial institutions are basically self-explanatory. An exception is the giro system, which is not part of the regular banking system but rather a supplement to it. Most payments in Switzerland occur by giro transfer. Two different types of giro systems function in basically the same manner: the giro system of the Post Office and the giro accounts at the Swiss National Bank. Both giro systems enable account holders to make payment without inconvenience and at nominal rates. In fact, the postal giro system substitutes for the check method of paying everyday bills for the average individual. A simple transfer form presented to the Post Office makes payment to and from giro accounts possible.

In addition, the Swiss National Bank giro system serves as a payment clearing system similar to that of the United States Federal Reserve. For example, giro transfers are used to make interbank payments using the giro balances maintained with the National Bank. This makes it unnecessary for banks to maintain clearing accounts.

Both giro systems are interrelated as payments may be effected between the National Bank giro system and the Postal giro system. These systems serve an important function in the country's economy.

LAWS AFFECTING BANKING

For many years, Swiss banks operated with a minimum of federal regulation. However, prompted by the economic climate of the 1930s, Switzerland enacted a codification of its banking customs, namely the Federal

Banking Law of 1934, which went into effect in 1935. This is the primary banking law in Switzerland. All Swiss institutions that accept deposits, including private banks, are subject to this Banking Law. In 1971 the Banking Law was amended to restrict the establishment of foreign-controlled banks in Switzerland. A reciprocity requirement was one of the main criteria incorporated into the Banking Law to limit the increasing numbers of foreign-owned banks and branches. The administration of this law is delegated to the Federal Banking Commission established thereunder. Minimum reserve requirements, as well as certain reporting requirements, were also established.

One of the most important provisions of the Federal Banking Law is Article 47, which codified the tradition of bank secrecy by making violations of bank secrecy a criminal rather than civil offense punishable by up to six months' imprisonment or a fine of 50,000 Swiss Francs. Limitations on Swiss banking secrecy will be further explored.

As previously mentioned, Swiss law requires banks under the supervision of the Federal Banking Law to submit periodic balance sheets to the Swiss National Bank, and all, with the exception of private banks, must also publish financial statements. In addition, reports on foreign currency positions are also filed. However, the confidentiality of statistical reports is preserved since only summarized and consolidated data is published. The Banking Law also provides for minimal liquidity requirements, which most Swiss banks easily meet. In fact, some Swiss banks are almost 100% liquid! On the whole, Swiss banks believe that maintaining sufficient liquidity is preferable to following a system of fixed reserve requirements.

Finally, it should be mentioned that there are additional legislative enactments affecting banks such as the Ordinances, the Federal Law relating to the Swiss National Bank of 1953, and the Federal Law on Investment Funds of 1966. However, let us now examine the regulatory bodies that supervise various sectors of the Swiss banking system. These include the Swiss National Bank, the Federal Council, the Federal Banking Commission, and the Bank for International Settlements (BIS).

SWISS NATIONAL BANK

Switzerland was one of the last industrialized nations in Europe to establish a central bank. Carefully monitoring the overall banking environment, the Swiss National Bank (SNB) is a central bank of unusual structure. The SNB was organized as a corporation under special Federal Law in 1905. The capital shares of the Swiss National Bank are held by private Swiss citizens and entities as well as by cantons, cantonal banks, and other public entities. The Federal Government, which does not subscribe to SNB capital shares, nevertheless retains statutory power to influence the composition of the Bank's direction and management.

The Swiss National Bank is similar in function to the United States Federal Reserve. First, it is responsible for the issuance and maintenance of currency. The SNB has been granted certain powers to regulate the domestic volume of money. Furthermore, the SNB sets annual money supply targets with the federal government.

Second, the SNB acts as a clearing bank both in the conventional sense and in its clearing of securities and giro (checks and payments of the Swiss banking sector) accounts. Certain reporting requirements call for the submission of certain reports to the SNB. The SNB does not, however, strictly supervise the banks of Switzerland. Instead, it issues advices. Thus, the Swiss system is very much a voluntary one, maintained by agreement and harmonious functioning with a common goal in mind. Nevertheless, the "advices" issued by the Swiss National Bank are strictly followed by the Swiss banks.

FEDERAL BANKING COMMISSION

The Banking Law of 1934 also gave limited amounts of supervision to the Federal Banking Commission. Its members are chosen by the Federal Council to whom they are responsible and to whom yearly reports must be filed. The Commission performs two functions. First, it is charged with overseeing compliance with the Banking Law. Second, the Commission oversees adherence to the law of investment trusts. The permission of the Commission is required to establish a bank in Switzerland. This Commission was originally established in order to remove responsibility for the control of the banking system from the Government. However, due to its link with the Federal Council there is still a connection with the government.

FEDERAL COUNCIL

The Federal Council is the executive branch of the Swiss Government whose members are elected for four-year terms by the Federal Assembly. Each of the seven Council members represents a separate department of the government. The Federal Council has promulgated orders affecting the maintenance of adequate reserves with the SNB. The Federal Council now directly controls liquidity rates and regulation of interest rates. It should be remembered, however, that interest rates in Switzerland are generally low compared with rates in other countries.

BANK FOR INTERNATIONAL SETTLEMENTS

Even though it is not a part of the Swiss banking system, the Bank for International Settlements (BIS) in Basel is an important institution. Established in 1930 to facilitate international transactions and to assist in the collection of war erparation payments, the BIS is somewhat similar to the International Monetary Fund, in which Switzerland does not participate. Much of the Swiss National Bank's contact with the world's other central banks is done through the BIS. For example, Switzerland has entered into swap transactions with the United States in which the BIS played an important role.

SELF-REGULATION

In addition to the regulatory bodies discussed, it should be mentioned that much of the regulation of Swiss banks occurs through trade associations of which the banks are members. This self-regulation covers areas frequently considered to be within the government's responsibility. One of the most important of these trade associations is the Swiss Bankers' Association, which generally protects the interests of both banks and their customers. Furthermore, the Association serves as the banking industry's main link with the Swiss Government.

In addition to the expertise and diversity of service available at Swiss banks, the protection offered to the finances of citizens from other war-torn nations established the stability and financial integrity of the Swiss system. In particular, Switzerland's political neutrality and custom of bank secrecy have contributed to Swiss preeminence in international banking.

BANK SECRECY

A great attraction to foreign capital has been Switzerland's highly regarded bank secrecy laws. Far from reflecting an effort to confound foreign law enforcement or to circumvent foreign tax or exchange control legislation, these principles reflect a Swiss concern for the economic liberties of the individual similar to American concerns for first amendment rights. The logical premises for treating bank secrecy with such respect have much to recommend themselves and go beyond the single observance of custom. As previously mentioned, Article 47(b) of the Banking Law of 1934 makes the violation of banking secrecy an offense punishable by fine or criminal prison term. Furthermore, negligent as well as intentional violations are covered by its provisions. It should be mentioned, however, that certain limitations on bank secrecy do exist under Swiss law. For example, banking secrecy will not extend to activities, either in Switzerland or abroad, that would constitute a crime under Swiss law. In addition, provision is made in certain specific instances for authorities to have access to bank records in case of inheritance or bankruptcy proceedings. Nevertheless, these limitations are narrowly defined to assure that the secrecy of individual banking matters is left intact. Similarly, certain provisions of the Swiss Criminal Law protecting confidential business information have also been invoked in connection with banking matters. Related to the concept of bank secrecy is the existence of numbered accounts. A great deal of mystery surrounds this relatively routine denomination of accounts by number code rather than by name. Rather than is commonly assumed, total anonymity is not provided by numbered accounts. Although true ownership of such accounts is concealed from the bank staff, a minimum of two bank officers are required to know the true identity of the beneficial owner of numbered accounts. Thereafter, the client's name is kept off papers generated in the servicing of the account, thus guarding the secrecy of the account-holder from staff and third parties. Finally, in the case of Swiss court order, information regarding the activities of a numbered account must be given just as in the case of a named account.

Concerns regarding taxation of an individual's assets have prompted many to seek jurisdictions that allow a maximum amount of retained earnings. On the international level, discrepancies between the tax rates of different nations have prompted tax jurisdiction shopping. Many have found havens in the Bahamas, the Cayman Islands, Liechtenstein, and the Netherland Antilles, but the ultimate haven for foreign investors has been and continues to be Switzerland. Many factors contribute to this preference, and not among the least is the fact that Switzerland is the most economically and politically stable of all developed Western nations. Economically, politically, and legally, Switzerland does not bother with the rest of the world; rather, it lets the rest of the world bother with her.

Switzerland also retains a high degree of economic neutrality, being neither a member of highly visible ecopolitical organizations such as the International Monetary Fund or the equally powerful low profile organizations such as the "Paris Club." Switzerland's philosophy has always been that one is most happy when one's hands are in one's own pockets. It is only natural to expect that money will flow to where it is allowed to function at its freest; anonymity for the investor and minimal government supervision of investments thus create a climate that favors capital attraction.

OTHER SYSTEMS BASED ON THE SWISS

The Swiss system's example of private regulation and minimal government supervision has inspired a small band of imitators worldwide. While this tends to give the individual greater choice, Switzerland remains the primary recipient of funds for anonymous accounts. The most interesting of these imitators is the Principality of Liechtenstein. Liechtenstein has taken the passive philosophy of the Swiss and, through variation and a great deal of ingenuity, has transformed it into an active international marketing technique for the attraction of capital. Liechtenstein has established a system where it benefits, and allows the beneficial owner to benefit, by using any one of the small number of bank secrecy nations, Switzerland being the primary example, as a safe harbor for the funds of its "entities." These "entities" are dummy corporations that Liechtenstein allows any individual to form, even if solely for the purpose, as most are, of avoiding the tax laws of another nation. Anonymity is retained by means of an agent acting for an undisclosed principal. This function is entrusted to a Liechtenstein attorney who signs the necessary papers in his fiduciary capacity. The name of the owner does not have to appear anywhere, and the real owners of the fiduciary enterprises do not have to be entered in the commercial register. The attorney handles virtually everything including the opening of a bank account for the entity in a place where bank secrecy is strong, such as Switzerland. The possibilities for illegal activities, particularly tax evasion, are limitless due to the fact that even if the bank reveals the account-holder's name, all that would be disclosed is the name of the entity and not its true source of funding.

Though the example of the Liechtenstein "entity" invites the equation of bank secrecy with illegality, this is not necessarily true. Many accounts are maintained for tax avoidance rather than evasion, and some are maintained simply because they offer a far wider range of services than their heavily restricted American banking counterparts. The question of legality aside, the key advantages to a Swiss, or any other secret account, is its security and its flexibility. The security of the account is self-evident, and the flexibility of the account derives from the fact that banks aren't highly regulated so that they can involve themselves more actively in investing, particularly in securities.

Austria's bank secrecy laws are equally or even more stringent than Swiss laws. Austrian banks are both financially and criminally liable for disclosing information about their clients' accounts. Bank secrecy laws also exist in the Bahamas, Cayman Islands, Panama, and Hungary, among others. However, these jurisdictions have recently been undergoing changes in their approach to bank secrecy in cases involving the United States. In particular, recent cases and agreements between the United States and bank secrecy jurisdictions indicate a relaxation of strict banking secrecy in specific instances involving taxation and securities law violations.

Switzerland's attitude toward taxation is relaxed to the point that domestic tax evasion is not a crime under the Swiss Penal Code and is only a minor offense under civil law. However, there is a lack of clarity as to just how severely domestic tax fraud will be treated.

The large majority of nations, particularly the United States, do not share Switzerland's relaxed attitude toward taxation law enforcement. The problems that Switzerland's bank secrecy laws and policies create with regard to international taxation, particularly when they act in disjunction with United States domestic laws, have plagued the U.S. Internal Revenue Service for many years. Surprisingly, the Swiss have made some very modest concessions to the United States, which they have rarely made elsewhere. For example, under Article XVI of the Convention between the United States and the Swiss Confederation for the Avoidance of Double Taxation with Respect to Taxes on Income, the Swiss are obligated to furnish information to the United States with regard to double taxation and with regard to fraud. However, even this disclosure is conditioned by secrecy. Though this may appear to be a small concession on the part of Switzerland, it is more than Switzerland has accorded to any other nation. Under the Treaty, as interpreted by two rulings by the Swiss Federal Supreme Court, Switzerland is not obligated under the Tax Convention's "fraud clause" to furnish genuine legal assistance in judicial proceedings, but is required only to furnish the IRS with an official report. More detailed assistance and findings, beyond such a report, would be needed to truly help the IRS.

There also appears to be problems with the so-called "concession" that Switzerland has made under Art. XVI(1) of the Tax Convention. Article XVI(1) provides in relevant part that, "Any information so exchanged shall be treated as secret and shall not be disclosed to any person other than those concerned with the assessment and collection of the taxes which are the subject of the present Convention." Since under the International Revenue Code, tax proceedings and reports may be inspected by third parties, and since the United States promotes a policy of broad public awareness of judicial and administrative proceedings, it is highly doubtful that this provision of the Tax Convention can be effectively complied with. Thus, with secrecy not assured, Switzerland would again have to deny information.

In addition to the Tax Convention, Switzerland has entered several bilateral and multilateral treaties for legal assistance in criminal matters. If such a treaty of mutual assistance exists and if compliance with its provisions is assured, the Swiss authorities will cooperate. However, as a general matter, foreign governments will be assisted only if the alleged criminal act would also be considered a violation had it occurred in Switzerland. Thus, assistance is not available in political or foreign exchange matters. Among these treaties are the European Convention on Mutual Assistance in Criminal Matters of 1959 and the Treaty between the United States of America and Switzerland on Mutual Assistance in Criminal Matters of 1977.

A significant recent agreement has been entered into for law enforcement cooperation in the field of securities trading on insider information. The Memorandum of Understanding for the Agreement of the Swiss Bankers' Association with regard to the handling of requests for information from the Securities and Exchange Commission of the United States on the subject of misuse of inside information was signed in August 1982. Pursuant to this agreement, the Swiss Banker's Association will appoint a Commission of inquiry to handle requests for information regarding holders of Swiss bank accounts. The Securities and Exchange Commission and/or the U.S. Department of Justice must satisfy preliminary conditions concerning the securities transactions claimed to have been made in violation of U.S. insider trading laws. For example, significant price and trading volume fluctuations within specified time periods prior to announcement of an acquisition or business combination (that is, merger, consolidation, or sale of substantially all of the issuer's assets) may be shown as justification for the inquiry. Other documentation and representations that the SEC will not make further disclosure of banking information, except in connection with investigation or actions by the SEC against alleged purchasers or sellers of identified securities or put or call options, must also be submitted to the Swiss Commission. Assuming all necessary items are submitted to the Commission, a report on the transactions involved will subsequently be called for from the Swiss banks concerned. Customers will be notified and given the opportunity to provide rebuttal evidence concerning U.S. insider trading laws. The parties agreed, however, that they did not intend to confer a right to judicial review in the courts of the United States with respect to decisions to disclose bank information. Finally, a report with all useful evidence will be returned as a rule within 45 days to the Commission.

This report will contain the name, address, and nationality of the customer, as well as details of the customer's transactions during the 40 days preceding the announcement. Thereafter, the Commission will furnish such information to the Federal Office for Police Matters to be forwarded to the SEC. In the event that the identity of the individual carrying out SEC-identified transactions was incorrect or that the individual does not meet the definitions of an insider found in the Agreement, such report need not be forwarded to the SEC.

Article 9 of the Agreement contains a stipulation that the Swiss bank shall immediately block the customer's account up to a sum equivalent to the profit (or loss avoided) if the threshold criterion is satisfied. Procedures for remittance of such blocked amounts to either the SEC or the customer are outlined and include consent as well as termination of SEC proceedings by final judgment, among others, Finally, the Swiss Bankers' Association will use its best efforts to keep the SEC informed of its members who agree to adhere to the terms of the Agreement. In light of the influence of the Swiss Bankers' Association exerts in self-regulation of the Swiss banking industry, the agreement will be widely accepted.

This agreement by the Swiss Bankers' Association to cooperate in the enforcement of United States insider trading laws by breaking the traditional bank secrecy is a significant development. Although certain safeguards are provided in order to prevent release of information except in specific areas of activity, these exceptions to bank secrecy were not previously granted. As mentioned earlier, requested assistance was conditioned on the requirement that the alleged activity constituted a violation under Swiss law. Therefore a shift in banking secrecy limits is evidenced by the agreement. The agreement's impact upon the Swiss banking industry remains to be seen.

Perhaps it would be useful to examine one of the main motivating factors for the Agreement between the Swiss Bankers' Association and the Securities and Exchange Commission. In *Securities and Exchange Commission v. Banca Della Svizzera Italiana*, 92 F.R.D. 111 (S.D.N.Y. 1981), an action was brought against a Swiss corporation to compel discovery of the names of parties allegedly involved in insider trading violations in purchases made on U.S. securities exchanges. The SEC alleged that defendants acted in bad faith by making deliberate use of Swiss nondisclosure laws to evade American securities laws against insider trading. The court held that, by making purchases on American securities exchanges, the Swiss corporation could be compelled to make discovery and answer interrogations concerning undisclosed principals despite the fact that such disclosure might subject it to criminal liability in Switzerland. The vital national interest in protecting the integrity of U.S. securities markets was mentioned by the court in its decision. The presence of the defendant in the United States through its subsidiary, as well as its participation in the U.S. securities markets by the purchase of call options and stock of a company, subjected the defendant to the court's jurisdiction. Furthermore, the lack of good faith of the defendant was cited by the court as the basis for distinguishing this case from the well-known *Societe Internationale Pour Participations Industrielles et Commerciales, S.A. v. Rogers*, 357 U.S. 197 (1958). Therefore, the Swiss nondisclosure laws were ineffective in shielding the defendant's activity within the United States.

This ruling raised serious questions regarding the future status of Swiss banking secrecy and prompted the agreement for cooperation in enforcement of insider trading laws previously stifled by Swiss law. At the least, the agreement serves to delineate the limits of bank secrecy in this area for both the United States and Switzerland, which were challenged by cases such as *Banca Della Svizzera Italiana*.

Thus we see that, within the United States, courts are moving away from the position that a foreign law's prohibition of discovery is an absolute bar. This trend away from honoring bank secrecy is also occurring in cases involving other jurisdictions, such as the Cayman Islands. This is not to say, however, that such secrecy provisions have not previously been subject to attack. For example, *Societe Internationale Pour Participations Industrielles et Commerciales, S.A. v. Rogers,* 357 U.S. 197 (1958) (or *Interhandel*) also involved an issue concerning Swiss banking secrecy. In *Interhandel,* litigation spanned both U.S. federal courts and the International Court of Justice. The action involved proper custody and control of assets seized by the United States during World War II pursuant to the United States Trading with the Enemy Act. The assets consisted of the cash and capital stock of General Aniline and Film Corporation (GAF), a Delaware corporation; they were seized by the Alien Property Custodian since the assets were found to be "owned by or held for the benefit of "I.G. Farbenindustrie," a German firm and then enemy national.

The plaintiff, a Swiss holding company known as I.G. Chemie or Interhandel, brought suit under the same statute to recover the confiscated assets. Interhandel claimed that it was the neutral owner of GAF stock and cash at the time of confiscation and thus entitled to recovery. However, the United States claimed that I.G. Chemie (Interhandel) was in fact beneficially owned by I.G. Farben, a German industrial corporation and by Sturzenegger and Cie., the Swiss bank that the chairman of I.G. Farben had founded. The bulk of the documentation, concerning ownership of various intermediary dummy corporations and showing the extent of I.G. Farben's ownership, was initially held by Sturzenegger. The Attorney General of the United States claimed that Interhandel was part of a conspiracy to conceal Farben's ownership and asserted that discovery of certain records concerning Interhandel's shareholders would prove the true ownership. Sturzenegger in turn claimed inability to produce such records, which were protected under Swiss bank secrecy laws and had been "confiscated" by the Swiss Federal Attorney. Nevertheless, subsequent to an order to dismiss Interhandel's complaint with prejudice if certain banking records were not produced for discovery as ordered within a six-month period, a total of 190,000 documents were released for inspection with the consent of the Swiss government and by waivers of confidentiality. The Supreme Court on appeal of the dismissal of plaintiff's complaint for failure to produce all requested documents, found that dismissal of plaintiff's complaint with prejudice was not authorized since it was established that failure to comply with the discovery order was due to inability, and not to willfulness, bad faith, or any fault of the petitioners.

Thus, the litigation in *Interhandel* wound on with no end in sight. A concurrent claim was brought by Switzerland for the release of GAF assets in the International Court of Justice in 1957. Among other objections, the United States asserted that the I.C.J. lacked jurisdiction since local U.S. remedies had not first been exhausted. In addition, the matter was claimed to be within the domestic jurisdiction of the United States.

The dispute was finally settled, aided by legislative amendments to the Trading with the Enemy Act, and the question of interference with American judicial procedures by Swiss bank secrecy laws was never litigated to termination.

Meanwhile, the United States continued to lose massive amounts of revenue, estimated to be as high as in the hundreds of millions of dollars, because of the obstacles presented by Swiss bank secrecy. Conversely, a selected few individuals gain by keeping their assets secret. Does this contribute to overall world market stability? Or does it tend to create an imbalance? On the one side, there are the economic interests of the protected individuals and the country whose secrecy protects them. On the other side, there are the interests of the nation being deprived of additional income. The struggle between the two sides continues.

WHY THE SYSTEM WORKS

Now that we have examined the basic functional components of the Swiss banking system, we should try to assess why it is able to work in the way that it does. To begin with, Switzerland has one of the lowest rates of inflation of any industrialized nation in the world. This naturally attracts outside capital since the shrinkage of the Swiss franc becomes less than that of other currencies. Furthermore, the Swiss have continued to maintain a low or practically nonexistent unemployment rate, thereby giving the Swiss National Bank room in which to maneuver in adjusting the money supply. Any short-term adjustments in the money supply that might cause unemployment are absorbed without causing too much concern for the overall economy.

These policies were employed in Switzerland extensively in the early 1970s when the U.S. dollar began to float after the demise of the Bretton Woods agreement. The exchange rate of the Swiss franc naturally has a great deal to do with the stability of Switzerland's economy. Since roughly 30% of Switzerland's GNP is exported, there is an abundance of available hard currency. Thus, the SNB can stabilize the franc with little difficulty when the need arises. Few countries are in so enviable a position. So long as the franc stays strong, Swiss banks will be besieged with a demand for franc denominated accounts and currency.

Maintenance of equilibrium among such factors as inflation, employment, GNP, hard currency holdings, and the strength of the franc is interrelated and essential for any economy. Should one link in the chain fail, the others are adversely affected. By carefully balancing each of these factors, the Swiss have created an extremely healthy economic environment.

The Swiss banking system has been selected to demonstrate some differences between American banking and Swiss banking. Space limitations do not permit a discussion of banking as practiced in other countries. Almost each country has its own particularity, regulations, customs and practices in banking. Thus, this book does not extend into geographical areas even though they might be closely related to the United States. Nevertheless, by showing the particularities of the Swiss banking system, readers will be able to appreciate in a general fashion how different banking can be in various countries.

Bibliography

Arthur Anderson & Co. *Tax and Trade Guide,* 5th ed. 1980.

Bär, Hans J. *The Banking System of Switzerland,* 3rd rev. ed. Zurich: Schulthess, 1964.

"Cayman Islands Case Shows How Courts in the U.S. Are Cracking the Secrecy of Foreign Banks." *Wall Street Journal* (October 14, 1982), p. 33.

H. R. Rep. No. 102, 96th Congress, 2nd Session. 1980.

Ikle, Max. *Switzerland: An International Banking and Financial Center.* Dowden: Hutchinson, Ross, 1972.

Interhandel Case (Switzerland v. United States of America). *I.C.J.* (1957), p. 105.

Kelder, James. *How To Open a Swiss Bank Account.* New York: Thomas Y. Crowell Company, Inc., 1976.

Meyer, Bernhard F. "Swiss Banking Secrecy and Its Legal Implications in the United States." *N. Eng. L. Rev.,* 14(Summer 1978), pp. 18–81.

Memorandum of Understanding between the United States of America and Switzerland, August 31, 1982.

Niederer, H. and M. C. Roesle. "Switzerland." In *International Banking Centers.* London: Euromoney Publications, 1982.

Noble, K. B. "Swiss Bankers Expected to Relax Secrecy on U.S. Stock Violations." *The New York Times* (September 1, 1982), p. 1.

Roethenmund, Robert. *The Swiss Banking Handbook: A Complete Manual for Practical Investors.* New York: Books in Focus, 1980.

Swiss Banks and Secrecy Laws: Hearings Before the House Committee on Banking and Currency on H.R. 15073. 91st Congress, 1st and 2nd Sessions. 364 (1969–70).

Swiss Code of Obligations, Act 97 (penalties for breach of bank secrecy).

27 U.S.T. 2019, T.I.A.S. 8302, entered into force January 1977.

Wirth, M. H. "Attachments of Swiss Bank Accounts: A Remedy for International Debt Collection." *Bus. Law,* 36(April 1981), pp. 1029–40.

12

The European Monetary System

Introduction

In March 1979, nine major European nations, members of the European Economic Community, formally launched the European Monetary System, an innovative plan of international monetary cooperation. The European Monetary System, commonly referred to as the EMS, is an arrangement among the member nations to limit fluctuations in their currencies and achieve monetary stability. It was thought that international trade between the participating nations would be improved if exchange rates were stable and predictable. It consists of a number of special features, such as a common currency unit, detailed regulation of permissible currency fluctuations among member nations, mutual credit facilities for participating countries, and the creation of a central reserve fund consisting of gold, dollars, and the currencies of the participating countries. Representatives of the central banks and ministers of finance administer the system and meet periodically in Brussels, Belgium.

Historical Background

The modern impetus for a European monetary alliance can be traced to the post-World War I era. In 1918, a visionary Austrian nobleman, Count Coudenhoven-Kalerghi, embarked on a project to create a "United States of Europe." Europe was ready at that time, after the destruction of World War I, for such an idea, and many hoped that future wars in Europe would be avoided by having a "United States of Europe."

Coudenhoven-Kalerghi put a lifetime of work into this project and indeed succeeded in obtaining the cooperation of most European countries. Committees were established in all major European nations to unite the continent. With the appearance of Mussolini and Hitler in Europe, however, this venture ultimately collapsed. Today the European Economic Community and the various multinational European organizations continue Coudenhoven-Kalerghi's efforts to bring the countries of Europe closer together.

In the post-World War II period, further steps were taken toward international financial cooperation. In 1950, the European Payments Union was created to foster settlement of commercial transactions among member nations. The establishment of the European Coal and Steel Community in 1951 further enhanced trade relations within the continent by removing most of the restrictions on the movement of these commodities.

In 1957, the six member nations of the European Coal and Steel Community—West Germany, France, Belgium, Luxembourg, the Netherlands, and Italy—signed the Treaty of Rome establishing the European Economic Community. The aim of the Community, or EEC as it is commonly designated, was to achieve economic and, to some extent, political integration and stability among European nations through the unrestricted interchange of goods and services, capital, and people.

Not until 1969 was the goal of establishing a monetary union with a common currency first approved in principle by the European Economic Community leaders. This plan was to have been finalized by 1980. If it had been achieved, it would have eliminated the fluctuations in exchange values among member nations' currencies by making it possible to have a common European monetary unit. By removing the risk of unstable money, it was hoped that greater economic, political, and social ties among EEC members would be fostered.

It was difficult even to imagine that various European countries with various political and social structures would be able to use the same currency. After all, by using a common currency, a major part of a country's independence is given up. Nevertheless, there are examples of independent countries that by choice use the currency of another sovereign nation. The Republic of Panama, for instance, uses the U.S. dollar as paper currency, even though it has its own Panamanian coinage. Similarly, the country of Liberia, an independent republic, uses the U.S. dollar as its official currency. Neither Panama nor Liberia have monetary exchange problems. If the U.S. dollar is in trouble, these countries will be adversely affected; if the dollar is strong and firm, it will reflect on their economies as well. Interestingly, in the tiny Caribbean island of Tortola, which is a British territory, the U.S. dollar is used as official legal tender.

Even if domestic currency and coinage are produced, many countries link its value to that of another, more widely recognized currency. For example, France, which long ago surrendered its colonial possessions in Africa, maintains very close ties with its former African territories. Fourteen independent African nations, which were once French colonies, link their currencies to the franc. Their currencies fluctuate accordingly, although all of them have their own independent currency systems.

In contrast, all former British colonies with the exception of Gambia have completely divorced themselves from the English pound. Although the United States is not a colonial power, the currencies of about forty foreign countries are tied to, and fluctuate with, the U.S. dollar. Finally, over twenty currencies are tied to so-called "baskets of currencies" of various types and with various degrees of rigidity.

The 1969 plan for a unified European currency was based upon a then existing structure governing international exchange rates known as the Bretton Woods international monetary system, which limited fluctuations of currency exchange rates of participating nations to within about 1% of the declared par value in terms of the dollar. With the collapse of the Bretton Woods system in 1971, however, a new framework was devised by the International Monetary Fund (IMF) member nations allowing for a wider range of fluctuation of 4.5% relative to the dollar. This new system would have permitted fluctuations among EEC members' currencies within a total range of 9% (4.5% upward and 4.5% downward).

In order to minimize these currency fluctuations and achieve the goal of economic stability, the European Joint Float Agreement was created in 1972, consisting of Belgium, Luxembourg, France, Italy, the Netherlands, and West Germany. Shortly thereafter, Denmark, Ireland, Norway, and the United Kingdom also joined. Out of this cooperation grew the so-called "Snake" and the "Worm." Within the "Snake," the exchange rates of a large number of European currencies moved up and down within a 2.25% spread (2.25% up and 2.25% down for a total of 4.5%). Because of their close economic relationship, the Netherlands and Belgium agreed between themselves to maintain the value of their currencies within about 1% of each other. This agreement became known as the "Worm," which was in the center of the "Snake." The currencies of all the participants in the Join Float Agreement were permitted to move *jointly* within the 4.5% range established by the IMF in 1971, and this 4.5% band became known as the "Tunnel."

The Snake functioned well for a very short time but began to disintegrate in June 1972, due to a decline in the exchange rates of the British pound. Ultimately, the currencies of Great Britain, Denmark, and Italy were forced to withdraw from the Snake framework, and in 1973 market pressure on the U.S. dollar caused further disintegration of the IMF agreements.

In April 1973, the European Economic Community established a European Monetary Cooperation Fund (EMCF) to facilitate the creation of a unified European currency.

Origins of the European Monetary System

Despite these initially unsuccessful efforts, the goal of achieving exchange rate stability and creating a unified European currency still remained. In July of 1978, a proposed new European Monetary System was presented to the nine European Council member nations and approved by a resolution of the European Council on December 5, 1978. The new European Monetary System was officially launched in March of 1979 under the sponsorship of German Chancellor Helmut Schmidt and French President Valery Giscard d'Estaing. There is some slight contradiction about the exact date, however.

Contrary to the original intentions of the Council, not all members of the European Common Market became full participants in the system. Great Britain was one of the very important members of the European Common Market to become a member of the EMS. However, it elected not to fully participate in the system since it did not want to subject its currency to restraint. Norway opted not to join the EMS either. On the other hand, Ireland did join, thereby divorcing the Irish pound from the English pound and establishing an independent exchange rate. Interestingly, however, the Irish currency decreased in value while that of Great Britain remained firm.

Seven of the nine European Community members became full participants in the EMS: Belgium, Denmark, France, West Germany, Ireland, Luxembourg, and the Netherlands. Italy also agreed to participate in the system under modified conditions due to difficulties it experienced with its currency. Germany is regarded as the strongest and most central of the EMS nations.

Features of the European Monetary System

THE EUROPEAN CURRENCY UNIT (ECU)

The European Monetary System is based on a central reserve that consists of gold, U.S. dollars, and the currencies of the countries participating in the system. The common denominator of the system is a newly created monetary unit called the *European currency unit (ECU)*. The ECU is not money and does not exist in a physical sense that currencies of participating countries do. It does, however, serve several important functions in the operation of the EMS: (a) as a denominator (numeraire) for the exchange rate mechanism; (b) as the basis for a divergence indicator; (c) as the denominator for operations in both the intervention and credit mechanisms; and (d) as a means of settlement among monetary authorities of the European Community.

In technical terms, the ECU is equivalent to a weighted average of a basket of currencies of EMS member nations, plus the British pound sterling. The ECU was defined as the sum of 3.66 Belgian francs, 0.217 Danish kronen, 1.55 French francs, 0.00759 Irish pounds, 109 Italian lire, 9.14 Luxembourg francs, 0.286 Dutch guilders. 0.0885 British pounds, and 0.828 German marks. Since revaluations and devaluations of these currencies occur, these figures are constantly changing. The weights assigned to each currency are based upon the relative economies—or upon the gross national product of each participating country as well as its share in intra-European trade. These weights are to be reexamined every five years, or upon request if the value of any currency changes by 25%.

The dollar value of the ECU, equivalent to approximately $1.40 at the inception of the EMS, can be calculated by multiplying the exchange rates of the EC currencies by their weighted value in the basket of ECU currencies. Therefore, the dollar value of the ECU will vary with the daily fluctuations in the exchange rates of the European currencies relative to the dollar.

The ECU serves as a monetary asset, which the central banks of participating EMS nations can hold as reserves, lend or borrow, or use as a means of settling debts among themselves. It is expected that the ECU could eventually be used by nonmember central banks as an international reserve asset similar to the SDR (special drawing right), which is issued by the international Monetary Fund in Washington, D.C.

Additionally, the ECU serves as an accounting unit for the calculation of the central exchange rates of the individual currencies of EMS members. Thus, at the inception of the EMS, each of the central banks of participating countries formally defined the value of its currency in terms of the number of units of that currency which would equal one ECU. The currency rates in relation to the central ECU are reexamined every six months; the examination includes a thorough evaluation of the balance of payments of the respective countries and the general economic conditions.

The conversion of EMS member currencies into their ECU equivalencies serves a twofold purpose: It contributes to the establishment of a central rate for each currency, which is then used to calculate a system of ECU-based exchange rates linking all member currencies. It also provides a benchmark against which fluctuations in exchange rates can be measured to determine when the "threshold of divergence" of the currency is reached. Thereafter, the government of that country must take action to maintain the value of its currency within agreed-upon limits. This may include adjustment of domestic economic policies to affect interest rates, intervention in foreign exchange markets, or devaluation (or revaluation) of its currency.

PERMISSIBLE CURRENCY FLUCTUATIONS

The countries participating in the European Monetary System agreed to maintain the exchange rates of their currencies within a 2.25% margin of the established central rates of the other EMS currencies. This actually means a total maximum fluctuation range of 4.5%. The Italian economy was not strong enough to maintain this limit; thus its lira was permitted to fluctuate within a 6% range of the other EMS currencies, for a total of 12%, which is a very considerable range for exchange rate movement. The participating countries agreed, however, that this exceptional range should be reduced if and when economic conditions would permit it. This was not the case as of 1984.

Intervention in participating currencies is compulsory when the limits defined by the fluctuation margins are reached. If an EMS currency reaches the upper or lower limits of its 2.25% (6% for Italy) maximum deviation due to underlying market forces, the nations whose currencies are involved must intervene in their national foreign exchange markets to alter supply and demand conditions causing such fluctuations. For instance, a nation whose currency appreciates 2.25% above the central rate of one or more EMS currencies must offer its own currency in unlimited amounts in exchange for the currency against which it is rising. Conversely, a member nation whose currency has depreciated to its lower limit below that of another EMS currency must buy its own currency in unlimited amounts in exchange for that currency against which it has fallen. In this respect, the daily exchange operation of the EMS is similar to the Snake arrangement that preceded it.

THRESHOLD OF DIVERGENCE

An added feature of the EMS that limits currency fluctuations, called the *threshold of divergence*, is designed to avoid certain problems associated with the old Snake system. Under this provision, not only do EMS member nations agree to limit the fluctuation in their currencies within 2.25% (6% for Italy) of its ECU-based central rate, but they also agree to various other forms of intervention by other central banks in the event that their currency deviates by 75% of their agreed maximum divergence values allowed against its ECU value.

The importance of this provision is evident when compared to the conditions that occurred under the old Snake system. Often the exchange rate of one member currency, particularly the German mark, due to internal developments in Germany's economy or speculative movements in the foreign exchange market, would rise relative to the dollar. The appreciation of the mark, for example, was part of a normal market adjustment that would reduce Germany's trade surplus by increasing the price of German goods in terms of foreign currencies. As one member's currency rose, however, other participants in the system were obliged to intervene to maintain the required exchange rate relationship between their currencies and that which was rising, often to the detriment of their own economies. The resulting rise in the value of Snake member currencies relative to the dollar and other non-Snake member currencies in many cases worsened their trade balances and affected domestic employment, and possibly undermined their ability to export.

The threshold of divergence feature of the new EMS was intended to guard somewhat against such recurring conditions. As previously noted, the ECU is composed of a weighted average of the external values of EMS member currencies. As EMS currencies rise or fall jointly in value relative to the dollar, the external value of the ECU also rises or falls relative to the dollar, thus leaving the ECU-based central rates of member currencies undisturbed, and no intervention is necessary.

If the value of only one EMS currency rises or falls, the external value of the ECU may remain relatively stable. When that currency deviates from its ECU-based central rate by 75% of the 2.25% limit, or 1.69% (4.5% for Italy), then the threshold of divergence safeguard is triggered. Other participants in the system are no longer required to adjust their exchange rate policies to keep pace with the currency that is out of line. Rather, the nation whose currency has reached its threshold of divergence is required to intervene with corrective measures aimed at eliminating the market pressures causing such deviation, or to explain to the other members why in its view no action was necessary.

Apart from intervention in foreign exchange markets, other remedies that a nation might employ include adjusting interest rates and adopting policies to correct internal conditions such as inflation, recession, or certain kinds of trade barriers that fostered such currency movements. Alternatively, a nation may be required to officially revalue or devalue its currency.

STRATEGIES FOR MARKET INTERVENTION

A nation has various means to finance intervention in support of its currency:

An EMS nation may use its foreign exchange reserves, which probably consist primarily of dollars.

The nation may avail itself of special credit facilities available to meet the requirements of the EMS. These facilities include three types of loans, structured according to their maturity dates:

The first and shortest-term tier consists of currencies that may be borrowed from the other EMS participants to satisfy the nation's immediate intervention needs. These loans are available for up to 45 days after the end of the month in which they were borrowed. Such loans can be extended for three months from the maturity date, but the amount that may be extended is limited. If it is mutually agreeable to the parties, a second three-month rollover is possible.

The second tier of loans consists of *short-term credit facilities* that may also be borrowed from the other EMS participants for three months and that can be extended up to six months past the initial maturity date. The amounts that can be borrowed are limited by the size of the pool of credit maintained on the books of the European Monetary Cooperation Fund and by the member's quota in the pool, which is determined by the size of their economy.

The third tier of borrowing is referred to as a *medium-term credit facility* wherein a nation may borrow for a term of two to five years from a pool of multibillion ECU funds. A member's access to medium-term credit is again determined by that member's quota in the multibillion ECU pool. However, borrowing under this facility is contingent upon the member's willingness to adopt internal economic policies designed to reduce those domestic conditions that necessitated financial assistance.

PAYMENT PROCEDURES AMONG CENTRAL BANKS

The countries participating in the EMS are expected to extend short-term credit facilities to members that, due to monetary developments, require such support.

When an EMS member finds it necessary to intervene to maintain some degree of stability in its exchange rates in relation to the other members of the system, the intervening country must so advise the central banks of the other member countries. In the past, member countries, and especially Germany, have been called upon to support the currencies of weaker nations. These efforts notwithstanding, member countries had to apply for permission to adjust their exchange rates due to their inability to maintain the previously established exchange rate of their currency in relation to those of others in the system. Of course, when intervening and making funds available, the lending central banks generally view these interventions as short-term financing and charge the going rate of interest, which creates an additional burden for the borrowing country.

When a participating country borrows a currency for the purpose of intervention, its debt is denominated in ECUs. The debtor nation can repay the debt in either ECUs or the borrowed currency. However, the central bank of the creditor country is not obligated to accept payment in ECUs in excess of 50% of the amount due. The balance of the repayment can be made in the currency borrowed or by transferring other reserve components, such as gold and U.S. dollars. Central banks among themselves, however, can agree on other methods of payment if they so wish, including SDRs to a certain extent.

If gold is transferred from one central bank to another in settlement of a debt, the price of gold is subject to acceptance by the creditor central bank.

If the debtor central bank no longer possesses ECUs and wishes to acquire some, it may apply first to the central banks, which are net accumulators of ECUs, or to the European Monetary Cooperation Fund (EMCF), which was established in 1973. In the latter case, ECUs are acquired from the Fund in return for a contribution of an equal percentage of the gold and dollar reserve holdings of the central bank.

The gold portion of the reserve is valued at the average of the prices recorded daily at the two London fixings during the previous six calendar months, but it does not exceed the average price of the two fixings on the penultimate working day of the period. For the dollar portion, the market rate of two working days prior to the value date is the basis.

ECU assets are used in intracommunity debt settlement within the limits and upon the terms set out in the agreement between the respective countries and their central banks. This agreement can be liquidated only by unanimous decision. The agreements are drawn up in English, French, and German, and all three are binding texts. The central banks may transfer ECUs to one another against U.S. dollars, EEC (European Economic Community) currencies, SDRs, or gold. For the purpose of meeting a decline in its dollar reserves, a central bank may acquire dollars against ECUs from the EMCF.

The percentage of participation in credit arrangements under the EMS depends on the size and strength of the economies of the participating countries. Germany and France, for example, have the largest participation; Ireland and Denmark have the smallest. Each participating central bank is assigned a debtor quota and a credit quota beyond which they are not obliged to go. The *debtor quota* determines the amount of support that each central bank may receive under the terms set forth in the agreement, and the *creditor quota* determines the amount of support that each bank undertakes to finance under these same terms. Every five years, the governors of the central banks must examine the quotas to determine if they should be revised. They may, however, conduct such examination before the expiration of the period.

The Chairman of the EMS must inform the participating central banks and the Commission representatives of any application for financial support. Whenever a central bank so requests, a meeting of the participating central banks may be held. A central bank might wish to inform the other central banks that its country's balance of payments is facing a deficit and has a disturbing decline in its foreign exchange reserves. In such case, the other central banks might decide, in proportion to their participation in the system, to refinance the suffering member.

European Monetary Cooperation Fund

The European Monetary Cooperation Fund (EMCF) is the institution that administers the various credit arrangements under the EMS. The Fund, which is also known as FECOM for its French initials, was established in April of 1973 with the original intention of creating a unified European currency in the wake of the collapse of the old Snake system.

Under the EMS, central banks of the member nations participating in the exchange rate and intervention arrangements were required to contribute 20% of their gold and U.S. dollar holdings to create a "reserve deposit" with the EMCF in return for an equivalent credit in ECUs. These arrangements are referred to as *revolving swaps*. This level of contribution to the EMCF is maintained by quarterly adjustments that reflect changes in the volume of a member nation's reserves and fluctuations in the price of gold and U.S. dollar exchange rates. The use of gold is a new development for in practice this asset was never used under the old Snake arrangement. As noted in the preceding section, regulations permit the EMCF to receive monetary reserves and issue ECU certificates to the monetary authorities of the member states, which may use them as a means of settlement of accounts.

An EMS member country is paid interest on its holdings of ECUs that exceed its quota, and it is charged interest on its deficiency if the member holds less than its quota of ECUs. The interest rate is equivalent to the weighted average of the discount rates prevailing with the EMS member nations.

Function of the EMS to Date

Shortly after its inauguration, the EMS witnessed a steady rise in the exchange rate of the German mark relative to the U.S. dollar. This in turn necessitated corrective action on the part of Germany and the other EMS nations to keep the value of their currencies within agreed-upon margins. Despite these measures, the external value of the mark continued to rise, threatening increased inflation in Germany and forcing other EMS members to raise interest rates to keep pace with the German rates, although their domestic economies would have benefited from a less restrictive monetary policy.

At the same time, the external value of the ECU was also rising due to the increased value of the British pound and the Italian lira on foreign exchange markets. Thus the value of the mark remained technically below the stipulated threshold of divergence level relative to the ECU. This situation came to typify one of the weaknesses of the system: the absence of Great Britain from the exchange rate maintenance system, despite its membership in the EMS and the use of its currency in computing the value of the ECU.

Ultimately the impasse was broken in September of 1979 when a decline in the value of the pound on foreign exchange markets caused a reduction in the external value of the ECU. The German mark was then impermissibly diverging from its ECU central value, and the threshold of divergence mechanism was triggered. Corrective action took the form of a 2% revaluation of the German mark and a 3% devaluation in the Danish krone, the weakest currency of the system at that time.

In late November of 1979, the krone was again devalued by 5% in response to domestic economic pressures caused by Denmark's rising interest rate.

The central exchange rates of the participating EMS countries remained unchanged until 1981. In March of 1981, the Italian lira was devalued by 6% against the other member currencies and the following October, currencies were again realigned.

This readjustment was precipitated by a substantial rise in the value of the dollar against the EMS currencies, beginning in the latter half of 1980, which worsened inflation in all the EMS nations and caused a large outflow of capital from Europe. By late 1981, the value of the German mark had begun to rise relative to the dollar, thus placing a strain on the entire European Monetary System. Because of these events as well as intra-European inflation rates, the French and German governments urged readjustment of the central rates. The German mark and the Dutch guilder were revalued by 5.5% relative to the Danish krone, the Belgian and Luxembourg francs and the Irish pound, while the French franc and Italian lira were devalued by 3% against these same currencies.

In June of 1982, member currencies were again realigned to accommodate divergent inflation rates and trade balances.

These currency realignments were made with minimal dislocation and, of course, were permissible under the agreement that established the EMS. Intra-European exchange rates have maintained a favorable level of stability even during periods of external crisis, such as the OPEC oil price increases and the rapid rise of the U.S. dollar in late 1980. Fluctuations in the value of EMS currencies relative to the dollar have been much less pronounced than that of the yen or the pound, for example.

Because of the relative stability of exchange rates that the EMS has achieved, trade among the participating nations has been fostered significantly over the last several years.

Influences of the U.S. Economy

The U.S. dollar has been, and continues to be, an important factor in the function of the EMS in several respects. When the dollar falls, the German mark is strengthened due to its position as a reserve asset. This in turn places a strain on the other EMS currencies, which must maintain the agreed-upon margins relative to the value of the mark. On the other hand, since oil and many other imports are paid in U.S. dollars, a rise in the value of the dollar on foreign exchange markets may lead to balance of payments troubles for the European nations.

At present there is no common dollar policy among the EMS nations, though daily consultation among the central banks does take place. While a common dollar policy is viewed as desirable, it is generally acknowledged that agreement in this area would be difficult to achieve.

The EMS is also subject to the effects of high interest rates in the United States, a sensitivity that places strains upon the European economies. The appropriate response to high U.S. interest rates has been a matter of some disagreement among the EMS nations. France, for example, has favored a lowering of European interest rates and has taken unilateral action in this direction even when other EMS members have not supported such policies.

Future Trends

When the EMS was adopted in 1979, the present exchange rate mechanism was envisioned as only a first step. After two years, in March of 1981, a new European Monetary Fund (EMF) was to be established, replacing the present support fund, which would function as a European central bank in which reserves would be pooled. The ECU was to become a full-fledged reserve and settlement currency that would be issued by the EMF.

The EMS central bankers and EEC council of ministers have agreed to defer this second stage until at least March of 1983. Both economic factors, such as high interest rates, and political considerations were responsible for this decision.

Establishing a European central bank would, of course, require the EMS members to surrender a great deal of control over domestic monetary policy to the EMF. Some members, particularly Germany, may be unwilling to do so. Additionally, the EMS nations have not resolved important issues concerning how the EMF should be set up and administered.

As an interim measure, the EEC's monetary committee members had hoped to create a swap-credit arrangement between the EMCF and the United States Federal Reserve Bank in order to relieve pressure on European currencies, particularly the German mark, from fluctuations in the dollar. Swap credits are used to finance intervention in the exchange markets during periods of currency instability. However, this arrangement was not supported by the Reagan administration, which favors the free movement of exchange rates.

One of the goals of the EMS, that of wider use of the ECU, has received wide support from the members. Some of the European banks now accept deposits and grant credits in ECUs. ECU bonds have been issued in France and Belgium, and in London the first certificate of deposit was issued in ECUs. Many new uses for the ECU are being discussed, perhaps the most ambitious of which is the idea that OPEC may be persuaded to accept payment for oil in ECUs.

It has been hoped that Great Britain may join the EMS exchange rate mechanism at the appropriate time, as was its announcement at the inception of the new system. To be admitted to the EMS, each country must have a certain level of monetary stability and lift foreign exchange restrictions. However, the decision by British officials has been postponed for the present due to unresolved issues, such as Common Market agricultural policy, budget payments, and—as some have suggested—inability to fix the rate at which the pound would enter the arrangement. It should also be mentioned that France, without the support of other EMS members, has tightened exchange controls and thus restricted free capital movement within the EMS.

Some commentators have noted that, despite the exchange rate stability that has been maintained, other projected benefits of the new system have not materialized. One of the goals expressed in the European Council's resolution establishing the EMS was that of uniting the divergent economic policies of the member nations to achieve economic stability. In practice, however, the EMS cannot force coordination of economic and monetary policies. Thus, the usual response to financial difficulties has been intervention by means of the credit facilities available to the participants, rather than a realignment of domestic economic policies to attack the source of a nation's financial problems.

Some commentators have stated that a convergence of inflation rates would indicate a coordinated monetary policy on the part of the EMS nations. Although participating countries have made efforts to prevent differences in the rate of inflation from widening, it appears that inflation rate disparities have increased. Yet it has been suggested that without the EMS, European inflation rates would be much worse.

Conclusion

The overall assessment of the EMS is that it has functioned well in maintaining the exchange rate stability that was desired at its inception. Trade among participating nations has also benefitted as a result of the new system.

Difficulties arise, however, in attempting to coordinate the various and often conflicting social, political, and economic aims of the member nations into a cohesive union. In additon, the need for a common dollar policy has been stressed.

It remains to be seen whether the EMS will achieve the desired unity of economic and monetary objectives needed to move onto the second stage of creating the EMF and utilizing the ECU as a full-fledged European currency.

Bibliography

"Banks Warm Up to the ECU." *Business Week* (October 18, 1982), p. 146.

"A Boost for the Boa? Beware." *The Economist* (March 14, 1981), p. 48.

Davies, G. "The EMS: One Spring Clean Will Do." *Euromoney* (April 1983), p. 27.

Dixon, J. "The ECU: A New, International Currency." *Europe* (March–April 1983).

"EMS: What Will You Swap for an ECU?" *The Economist* (June 13, 1981), p. 50.

"The European Monetary System." *Fedpoints*, 25(October 1979, rev. November 1983).

Kollar. "Despite Early Criticism, Monetary System Proves Advantageous." *International Banker* (December 16, 1981), p. 26.

Llewellyn. "EMS Helps to Check Spread of Disorder." *International Banker* (December 16, 1981), p. 23.

"The Next 90 Days." *Business International* (July 9, 1982), p. 220.

Pearlman, E. "The Troubled Future of the European Monetary System." *International Investor* (November 1981), p. 269.

13

International Lending Agencies

The need for financial assistance of developing nations is larger and generates a higher degree of risk than is normally encountered in traditional commercial lending situations. At the same time, balance of payments difficulties may call for massive infusions of funds often beyond the lending capability of commercial banks. International lending agencies have been established to fill the needs of developing and other countries, as well as to finance projects and economic development of the borrowing nations. These agencies are numerous and each has its own variety of programs and lending criteria. The aim of this chapter is to illustrate the objectives of selected major lending agencies by examining their organization, major programs, and policies. In particular, the discussion will focus upon:

- the International Monetary Fund (IMF),
- the International Bank for Reconstruction and Development (IBRD), otherwise known as the World Bank,
- the Export-Import Bank of the United States (Eximbank),
- the Foreign Credit Insurance Association (FCIA),
- the International Financial Corporation (IFC),
- the Inter-American Development Bank (IDB),
- the Overseas Private Investment Corporation (OPIC),
- the Asian Development Bank (ADB), and
- the Agency for International Development (AID).

Generally, the type of project for which financing is sought will play a major role in determining which of these agencies will be the appropriate source of funding. Each institution has established lending requirements and project guidelines that define the size and the duration of the loan. It is of major importance, therefore, that prospective borrowers and exporters familiarize themselves with the available programs of these agencies in order to identity those offering the greatest likelihood of funding. The variety of purposes, as well as the range of borrowers for whom assistance is available, is reflected in the following discussion of agency policies.

International Monetary Fund

The International Monetary Fund (IMF) is an international organization, the members of which are admitted in accordance with the Resolutions adopted by the Board of Governors of the IMF. The Articles of Agreement of the IMF were drafted at the Bretton Woods Conference in 1944 and took effect in December of 1945. The mebership as of June of 1983 totalled 146 nations. IMF policy decisions are made by a Board of Governors to which a governor and an alternate are appointed by each member country. A Managing Director and Executive Directors are responsible for daily operations. The IMF is recognized as a legal entity, with the capacity to enter into contracts, acquire property, and institute legal proceedings. Furthermore, the IMF is accorded certain privileges and immunities including freedom from search or from attachment of assets and an exemption from certain forms of taxation.

The principal purposes of the IMF include the promotion of international monetary cooperation and exchange stability, the expansion of international trade, the maintenance of orderly exchange arrangements as a curb on competitive depreciation of currencies, and the alleviation of balance of payment disequilibria, both in duration and degree. Its significance, however, lies in the assistance it gives member nations experiencing steeply rising current account deficits. By making resources temporarily available to meet balance of payment shortages, and by promoting adjustment of foreign exchange rates, the IMF fosters the smooth functioning of members' monetary positions in international markets.

In order to meet these goals, a wide range of programs monitor the currency positions of member nations, alleviating liquidity problems caused by temporary budget deficits. Loans and reserve arrangements often are used to create a "pool" of resources to meet the short-term currency needs of its members. Funds are frequently provided on an unconditional basis, through the allocation of *special drawing rights* (SDRs) and occasionally through the creation of reserve positions in the

Fund; alternatively, conditional funding may be accomplished by extending credit directly to the member country subject to use or operating restrictions.

INTERVENTION ACTIVITIES

Basic IMF funding is supplied by the quota subscriptions of members. These resources are contributed in the form of gold, SDRs, and currencies in accordance with the quotas assigned to them upon entry into the IMF. These quota amounts are subject to periodic review. In turn, contribution quotas determine the nation's rights and obligations in the IMF, as well as its voting strength.

Within recent years, several economic factors have joined to create immense drains on the IMF funds, raising the possibility that the resources of the IMF supplied by members' quotas will soon become insufficient to meet the demands of borrowing nations. As a result, proposals for increasing quotas have been acted upon by member nations at recent annual meetings. For example, the United States at the beginning of 1983 considered an increase in its IMF quota of $8.4 billion U.S., a proposal subject to the approval of the U.S. Congress. This increase, in addition to the proposed increase in the U.S. contribution to the General Agreement to Borrow program from 4.5 billion SDRs to 17 billion SDRs, has been promoted as a necessary support to the international monetary system during the recent times of crisis. Without an increase in available short-term funds, it is feared that many countries would default on loans and be unable to service their debt, bringing grave consequences to the banks of the Western world. The IMF is able to replenish its resources by increasing quotas in this fashion. Quota subscriptions remain the basic source of financing for the IMF. Much of the currently proposed increase in quota contributions is intended for third world countries whose debt to creditor nations has grown to more than $600 billion as of the beginning of 1983.

In addition to adjustments to quotas, however, the IMF may supplement its resources by borrowing from a certain group of its member nations and banks. Borrowing activities have increased as the IMF's role in financing balance of payments deficits have expanded.

Two basic arrangements have developed for use of IMF resources: the systems of "drawing" and "stand-by arrangements."

In making a *draw* on IMF resources, members purchase or sell currency needed for the alleviation of short-term balance of payment difficulties. In order to assure the short-term nature of the draw, the transaction undertaken by the member nation (that is, the purchase or sale) must be "closed" by a corresponding resale or repurchase of the same currency at a date in the future normally within three to five years of the drawing. When the currency of another member is desired, a transfer of an equivalent amount of the purchasing country's own currency to the IMF is required to "cover" the amount of the transaction. The amount of currency that each member may draw is set within variable limits to control and allocate available resources.

A program known as the General Agreement to Borrow Program (GAB) permits participating countries to draw sums when needed to adjust to difficulties in the international monetary system. This program was originally concluded between the IMF and ten industrial member countries in 1962 for four years; subsequent renewals have extended its life to October of 1985. The maximum credit amount provided for use of GAB funds was set at approximately 6.4 billion SDRs as of April 30, 1982. Other special borrowing facilities are also available including the "oil facility" and the "supplementary financing facility."

The IMF also provides *stand-by arrangements* for countries that are not in immediate need of currency but that nevertheless wish to have the assurance that immediate access will be available at a future time. A stand-by arrangement provides the potential borrower with a commitment for funds from the IMF if, in fact, the need for additional resources arises.

IMF funding is provided to members either on an unconditional basis or subject to restrictions. Funds are made available through the allocation of SDRs and by the generation of reserve positions at the IMF. Depending upon the type of credit and its amount in relation to an IMF member's quota, different conditions may be imposed by the IMF.

A major portion of IMF operations involve transactions from the General Resources Account through which purchases of funds are made principally in the reserve tranche and credit tranche as well as under the extended IMF facility. *Reserve tranche* purchases represent a member's use of liquid reserves held at the IMF. Reserve tranche positions totaling approximately 1 billion SDRs were utilized during 1981/1982, and they were for the most part used to meet general balance of payments needs. Most of the purchases in the credit tranches were connected with high-conditionality drawings. Numerous other purchase facilities have also been established by the IMF for purposes of providing financing for member nations. Among these are the compensatory financing facility, which requires that the borrower cooperate with the IMF to resolve balance of payments difficulties.

Clearly, the general liquidity of the IMF depends upon the availability of the currencies that are considered usable. These currencies come from member countries having balance of payments and gross reserve positions that the Executive Board considers to be strong enough to be sold by the IMF to finance other members' drawings.

Intervention in the international currency markets, as described, is only one of the IMF's activities. No less significant are its efforts at monitoring its members' compliance with the currency exchange guidelines imposed upon them by the Articles of Agreement. This surveillance reflects the importance attached to the relationships between exchange rates, interest rates, and domestic budgetary policies. Ultimately, it reflects the significance of their combined effect on a nation's balance of payments. These attempts to identify and control potentially harmful trends at an early stage through the coordination of monetary and fiscal policies has met with varying degrees of success. This is particularly so in Latin America, where a combination of adverse economic conditions and inadequate governmental response to deficit growth are threatening to undo economic gains already achieved. Indeed, surveillance efforts alone appear often to be an insufficient means of resolving the economic difficulties of individual member nations when no corresponding change occurs in their fundamental economic policies and practices; these policies, implemented on a domestic level and international level, hold the greatest responsibility for the nation's economic health.

Closely related to its scrutiny of exchange rates, and other economic developments, the IMF is responsible for monitoring trade practices under the General Agreement on Tariffs and Trade (GATT). These duties include the collection of data concerning balance of payment amounts and monetary reserves.

The results of IMF operations for the fiscal year ended April 30, 1982 amounted to a net income of 92 million SDRs, a significant increase from 80 million SDRs in 1980/81. The SDR, or *special drawing right*, is a unit of account established and recognized at the IMF, and it is comprised of the weighted values of several currencies in stipulated proportions. It exists merely as a bookkeeping entry, maintained by parties to an SDR transaction. As of January 1, 1981 the number of currencies in the SDR valuation basket was reduced from 16 to 5; currently included are the United States dollar, the Japanese yen, the British pound, the Deutsche mark, and the French franc. The share of the U.S. dollar in the SDR value has declined from 78% in 1973 to 56% in 1980. According to the IMF Annual Report for 1982, the main suppliers of SDRs were Canada and the Federal Republic of Germany. Notwithstanding their purely "paper" existence, the variety of uses to which SDRs may be put suggests their resemblance to actual currency. In particular, the acquisition of SDRs enables purchasing nations to meet obligations owed to the IMF, such as charges in the General Resources Account. The IMF also permits:

- the purchase and sale of forward SDRs;
- the lending, borrowing or pledging of SDRs;
- the use of SDRs in swaps; and
- the making of donations (or grants) of SDRs.

Outside the IMF-related transactions, the SDR is used to denominate diverse private financial investments and obligations, principally as a means of diversifying the risk of exchange fluctuations.

The risk-reducing quality is one of the SDR's chief attractions. Briefly stated, the change in the value of an SDR is likely to be less extreme than changes in its constituent currencies because it represents an average of those fluctuations. For this reason, the SDR plays a modest but growing role as a unit of account in private transactions where currency fluctuations are anticipated. In order to supply the increased demand for SDRs, banks now offer SDR denominated accounts and CDs. Furthermore, a modest international market for SDR denominated instruments is developing abroad. Thus, the SDR has developed into a unit of account with purposes other than that of serving as a source of available resources to IMF members.

OTHER SERVICES

Finally, in addition to some of the numerous programs already discussed, the IMF offers training and technical assistance upon the request of members. Various courses and informational services are made available with the aim of improving the skills and knowledge of member countries in the sphere of economics and data collection. The IMF consistently seeks to coordinate its activities and cooperate with international and regional organizations, especially those concerned with economic matters and world trade.

World Bank

The International Bank for Reconstruction and Development, better known as the World Bank, was created in 1945. The Bank is an intergovernmental institution organized in corporate form, all of the capital stock of which is owned by the member governments (which totaled 142 in 1982). The World Bank is granted full legal status as well as protective privileges and immunities. Membership in the IMF is a prerequisite to membership in the World Bank. An overview of two of the World Bank's affiliates, the IFC (International Financial Corporation) and the IDA

(International Development Association) will also be included in the discussion that follows.

The principal emphasis of the World Bank is the making or guaranteeing of loans for productive reconstruction and development projects. Toward this goal, it uses its own capital funds and organizes private capital or financing.

The annual lending program of the World Bank has increased from $2 billion in 1973 to $11.2 billion for the fiscal year 1983 (this does not include its two affiliates, the IFC and the IDA). World Bank net income for 1982 was $598 million. Demands for financing have increased in recent years. As a consequence, the subscribed capital of the Bank was increased from $30.4 billion in 1973 to $49 billion in 1982, with callable or authorized capital of $77 billion.

The World Bank grants or guarantees project loans for eligible projects within the territories of member governments. Typically, the projects involved are substantial and require sizable funding. Loans were made either directly to the government or to private enterprises for use on approved projects. Participation by others is necessary since financing of the whole project cost will be undertaken by the World Bank.

The amount of foreign exchange normally lent covers the costs of imported goods and services. Furthermore, the use of loan proceeds typically need not be limited to one particular country, although purchases must be made in one of the member countries or in Switzerland. Nevertheless, borrowers are encouraged to obtain supplies through competitive bidding so that funds are economically utilized. For the year 1982, India, Indonesia, and Brazil were the largest borrowers of funds from the World Bank.

If the loan is not made directly to a government, the government must still guarantee the loan principal, interest, and other charges. Such loans are extended for medium to long terms at a rate of interest based on the cost of money to the Bank plus expenses and a small commission. The Bank raises funds for operations through bond sales and sales of its loan portfolio, primarily to large institutional investors. In addition, discussions are under way concerning the recycling of assets in the international monetary system by means of World Bank acquisition of international loan portfolios of commercial banks in exchange for long-term notes issued by the Bank. Sovereign risk would thus be transferred from commercial banks to the World Bank. Finally, the Bank is involved in other miscellaneous operations, mainly offering advisory and technical development services. Advisors and assistants are provided in several specialized areas to assist in the economic development of member countries.

International Development Agency

The International Development Agency (IDA) is an affiliate of the World Bank. Although the two entities share a common administration and management, their financial resources are separate. World Bank membership is a prerequisite to membership in the IDA. Established in 1960, IDA programs are aimed at the economic development of less developed nations through the granting of loans with liberal repayment terms. Loans may be made only to member governments, which totaled 130 as of 1982.

The principal beneficiaries of IDA programs are countries that need a supplemental source of development capital but that have weak balance of payments precluding the possibility of obtaining credit on conventional terms. Liberal repayment terms are usually applied. The IDA must be satisfied that the project is economically viable before credit is granted. An important criterion is that assistance is destined for the specific sector of the national economy where it will have the greatest overall effect. In 1982, India, Bangladesh, and Pakistan were the most active borrowers from the IDA. Overall, the agricultural sector obtained the highest proportion of funding with 44%, followed by transportation and power-related industries.

The IDA must call on its members from time to time to replenish its resources. For 1982, the IDA had usable cumulative resources of approximately $25.3 billion. The resolution authorizing the Sixth Replenishment of the IDA provides for funding from donors' contributions of an amount equivalent to 9.15 billion SDRs over the three-year period of 1981–1983.

It is significant that a large percentage (40%) of IDA and World Bank projects involved cofinancing in an amount totaling $7,424 million for 1982. Moreover, the IDA has expanded the methods for cofinancing to include participation with official aid agencies, export credit institutions, and commercial banks.

International Financial Corporation

The International Financial Corporation (IFC), also an affiliate of the World Bank, was established in 1956. Since the IFC has its own funds and staff, it is formally considered an independent institution. World Bank membership is a prerequisite to IFC membership, which totaled 122 countries as of 1982. Resources of the IFC are derived from the capital subscriptions of members, determined according to the nation's economic strength, as well as from earnings, borrowings, and participations. Assets for 1982 totaled approximately $1.2 billion while the net income for that period was $21.6 million.

The IFC was established for the purpose of promoting private investment in developing countries. Within the private sector, the IFC is designed to promote the international flow of private capital, to develop the capital markets of member countries, and to establish new private enterprises and investment opportunities. Monetary conditions during the last few years have accentuated the debt problems found in developing countries that borrow from international financial markets. The IFC is intended to complement World Bank lending activities by making loans to enterprises not owned or operated by member governments. In this respect, it stands in contrast to the World Bank, which requires direct borrowing by the government or borrowing with government guarantees. Thus, the IFC's main purpose is to aid the international "private sector."

The IFC is permitted to subscribe to or purchase capital stock— another feature distinguishing it from the World Bank. The investment activities of the IFC are centered in manufacturing, agribusiness, and financial institutions. Efforts are being made to increase development in smaller and poorer member countries, particularly in Africa. Overall, the investment portfolios of the IFC are well diversified in terms of country and type of investment. In addition, the IFC obtains the participation of private investors through portfolio sales normally in segments of $100,000. This enables the IFC to recycle its funds for additional projects. Furthermore, the IFC also continues to syndicate approximately one-third of its loans with commercial financial institutions. The average length of the IFC loan is seven years with a grace period of three years, although terms are flexible within a range of 5–15 years for an average loan amount of $1.25 million. The IFC follows certain basic criteria when making its investment decisions. It generally invests only in ventures that make a contribution to the economic development of the country; only projects that offer the chance of an adequate financial return are considered. Perhaps of most importance, it must be shown that without IFC assistance the project would not be able to attract adequate financing on reasonable terms within an acceptable time frame. Finally, while providing technical assistance and financing, the IFC consults and cooperates with a large number of international and bilateral agencies, particularly the World Bank. In fiscal year 1982, lending commitments by the World Bank, the IDA and the IFC totaled approximately $13,625 million (an increase of about $525 million from 1981).

Export-Import Bank (Eximbank)

The Export-Import Bank is an international agency of the U.S. government established in 1945 to supplement private institutions in financing world trade and investment. Eximbank provides supplementary commercial financing of U.S. export by making direct loans and guaranteeing the repayment of loans provided by other institutions. U.S. manufacturers are thus encouraged to increase foreign sales by helping them to obtain financing for their customers.

Eximbank is granted various powers by statute, including general banking powers, such as the power to purchase or guarantee negotiable instruments and make direct loans, or the power to guarantee and insure exporters against certain political and credit risks encountered when exporting. So as not to compete with private sources of capital, financing is more frequently supplied for exporting than for importing, reflecting the fact that imports are usually financed by domestic commercial institutions.

Operating funds come from four main sources: capital stock of $16 billion by the U.S. government; borrowings from the U.S. Treasury, currently authorized up to $6 billion; retained earnings; and proceeds from the sale of participations in Eximbank's portfolio. Unlike other similar organizations, Eximbank does not receive any appropriated funds.

Several types of financial assistance may be available to those engaged in international business. Direct loans are made when established criteria are met by the potential borrower. In addition to the lender's meeting sound lending criteria, it must be shown that adequate financing is unavailable from private sources on reasonable terms. For example, in 1982, Eximbank provided $5 billion in long-term financing for major U.S. export sales through so-called Direct Credits to foreign purchasers and $890 million in so-called Financial Guarantees to private lenders. The major areas of investment financed by Eximbank include: (1) electric power exports (worth $1.3 billion in 1981), (2) aircraft, (3) construction equipment, and (4) communications. For fiscal year 1984. Eximbank's budget includes authority to extend $3.865 billion in loans and $10 billion in guarantees and insurance to promote U.S. export sales.

Additional types of assistance may be suitable for a particular project. Project credits are made directly to public or private entities located abroad for the purchase of U.S. commodities, goods, and services. Generally, the foreign purchaser enters into an agreement with Eximbank to use the credits for specified items. Disbursements are made either to the borrower upon evidence of proper invoices for reimbursement or to a U.S. commercial bank as reimbursement for payments made under a letter of credit in favor of a supplier that was issued at the borrower's request and guaranteed by Eximbank. A grant of credit may also be made to foreign lending institutions for relending to foreign importers. Typically, these loans are made to foreign development banks, which in turn relend funds to small foreign enterprises. Loans are also made to U.S. producers to enable them to compete effectively. For example, the so-called medium-term discount loan program enables U.S. suppliers to obtain the fixed-rate financing needed to compete with subsidized foreign exports. Emergency foreign trade credits usually are made only in conjunction with the IMF, typically when the country is experiencing a serious shortage of U.S. dollars that will affect the continued purchase of U.S. goods. For obvious reasons, financing is restricted to export of U.S. goods and services. Another type of assistance is the agricultural commodity credit, under which a guarantee-type arrangement is made with the commercial banks that actually supply the financing.

Among the most important programs offered by Eximbank are the guarantees and insurance issued to commercial banks or exporters. Guarantees cover the political and credit risks encountered on medium-term transactions according to defined terms. Guarantees take the form of commercial bank guarantees and exporter guarantees. Under a commercial bank guarantee, a certain amount of the early credit risk is assumed by the commercial bank, while Eximbank assumes all political risks and credit risk present on later installments. On the other hand, exporter guarantees are issued directly to the exporter and cover most types of default with the exception of nonacceptance of goods (or default caused by the exporter). This form of guarantee is available only if a commercial bank guarantee or insurance policy cannot be obtained. Generally, the exporter is required to retain a certain portion of the investment risk by the terms of the guarantee.

Foreign Credit Insurance Association

For several years, a serious problem of nonpayment prevented the expansion of U.S. exports into international trade; indeed, the lack of growth into international markets eventually began to affect the U.S. balance of trade. This prompted the U.S. government to develop a program to provide competitive credit for international markets.

The Foreign Credit Insurance Association (FCIA) operates in conjunction with Eximbank to cover credit and/or political risks for short- and medium-term transactions; while Eximbank underwrites the political risks, it shares the credit risks with the FCIA.

The FCIA was created in 1961 to increase the U.S. export trade by providing insurance for export transactions. It is currently comprised of fifty of the nation's leading insurance companies. The FCIA offers an extensive range of policies covering repayment risks on short- and medium-term sales. Insurance coverage is intended for commercial as well as political risks. FCIA policies are guaranteed by the U.S. government, and, in the event of a FCIA insured default, repayment of the receivable is certain. Proceeds under FCIA policies may be assigned to commercial financing institutions as security against discounted receivables. Thus, their favored status enables the exporter to obtain financing of foreign receivables more easily and permits the exporter to offer more competitive terms.

FCIA member companies generally underwrite commercial credit risks, leaving to Eximbank the insurance of political risks and the reinsurance of excess commercial risks. The types of losses covered by FCIA are extensive. For example, commercial losses include those due to bankruptcies, market changes, expense increase, natural disasters, insolvencies, and nonacceptance of products. These are to be distinguished from political risks such as war, revolution, insurrection, shipment detention, license revocation, nationalization, confiscation, and currency controls. Although percentages may vary, usually 90% of commercial losses and 100% of political losses are covered. The exporter must participate as a coinsurer and retain a percentage of the risk, which may range from 5 to 15%.

Virtually any U.S. product is eligible for coverage by an FCIA policy. The goods must be sold for U.S. dollars in order to qualify. Any company that is registered to do business in the U.S. or that receives prior approval from the FCIA may be covered by FCIA programs. Coverage is also extended to commercial banks and other financing institutions that support U.S. exports.

When selecting a policy, care should be taken to examine its terms in detail. Two categories of policies give coverage for short- and medium-term sales protection. Single-buyer policies cover capital and quasicapital goods ordered by a specific customer, manufactured in the U.S., and sold in international trade on terms from six months to five or more years. Multibuyer policies cover all (or a reasonable spread) of an exporter's overseas business, normally shipped with payment terms of up to five years depending upon the product type. The master policy is for short-term (180 days or less) or medium-term (181 days to 5 years) sales. Commercial losses are covered to 90%, while political losses are covered 100%. Medium-term coverage requires a minimum down payment for the goods of at least 15% on or before delivery so that the percentages covered include only the balance or the financed portion. Special coverages, such as preshipment insurance or coverage for consigned goods against political risk, are also available.

Another useful policy offered is the service coverage. This is important for such companies as management consultants, engineering firms, and computer programmers. A small business policy offers qualified companies more liberal coverage, with 95% of commercial risk covered with no deductible. Various criteria regarding net worth and business volume must be satisfied by the entity seeking such coverage. Finally, the bank coverage is available for U.S. commercial banks, Edge Act Corporations, and U.S. subsidiaries and agencies of foreign banks. Coverage for default of a foreign receivable for 90% of commercial and 100% of political risk is provided with no deductible at the present time. This permits banks to increase foreign exposure through letter of credit and direct financing activities, thus encouraging international trade.

Overseas Private Investment Corporation

The Overseas Private Investment Corporation (OPIC) was created by the Foreign Assistance Act of 1969 and organized in 1971. Its general purpose is to foster privately financed development efforts by enabling U.S. private capital to invest in the economic and social development of friendly less developed countries. The OPIC currently operates in approximately 100 developing nations. Agreements are reached between these nations and the United States for the operation of OPIC programs. In 1982, with total assets of approximately $775 million, OPIC's net income was $83.5 million. The OPIC operates two main programs: the financing of projects by U.S. investors in less developed countries, and the insuring of private investments against certain political risks in those countries. OPIC management is structurally diverse, with the members of its Board of Directors drawn from both private and government sectors. U.S. investors are relying upon OPIC more than ever before for political risk insurance, as well as for direct loans and loan guarantees.

The OPIC financing program encompasses a variety of loan and loan guaranty plans, which extend medium- and long-term funding for projects having substantial U.S. equity and management participation. Frequently, such funding takes the form of *project financing*. The size of the loans range anywhere from $100,000 to $4 million. On the other hand, loan guarantees issued to private U.S. financial institutions making eligible loans range up to $50 million. In 1982, direct loan and loan guaranty commitments of $108.7 million were made.

On a regional basis, for 1982–83, the largest percentage of projects will be located in the Near East, followed by Latin America, East Asia, Africa, and South Asia. Numerous types of projects are undertaken with the backing of OPIC, and the areas of investment include: agribusiness (including agricultural production of food processing techniques), the oil and gas sector, medical services, and construction and development of financial institutions. Before OPIC assistance is extended, the anticipated effects of the investment on the U.S. economy are assessed. It is generally felt that OPIC-assisted investment ultimately benefits the U.S. economy by generating markets for U.S. exports and increasing domestic employment.

A program designed to increase small business participation in Third World Markets is the so-called small contractor's program. Under this program, OPIC provides partial guarantees (currently up to 75%) to financial institutions issuing stand-by letters of credit, as well as other forms of guarantees, on behalf of small business contractors entering these markets.

INSURANCE

OPIC's other main program consists of insuring U.S. private investments against certain foreign political risks. OPIC's political risk insurance coverage for eligible investors was at one time limited to three broad areas of risk:

1. the inability to convert local currency received by the investor as profits, earnings, or return of the original investment back into U.S. dollars;
2. the loss of investment due to expropriation, nationalization, or confiscation by action of a foreign government; and
3. the loss of investment and physical damage due to war (whether declared or undeclared), revolution, or insurrection (referred to as WRI coverage).

OPIC has subsequently expanded its political risk insurance package to include risk of loss due to civil strife. Formerly, WRI coverage was applicable only to damage resulting from attempts by organized groups to overthrow government authority or to oust it from a particular geographic region. However, in many cases, damage to investments caused by politically motivated acts was not compensable. For example, damage caused by terrorists seeking to destroy American property, but not necessarily to overthrow or oust an existing political regime, was not covered under regular WRI coverage. Coverage for civil strife damage is greatly needed in many areas of the world, especially since damage caused by such actions has increased dramatically in the seventies and early eighties. The lack of coverage for such risk puts American investors at a disadvantage since several major U.S. trade competitors offer such coverage. Furthermore, the risk of damage from civil strife is generally not insurable on the private insurance market.

As a result of the gap in WRI coverage, civil strife coverage was offered since late October of 1982, in conjunction with the regular WRI policy. Numerous types of damage caused by several individuals or terrorists are included within the terms of civil strife coverage, with the exception of damage caused by individuals or groups primarily oriented toward promoting the demands of labor or student groups. The burden of proof rests with the insured to demonstrate that the damage resulted from a politically motivated event. As with regular WRI coverage, actual premiums are likely to vary according to the risk involved in the individual project. Depending upon the coverage selected, coinsurance or self-insurance requirements will be imposed, normally at a minimum of 10% of the risk of loss based on total investment figures. Overall, OPIC coverage enables U.S. investors entering markets in developing countries to obtain financing and more complete insurance programs to facilitate business.

Inter-American Development Bank

The Inter-American Development Bank (IDB) was established in 1959 by agreement among the organizing nations. Originally, the IDB consisted of 19 Latin American nations and the United States. Membership has expanded to 43 nations as of 1982. The general purpose of the IDB is to accelerate the economic and social development of member countries. Toward this goal, the IDB promotes public and private investment for development projects and assists in the development of economic policies. In addition, IDB utilizes its own capital and the contributions of members to finance developments and provide technical assistance for projects.

Sources of IDB funds include (1) ordinary capital, which is used to make normal loans that are repayable in the currency loaned, and (2) funds for special operations, which are used for making more liberal loans on special (or soft) terms provided that special conditions are met. Generally, in the case of loans falling into the latter category, balance of payments problems are present, indicating a lack of hard currency, which will prevent repayment on usual terms. Some members have made special contributions toward establishing particular regional development.

As a general matter, participation in the IDB gives both tangible and intangible benefits to its members. While the borrowing countries gain revenues, nonborrowing countries frequently experience an increased demand for exports to execute development projects. For example, the IDB has established a Social Progress Trust Fund, which provides funds and technical assistance for social development in Latin America. Specific lending guidelines and criteria have been formulated to govern IDB loan application procedures relating to borrower eligibility. The government of the project country must give its approval before funds are authorized to be lent. Thereafter, control procedures are implemented to assure that funds are in fact being used for authorized purposes.

Financing for many different types of projects is arranged by the bank. For example, funds have been provided for projects involving agriculture, industry, energy, mining, transportation, communication, health, education, tourism, science, and urban development. Despite these high levels of assistance, the external sector of Latin American economies has greatly deteriorated due to the loss of foreign exchange while high interest rates and increased needs for financing have placed additional demands on them. The IDB also engages in cofinancing operations with several other international financial organizations.

Agency for International Development

The foreign assistance program of the United States, known as the Agency for International Development (AID) serves an important role in financing international transactions. Established in 1947, AID is a semiautonomous agency now affiliated with the International Development Corporation Agency. The main goal of AID is the development of the lesser developed nations. While during the time of the Marshall Plan AID activities were concentrated on Europe, the emphasis is now on the less developed countries of Asia, Africa, and Latin America.

One of the principal means of encouraging private enterprise to contribute to the economic development of less developed areas is the guarantee program. Three main variations of this program promote the involvement of private enterprise in the economic development of less developed areas.

First, the *convertibility guarantee* contract with the U.S. government offers protection against the risk of inability to convert local currency received on investments into U.S. dollars within a certain range of exchange rates. This protection extends to the transfer of earnings as well as to the repatriation of capital. In order to obtain this coverage, the U.S. government must have entered into a so-called investment guaranty agreement with the country where the investment is located. It should be realized that this coverage is not for depreciation in currency values.

Second, the *investment guarantee* program protects direct investments abroad against noncommercial risks. Certain investments can be insured against certain losses such as expropriation, confiscation, war, revolution, and insurrection. However, the investors, as well as the project, must meet all applicable eligibility requirements, such as obtaining foreign government approvals. In addition, limitations are imposed on the percentage value of the investment that may be covered.

Policy requirements depend upon the type and duration of coverage sought, and they will vary.

The third type of guarantee offered by AID is the *expropriation guarantee*, which provides compensation for property that is expropriated without adequate compensation. The claimant must show that the specific conditions exist involving control by the foreign government for the requisite time period in order to receive compensation under the terms of the policy. In addition, a percentage limitation is imposed on the amount of coverage provided on the original investment. No allowances for anticipated future earnings are calculated into coverage figures.

In addition to these guarantees, AID offers development loans for the most part aimed at financing projects, as opposed to merely encouraging the importation by foreign countries of capital goods and commodities. Special application and loan review procedures must be followed in order to obtain AID funding. Many statutory requirements also must be met by the applicants. For example, the impact of the project on economic development must be shown to be favorable to the U.S. economy. In addition, the project must offer a return adequate for loan repayment. In order to prevent the aggravation of balance of payments difficulties, AID makes loans available on "soft" terms to lessen the pressure on the foreign exchange resources of less developed countries. Restrictions on the use of proceeds are imposed by AID to assure that the funds are used for financing goods and services produced in the United States. In addition, the approval of construction and other project-related contracts must frequently be obtained before funds are dispersed. Finally, AID offers risk coverage to certain projects in developing countries. However, insurance coverage is frequently or more easily obtained through FCIA and Eximbank, since AID eligibility requirements are more stringent.

Asian Development Bank

The Asian Development Bank (ADB) was founded in 1966 for the purpose of promoting the economic and social development of the Asian and Pacific region. This institution, the membership of which totaled 44 nations in 1981, had subscribed capital resources of about $8.3 billion and paid-in capital of about $1.6 billion for the period ended December 31, 1981. The ADB is engaged in four main areas of activity: It (1) extends ordinary loans, (2) offers special fund loans, (3) provides technical assistance (grants), and (4) encourages regional activities (grants). Thus, the bank plays a very important role in the economic development of these nations. Technical assistance goes toward designing development projects for which the bank or other institutions provide financing. The ADB provides additional support for its developing member countries through cofinancing arrangements and through borrowings in international capital markets. During 1981, the bank made borrowings equivalent to $668.5 million. Due to the favorable terms prevailing in the Japanese market, about half of the amount borrowed was denominated in Japanese yen. The bank emphasizes the cofinancing of development projects to assure a large supply of other resources in addition to its own. For example, during 1981, 23 projects involved cofinancing funds amounting to $627 million with ADB contributions of $827 million. In addition, the bank has increased its involvement with other international institutions involved in the Asian and Pacific region, including the World Bank, the United Nations, the International Fund for Agricultural Development, and, most recently, the International Monetary Fund, which has also increased its activities and assistance to member countries in the area. Overall lending operations in 1981 amounted to over $1.6 billion, with an average loan size of $29 million (this includes both ordinary and concessional loans). Concessional loans comprised about one-third of the total loans made. Asian Development Fund resources amounting to about $3.2 billion finance the bank's concessional lending program. For ordinary loans approved after January 1, 1982, the interest rate charged was 11%. After making special appropriations, the bank's net income for 1981 was approximately $139 million.

ADB concentrated its lending activities among three priority sectors for the year 1981. Agriculture and the agroindustry (particularly food production) accounted for approximately one-third of ADB lending activities, followed by the energy sector and social infrastructure projects that include water supply, education, housing, urban development, health care, and population planning. In fact, the social infrastructure sector experienced the largest increase in lending activity, amounting to about 21% of the total lending in 1981. Several specialized funds exist at the ADB and are aimed at funding specialized needs and priority projects of borrowing nations. The funds lent by the bank are ordinarily matched with investment funds from the borrowing country. Cofinancing with borrowing nations, as well as with other lending entities, has thus become an important element in ADB lending.

In addition to providing the foreign exchange needed for financial projects, the bank has also financed portions of local currency costs. Due to economic constraints placed upon developing member countries, several of these countries have tried to lessen the impact of foreign exchange shortages on their economic development by taking such measures as devaluing their currency. Nevertheless, serious reductions in GNP growth rates have compounded the problems faced by developing member countries. For this reason, the ADB is seeking to increase the cooperation of other agencies in lending to this area. A majority of these member nations have therefore assigned industry projects a high priority in their scheme for quickly achieving a balanced socioeconomic development.

Conclusion

International lending agencies are meeting the ever increasing demand of member nations for development funds and financial expertise. The specialized activities of these organizations are directed at reducing the problems characteristic of developing economies. By providing huge amounts for funding, the more industrialized nations are able also to recycle assets internationally in order to create a larger marketplace for their own goods and services and promote economic development.

Bibliography

Agency for International Development. *Annual Report.* 1982.

Asian Development Bank. *Annual Report.* 1982.

deVWragg, L. "Documentation of the Commercial Special Drawing Right." *Int'l Fin. L. Rev.* (February 1983), p. 22.

Export-Import Bank of the United States. *Annual Report.* 1982.

Foreign Credit Insurance Association. *Annual Report.* 1982.

Grant, C. "Don't Call the IMF: It's Running Out of Quotas." *Euromoney* (August 1982), pp. 51–52.

Inter-American Development Bank. *Annual Report.* 1982.

International Bank for Reconstruction and Development. *Annual Report.* (World Bank.) 1982.

International Financial Corporation. *Annual Report.* 1982.

International Monetary Fund. *Annual Report.* 1982.

Kammert, James. *International Commercial Banking Management.* New York: AMACOM, 1981.

Mason, Edward and Robert Asher. *The World Bank Since Bretton Woods.* Washington, D.C.: Brookings Institute, 1973.

Mathis, Ferdinand J., ed. *Offshore Lending by U.S. Commercial Banks.* Washington, D.C.: Bankers Association for Foreign Trade, 1975.

Norton, R. "Wading Through the Alphabet Soup of World Finance." *American Banker* (July 18, 1983), p. 1.

Overseas Private Investment Corporation. *Annual Report.* 1982.

"Those Who Pay the Piper Are Calling a Dreary Tune." *The Economist,* 281(October 3, 1981), pp. 81–82.

Yohai, S. A. "How the World Bank Might Recycle Assets." *Euromoney* (January 1983), pp. 47–48.

Glossary

Accepted Draft. Draft accepted by the drawee by affixing a signature or official stamp in the case of a bank. The draft is then subject to the provisions of the law regarding bills of exchange and becomes the primary obligation of the acceptor.

Agio. Premium paid or quoted over and above certain prices.

Agreement Corporation. International banking corporation chartered by state banking authorities and regulated in their activities by the Federal Reserve Board.

Arbitrage. The purchase or sale of securities or of commodities in one market for simultaneous sale or purchase in another market at a profit or in expectation of profit.

Arbitrageur. An individual seeking to take advantage of price differentials through arbitrage.

Ask. Price at which sales are offered.

Assignable Letter of Credit. Letter of credit that permits the right to proceeds to be assigned; the beneficiary remains responsible for presentation of proper documents.

Back-to-Back Letter of Credit. A letter of credit opened on the strength of another letter of credit with identical documentary requirements for the same merchandise, but for a different payable amount.

Balance of Payments. The measure of the totality of a nation's economic transactions with the rest of the world during a certain time period.

Balance of Services. The measure of the amount of service items purchased and sold by a nation during a specific time period.

Balance of Trade. The difference between a nation's imports and exports of merchandise during a certain time period.

Bank Draft. A check drawn by a bank against its account in another bank.

Bank Examiner. An official representative of a federal or state regulatory body who examines the finances, policies, and management of banks under his jurisdiction to assure compliance with statutes and regulations.

Bank Holding Company. A company that controls a bank or banks, as defined by the Bank Holding Company Act.

Banker's Acceptance. A draft payable at a future date drawn on and accepted by a bank.

Bearish. The anticipation that prices will decline.

Bid. The price at which purchases are sought (such as for an option contract or foreign exchange).

Bill of Exchange. A draft written by one party to another directing the payment of a specific sum of money to a third person on a specific date; a promissory note wherein the issuer promises to pay a specific sum.

Bill of Lading. A document representing title to goods to be shipped, which is signed by the shipping company (or its agent) and which serves as receipt of goods shipped pursuant to its terms.

Board of Governors of Federal Reserve System. A federal body that monitors and controls the activities of the Federal Reserve banks and that has regulatory power over member banks.

Bond. A certificate of debt that normally bears interest and obligates the issuer to pay the principal at the specified time and to pay interest as agreed.

Broker. An intermediary who does not trade for his own account.

Bullish. The anticipation that prices will appreciate.

Buyer's Option. The purchase of foreign exchange with an option enabling the buyer to determine the date of performance within certain limits.

Capital (of a bank). The amount paid in cash by stockholders to permit a bank to function. Bank capital requirements are set by the appropriate governmental agency.

Capital Resources (of a bank). Includes the bank's capital, surplus, reserves, and undivided profit (or retained earnings).

Cashier's Check. A check issued by a bank and drawn upon itself. It represents an obligation of the bank and is used to pay bank obligations and to pay the proceeds of loans to the bank's clients. It is also sold to bank customers for use where a personal check is not acceptable.

Central Bank. An agency formed by a national government to regulate currency and set monetary policy. In the United States the Federal Reserve System serves this function.

Certificate of Deposit. A receipt for funds deposited with a bank.

Certificate of Inspection. A certificate issued by an independent inspector indicating the condition of goods inspected before (or after) shipment.

Certificate of Origin. A document certifying the country of origin of goods shipped.

Certified Check. The check of a depositor drawn on a bank and for which the bank assumes responsibility for payment by placing the certification stamp on the check. Regulations require that the amount of the check be charged immediately to the depositor's account.

Check. A draft drawn on a bank for a specified sum payable from available funds to a specified party or bearer and payable on demand.

Chips. The Clearing House International Payment System is a recently enacted system that provides same day settlement of clearing house funds.

Clean Bill of Lading. A bill of lading without a superimposed clause or annotation that declares a defective condition in the goods and/or packaging.

Clean Letter of Credit. Letter of credit that does not call for presentation of any documents besides the draft for payment.

Collateral. Property pledged to assure payment of a loan or secure an obligation.

Collection. The process of presentation of documents upon payment or acceptance of a draft for payment at a later date.

Commercial Bank. A bank chartered by the Comptroller of the Currency (a national bank) or by a state. A commercial bank usually specializes in demand deposits and short-term commercial loans. It is also authorized to accept savings and checking accounts of individuals and to grant personal loans and mortgages.

Comptroller of the Currency. The Office of the U.S. Comptroller of the Currency, under the direction of the Secretary of the Treasury, is responsible for coordinating the examination of all national banks and for the regulations governing national banks.

Confirmed Letter of Credit. A letter of credit to which the obligation for payment of the second (confirming) bank is added to that of the issuing bank.

Consular Invoice. An invoice for goods containing certification of the consulate of the exporting nation usually issued on a special form.

Contract Rate. The rate of exchange specified in a foreign exchange contract.

Conversion. The actual exchange of the currency of one country for that of another. Conversions usually pass through banking channels.

Convertibility. The ability to freely exchange currency for that of another country.

Correspondent Bank. A commercial bank with which another bank has an account relationship. The correspondent bank provides banking services mostly in the region where it is located.

Cost and Freight (C&F). A shipping term indicating that the seller bears the cost of transportation to the special point of destination.

Cost, Insurance, and Freight (CIF). A shipping term indicating that the seller bears the cost of transportation and insurance of the goods to the specified point of destination.

Coupon Bond. A bond with coupons attached, which are presented for interest payment on due dates.

Covering a Position. The purchase or sale of foreign currency (or of securities or commodities) to balance open positions.

Cross Rates. The exchange rate between two foreign currencies, neither of which is the U.S. dollar.

Dealer. Someone (1) who buys and sells foreign exchange (or securities or commodities) for his own account, (2) who holds positions for his own account, and (3) who does so for resale to others in the ordinary course of his trade or business.

Demand Deposit. A deposit payable on demand with no notice of withdrawal required. Member banks of the Federal Reserve system are required to maintain higher legal reserve balances on these deposits than on other kinds of deposits.

Depository. A bank designated as the receiver of funds.

Devaluation. Government action that changes the value of a country's currency downward in terms of other currencies.

Disagio. A discount from a price.

Discount. A rate lower than the normal spot rate (such as when a foreign currency sells for less than the spot rate).

Discount Window. The lending of funds by the Federal Reserve to member banks at the discount rate.

Documentary Letter of Credit. A letter of credit that calls for presentation of conforming documents to be made for payment.

Documents Against Acceptance (D/A). Documents representing title to goods shipped will be delivered by the bank only against acceptance of the draft stipulating payment at a future date. Used in connection with collection or letter of credit transactions.

Documents Against Payment (D/P). Documents representing title to goods shipped will be delivered by the bank only against payment in full. Used in connection with collection or letter of credit transactions.

Draft. An order in writing by one party instructing a second party to make payment of a specified amount on a specified date.

Due from Account (Nostro). A deposit account held at one bank by another.

Due to Account (Vostro). A deposit account held by a bank at another.

Edge Act. An act, passed by the U.S. Congress in 1919, that enables banks to be chartered by the Board of Governors of the Federal Reserve System to aid in financing foreign trade.

Edge Act Corporation. A special corporate entity that is permitted to engage in international banking or financial operations pursuant to Section 25(a) of the Federal Reserve Act.

Eurocurrency. A currency placed on deposit with a bank outside the country that issued the currency.

Eurodollars. U.S. dollars placed on deposit with banks outside the United States.

Expiration Month. A month in the foreign currency options expiration cycle, such as March, June, September or December. The months depend upon the terms of the deal and market practice.

Federal Deposit Insurance Corporation (FDIC). A government corporation, created by the Bank Act of 1933, that insures the deposits of all banks entitled to insurance benefits under the Federal Reserve Act. All member banks of the Federal Reserve System are required to be members of the FDIC. Other banks may become members upon approval of the FDIC.

Federal Funds. Excess funds held at a Federal Reserve Bank, which are loaned out to other banks to help them meet reserve requirements.

Federal Reserve Banks. Twelve regional reserve banks created by and operated under the Federal Reserve System.

Federal Reserve Note. A note issued by Federal Reserve banks to member banks to meet the demand for currency. When the demand decreases, the notes are retired.

Federal Reserve System. The central banking system of the United States created by the Federal Reserve Act of 1913 to regulate the money supply of the United States, to set and hold the reserves of member banks, to examine member banks, and to promote and facilitate the clearance and collection of checks for all banks.

Fiduciary. An individual or corporation—that is, a bank—to whom property is entrusted according to a trust agreement. The property is invested or utilized in the interest of the owner to the best ability of the fiduciary.

Fixed Rate of Exchange. When the official exchange rate of a country's currency is maintained within a specified small range of fluctuation by the government (contrary to floating).

Float. Funds in the process of collection by one bank but drawn on another bank.

Floating. When a country's central bank does not protect either upper or lower currency fluctuation limits, the exchange rate is said to be "floating." In other words, market forces determine the currency's value. When the government interferes with free market forces, it is termed a "dirty" float. If the government does not interfere, it is termed a "clean" float.

Foreign Currency. The official medium of exchange of a government other than the United States government.

Foreign Currency Account. An account carried in foreign currency.

Foreign Currency Futures Contract. A foreign exchange contract that is standardized as to size and settlement date and that is traded on a commodity exchange.

Foreign Currency Letter of Credit. A letter of credit denominated in a foreign currency, payment for which is usually made on the settlement date or date on which the beneficiary receives payment.

Foreign Exchange. The exchange of foreign currencies. Rates of exchange are determined by supply, demand, and the stability of the currency.

Forward Contract (SEE *Future Exchange Contract*). A contract for the purchase or sale of foreign exchange from a bank at a fixed rate with delivery at a specified date.

Forward Transaction. A transaction for settlement more than two business days after the transaction date or more than one business day in the case of a Canadian dollar transaction. Such transactions are arranged mostly through banking channels.

Free Alongside (FAS). A shipping term indicating that the seller bears the cost of transportation of the goods within reach of the loading tackle alongside the ship that will deliver the goods.

Free on Board (FOB). A shipping term indicating that the seller is responsible for arranging for goods to be loaded onto the transportation vehicle furnished by the buyer. The price quoted FOB thus includes only costs up to this point of shipment.

Full Up. When the limit on trading in a particular currency or with a particular customer has been reached, thus preventing the trader from dealing further.

Future Exchange Contract. A contract concluded at commodity exchanges for the purpose or sale of foreign exchange at a fixed rate with delivery at a specified date. Future exchange contracts are entered to preclude risks of fluctuations in rates. They are also used for speculation.

Give. Sell.

Good Date. Date when banks are open in both markets.

Good Funds. Funds unconditionally and freely available for use.

Gross National Product (GNP). An economic indicator that measures the total of goods and services produced within a nation plus expenditures by consumers and government, as well as private investment during a certain time period.

Hedge. Purchase or sale of foreign exchange or of other commodities to protect an asset or limit exposure to liability by fixing the rate.

Holding Company. A company that owns the shares of another company.

International Banking Facility. A separate record keeping division of a domestic or foreign bank, located in the U.S., that is accorded regulatory treatment similar to that of an offshore branch by the Federal Reserve Board.

Interbank Market. The market for foreign currencies and options. International banking institutions and multinational corporations are participants.

International Monetary Market. The largest market for trading foreign currency futures contracts, located at the Chicago Mercantile Exchange.

Irrevocable Letter of Credit. A letter of credit that may not be cancelled, modified, or amended without the prior consent of all the parties involved in the letter of credit transaction.

Lay Off (or reverse, unwind). To offset a position by reselling what has been purchased and vice versa.

Lending Limit. The amount or percentage of capital and surplus that a bank is legally permitted to lend to a single borrower. Currently, the regular lending limit for national banks is 15%; in certain cases, where there is sufficient qualifying collateral, this is extended to 25%.

Letter of Credit (commercial or documentary). An instrument issued by a bank at the request of its customer to pay an indicated amount to the beneficiary against certain documents in accordance with specific terms. The acceptance by the bank of drafts darwn under a letter of credit satisfies the parties involved in the transaction.

Limit. The highest or lowest price at which one may conclude particular transactions.

Line of Credit. A bank agrees to extend funds or to accept commitments up to an agreed maximum on behalf of its customer. The customer pays interest on the borrowed portion only. The bank regularly monitors the credit status of the customer and may withdraw from the agreement.

Long. A credit balance in foreign currency of dollars or commodities). When one owns spot or future contracts in commodities, foreign exchange, or securities in excess of one's commitments to deliver.

Long-Term Capital Movements. The measure of a nation's receipts and transfers of a monetary nature for a long-term duration, that is, longer than one year.

Margin. Funds required to carry a short position.

Member Bank. A bank that is a member of the Federal Reserve System. All national banks must be members. State-chartered banks may voluntarily join the Federal Reserve System.

Merchant Credit. Letter of credit issued by the buyer as opposed to a bank. The bank does not bear any obligation to make payment. (SEE ALSO Letter of Credit.)

Monetary Base. The measurement prepared by the Federal Reserve comprised of total reserves, currency outside the vaults of the U.S. Treasury, Reserve Banks and depository institutions, plus surplus vault cash at institutions other than commercial banks.

Money Supply. A measurement of the Nation's overall monetary position comprised of subdivisions that categorize monetary items according to specified characteristics as follows:

M_1. This includes currency, travelers checks, demand deposits, and other checkable deposits.

M_2. This includes all M_1 items plus overnight purchase agreements and Eurodollars, money market mutual fund balances, money market dollar accounts, savings, and small time deposits.

M_3. This includes all M_2 items plus large time deposits and term repurchase agreements and institution only money market mutual fund balances.

L. This includes all M_3 items plus liquid assets.

National Bank. A commercial bank under the jurisdiction of the U.S.

Comptroller of the Currency is also a member of the Federal Reserve System and the FDIC.

Negotiable Instrument. A written instrument, signed by the maker or drawer, that contains an unconditional promise or order to pay a sum certain in money. In addition, it must be payable on demand or at a fixed or determinable future date to order or to bearer. If the instrument refers to a drawer, he must be identified thereon with reasonable certainty.

Negotiation. Presentation of documents required under a letter of credit to the negotiating bank for payment.

Note. The recognized legal evidence of a debt that must meet the requirements of the Uniform Commercial Code.

Now Account. Negotiable order of withdrawal (a new form of interest-bearing demand deposit).

Offer. The price at which one is willing to sell an item such as an option contract or foreign exchange. (SEE Ask.)

On-Board Bill of Lading. Bill of lading indicating that goods have actually been loaded on the ship.

On-Deck Bill of Lading. Bill of lading indicating that goods have been loaded on the deck of the ship.

Open Position. A purchase or sale without an offsetting transaction.

Option. Right to make use of (or accept) an offer. Unlike stock options, the foreign exchange must ultimately be purchased or sold by a specified date. (SEE Buyer's Option or Seller's Option.)

Option Buyer. The party who by paying a premium acquires the rights conveyed by an option.

Option Seller. The option writer or grantor who is obligated to honor an option of exercised.

Overnight Eurodollars. Lending (or borrowing) Eurodollars for one ing day.

Overnight Repurchase Agreement. The lending of money overnight with the agreement to repurchase the next day.

Packing List. A list indicating the characteristics of goods contained in each parcel.

Pip. Refers to fractional decimal rate quotations. (SEE Points.)

Points. Fractional quotation. Though larger than pip, often mistaken for pips during trading.

Premium. A price higher than the spot rate.

Prime Rate. The rate of interest charged by a bank for its best or financially strongest clients.

Protest. Legal procedure establishing the refusal of the drawee to accept a draft (protest for nonacceptance) or to pay a draft (protest for nonpayment). This procedure is frequently required abroad to preserve recourse against the endorser.

Quote. The rates at which one will buy and sell.

Rate. A numerical expression of the value of one currency in terms of another at a given point in time.

Received for Shipment Bill of Lading. A bill of lading indicating that goods have been received by the shipping company for shipment. Goods may or may not be actually loaded on board.

Recourse. Right of claim for payment against endorsers and drawers of a check or a bill of exchange.

Red Clause. A clause in a documentary credit that authorizes the paying bank to advance funds to the beneficiary on an unsecured basis before actual shipment of the goods.

Reimbursing Bank. The bank from which the intermediary negotiating bank can claim payment.

Reserve. A portion of the profits allocated to protect against any depreciation in assets caused by bad debts or other contingencies.

Restricted Letter of Credit. Letter of credit restricted for negotiation at a specific bank.

Revaluation. Government action that increases the value of a country's currency in terms of other currencies.

Revocable Letter of Credit. A letter of credit that may be cancelled or withdrawn at any time prior to payment without prior notice to the beneficiary.

Revolving Letter of Credit. A letter of credit that is automatically reinstated for the original amount upon completion of payment and reimbursement of the bank. It is used for multiple shipments to avoid application for several individual letters of credit.

Rollover. A forward contract renewed or extended for delivery further in the future.

Savings Bank. A banking association specializing in savings accounts and investing in mortgages, long-term bonds, and other investments for the benefit of depositors. It also performs commercial functions.

Seller's Option. When the seller of the foreign exchange for future delivery can choose the delivery date within certain limits.

Settlement. Payment on closing out of contracts.

Short. When one has delivery commitments without owning the currencies or commodities.

Short-Term Capital Movements. The measure of a nation's receipts and transfers of a monetary nature for a short-term duration, that is, one year or less.

Sight Letter of Credit. A letter of credit that is immediately payable by the negotiating bank upon presentation of conforming documents.

Special Drawing Rights (SDRs). International monetary reserve assets created by the International Monetary Fund in 1970 for use by governments only in official balance of payment transactions. Currently, the SDR is composed of a "basket" of five major currencies: the U.S. dollar, Deutsche mark, French franc, Japanese yen, and English pound sterling.

Speculation. The purchase or sale of foreign exchange for the purpose of making a profit based on anticipated favorable price changes.

Spot. A foreign exchange purchase or sale transaction in which the value date is two working days following the trade date (except for Canada, which is one day).

Spread. A transaction in which one simultaneously buys a call option and sells a call option or buys a put option and sells a put option on the same currency but of a different option series. Also refers to the differential between the purchase and sale price of a commodity (such as foreign exchange).

Stand-By Letter of Credit. A letter of credit payable upon representation of specified documents in the event that a commitment is not honored by one of the parties.

State Bank. A banking association chartered under state laws. A state bank may become a member of the Federal Reserve System and subject to regulation by the Federal Reserve Board.

Swap. A simultaneous purchase and sale (or sale and purchase) of a foreign currency, usually against U.S. dollars. It can be made between two dates including spot and future dates. Swaps are a method for borrowing or lending foreign currency.

SWIFT. The Society for Worldwide Interbank Financial Telecommunications was established in 1977 and includes several hundred bank members. The system is based on standardized instruction language to facilitate payment transfers.

Take. Buy.

Test Key. A code used to authenticate bank messages transferring funds by cable, phone, computer, and the like.

Time Letter of Credit. A letter of credit payable upon presentation of conforming documents at a future date, which is maturity of the draft accepted by the negotiating bank.

Trade Bill of Exchange. Bill of exchange for a trade transaction, as opposed to a draft issued for financing purposes.

Trading Date. The date when a transaction is completed.

Transferable Letter of Credit. A letter of credit that permits a transfer of both the right to present documents and receive payment in accordance with the terms of the credit.

Transshipment. When goods are not shipped directly to their destination on one ship.

TT. Telegraphic Transfer. Expression used by banks and foreign exchange dealers and brokers indicating remittance by cable.

Value Date. A date on which "good fund" settlement is made.

Warrant. A draft that is not negotiable but that can be converted into a negotiable instrument. A warrant is evidence of indebtedness that can be redeemed when presented to the drawer of the warrant.

Yours. To sell to another.

Index

A

Acceptace, liabilities caused by, 79
Acceptance financing, Federal Reserve
   System role in:
  credit, 80
  discount by, 80
  dollar exchanges, 80
  eligible transactions, 80
Acceptance market, investors in, 82
Acceptances, discount eligibility of
   domestic, 81–82
  custodian of goods as employee, 81
  detachment of employee, 81
  field warehousing arrangement, 81
  Regulation A, 81
  securing title, 81–82
Acquisitions, by foreign banks:
  Bank Holding Company Act, 30
  Bank Merger Act, 30–31
  Change in Bank Control Act, 31
  disapproval of, reasons for, 31
  factors in application, 30
  failing U.S. institutions, 32
  foreign investors, 31–32
Advised/confirmed credits:
  advising bank, 51–52, 54
  compliance, proof of, 55
  confirmed, 52
  confirming bank, 52
  data required, 55

documents to present, 55
  example, 53
  reasons for, 52
  reconfirmation by local bank, 54
  terms and conditions, 54–55
Agency for International Development:
  convertibility guarantee, 268
  development loans, 269
  expropriation guarantee, 269
  investment guarantee, 269
  nature, 268
Agreement corporations. See Edge Act and
  agreement corporations
Alteration of checks:
  after certification, 104–05
  fraud, 104
  loss risk, 104
  materiality, 103–04
  nature, 103
  negligence, 104
Arbitrage:
  calculations, 133
  equalization, 133
  FASB statement 8, 118
  FASB statement 52, 118
  interest rates, 117, 134
  nature, 117, 132–33
  risk, 117–18
  short-term capital movements, 133–34
Asian Development Bank:
  activities, 269–70

local currencies, 270, 271
nature, 269–70
priorities of, 270–71
Austria, bank secrecy in, 232

B

Balance of payments:
  balance of services, 3, 7–8
  balance of trade, 3
  CIF valuation, 7
  components, 2
  currency controls, 9–10
  customs, 7
  dollars as commodity, 5
  double-entry bookkeeping, 4–5
  effects, 1–2
  equilibrium, 5
  errors and omissions, 2–3
  exports, 6–7
  factors in, 1
  figures, use of, 11
  firms, 4
  flight of capital, 8–9
  foreign transactions, 2
  high interest rates, 10
  long-term capital movements, 4
  military expenses, 7
  nature, 1
  negative, 5
  political problems, 9, 10
  positive, 5
  short-term capital movements, 3–4, 8–9
  statistical discrepancies, 1, 11
  theory, 148
  U.S. experience, 6–7
  valuation, 6, 7
Bank mergers, 32–33
Bank, role of in letter of credit:
  delay, 63
  issuing bank, 6–263
  obligations for, 63–64
  place of presentation, 63
  terms and conditions, adherence to, 63
Bank holding companies:
  activities not close to banking, 217
  Bank Holding Company Act of 1956,
    210–11
    Amendments of 1970, 211
    jurisdiction, 215–16
    purpose, 215
    Regulation K, 211
    Regulation Y, 211

basic limits, Section 4, 216
control, problems with, 212–13
  bank stock, attribution of, 213
  direct, 213
  indirect, 213, 214
  limits, 213
  presumptions of control, 214
  Regulation Y, 213, 214
  subsidiary relations, 213
  transferability, 214
definition, 212
  companies, 212
  exemptions, 212
  subsidiaries as banks, 212
exemptions for nonbanking activities,
  217
expansion, 220–21
5% rule, 217–18
foreign banks, 212, 220
  activities, 220
foreign bank holding companies,
  218–19, 220
  exemptions, 220
  limits, 219
and Federal Reserve regulations, 219
grandfather provisions, 215, 217
International Banking Act of 1978, 212
interstate branching, limit on, 215
laws about, 210
McFadden Act, 215
other activities of companies, 216
permissible activities, list, 216–17
Regulation K, 215–16, 219
  amendment, 219
Regulation Y, 216–17
and SEC, 211
Banker's acceptances:
  acceptance, discount of, 78
  acceptance, misuse, 79
  dollar, 77
  dollar exchange bills, 78–79
  and Federal Reserve, 75
  finance, 77–78
  limits, 76
  and letters of credit, 75
  nature, 75
  reasons for, 74
  Regulation D, 78
  Regulation Q, 77
  signature, 75
  trade-related, 76–77
    and acceptance by bank, 76
    rediscounting, 76–77

Banks, rights between, 67
Bills of lading:
  clean, 56, 57
  documentary commercial letters of
      credit, 56–57
  documentary letters of credit, 56
  full set on-board, 56
  on-board, 56
  order, negotiable, 56
  received-for-shipment, 56
  for ships, 56
  stale, 57
  straight, 56
  through, 56
  transshipment, 56
Bond portfolio:
  activity trends, discussion, 206
  capital, 205
  contingency liability, 205
  current liabilities vs. assets, 205
  evaluation of, 204–05
  federal funds, 206
  footing, 206–07
  liquidity, factors in, 206
  municipals, 205
  net earnings, 206–07
  prompt payment, 207
  very active accounts, 207

C

Cayman Islands, 231, 232
CDs:
  floating rate, 168
  LIBOR, 168–69
  negotiable, 168, 169
  TAP, 168
  TRANCHE, 168
Certificate of origin:
  credit terms, 59
  inspection, 58, 59
  limits, 59
  reasons for, 58
  shipment terms, 59
  through bill of lading, 60
  transshipment, 60
Checks:
  cashiers:
    vs. bills of exchange, 98
    defined, 97
    stopping of, 98
    validity, 98
  certified:
    certification, 96
    effects, 97
    factors, 96
    holders in due course, 97
    real defenses, 97
    revocation, 97
    third party liability, 96, 97
  defined, 95
  Eurocheques, 100
  foreign, 100
  money orders, 99–100
    bank, 99
    personal, 99, 100
  nature, 95
  risk, general, 100–01
  tellers, 98–99
  travelers, 99
  types, 95–96
Collections:
  acceptance D/P, 87
  bank, responsibility of:
    collecting, 89–90
    delivery and storage, 89
    duties, 89
    liability, 89
    and URC, 89
  cash against documents, 86
  collection with acceptance, 87
  collection order, 90
  documents, 86
  documents against acceptance, 87
  documents against payment, 86–87
  draft payment, 85–86
  import/export, 86
  intermediary banks, 86
  payment, 92–93
    and forwarding of proceeds, 93
    and funds transfer, 92
    partial, 93
    rights, 93
  presentation of documents, 91–92
    and buyer, 91
    draft, payment, 91
  procedure, general, 87–88
    and sellers' draft, 88
    and shipments, 88
  protest, 91
  terminology, 85–86
  Uniform Rules for Collection, 88–89
Contractual terms, for currency trading:
  bid, 143
  confirmation slip, 142

contract, nature, 142
contract date, 143
depreciation, 144
devaluation, 144
European practice, 143
exchange rates, nature, 143
flat quotes, 144
forward rates, 144
maturity dates, 143
offer, 143
recording, 142
revaluation, 144
settlement, 143
short-term trends, 144
spot, 144
spread, 143
U.S. practice, 143
Correspondent banks, 25
Covenants, 187–88
assets, preservation of, 187–88
by borrower, 187
pari passu, 187
Currency trading. See Contractual terms,
for currency trading

D

Dealers, international money market:
functions, 115
income/loss from holding of currency by,
116
positions, 116
speculation, 115
unusual currencies, 115, 116
Documents, conformity of:
delay in UCC, 68–69
discrepancies, delays caused by, 67
form vs. content, 68
minor discrepancies, 68
packaging list, 67
trust receipt, 68
Documentation, syndication:
example, 179–80
loan agreement, 182
mandate letter, 180
negotiation, 180
placement memo:
differed from prospectus, 180
EAB/Colocotronis loans, case, 181
information in, 181
judgement standard, 181–82
laws about, 180–81

Documentation, syndication,
definitions in:
agent, powers and duties of, 188–89
commitment to lend and borrow, 183
conditions precedent, 185–86
conflicting actions, 188, 189
costs, 189
default, 186, 187, 188, 189
distributions to banks, 188
drawdown, 183
enforcement, 189–90
fees, 184–85
agency, 185
commitment, 185
management, 185
indemnific action of agents, 189
indemnities, 185
information, liability for, 189
interest, 184
liability, agents', 189
maturity, acceleration of, 188
notes, 184
repayment, 183–84
representations, 186
taxation, 185
warranties, 186
Draft, defined, 95

E

ECU, European Currency Units:
calculations about, 243
defined, 243
functions, 243–44
and national currencies, 244
Edge Act and agreement corporations:
acceptances, security of, 16–17
activities range, 15–16
agreement corporations, 15
deposit restitution, 16
domestic branching, 17
equity positions, 17
examination, 18
foreign activities, range, 18
foreign branches, 17
limits, 15
nature, 15
Regulation K, 15, 16, 17
share holding, 17
EEC. See European Monetary System
Eurodollar lending:
minimum required statements, 165
syndication, 165

Eurodollar market:
    activities, 169–71
        growth, 170–71
        Regulation D, 170
        Regulation Q, 170
        tax, 171
    as bookkeeping entities, 166
    deposits, 166
    format, 166–67
    nature, 166
    other currencies, 166
    other locations, 166
European Monetary System:
    common currency, problems with,
        240–41
        British colonies, example, 241
        CFA France, example, 241
        Liberia, example, 240
        Panama, example, 240
    central banks, payment processes
        between, 246–48
        creditor quota, 247
        debtor quota, 247
        and ECUs, 247
        and exchange fluctuations, 246–47
        meetings, 248
    currency rate fluctuations, permissible,
        244
    and EEC, founding of, 240
    ECSC (European Coal and Steel
        Community), 240
    European Joint Float Agreement, 241
        failure of, 241
    European Monetary Cooperation Fund,
        248
    European Payments Union, 240
    and European unification, early work,
        239–40
    function to date, 248–50
    future of, 250–52
    market intervention, strategies, 245–46
    origins, 242
    threshold of divergence, 244–45
        and German mark, 245
    and U.S. economy, 250
Examination of banks:
    agencies:
        asset maintenance rule, 194
        FDIC, 193–94
        FFIEC, 195
        FRS, 193
        OCC, 193
        SEC, 194

analysis, 201–02
compared to audit, 200
CPAs, 200
discussion, 199–200
focus of:
    assets, classification of, 202
    bond portfolio, 203–04
    CDs, collateral, 204
    lending limits, 203
    loan files, 202
    loans, classification of, 202
    real estate, 202, 203
    stock as collateral, 204
    warning signs, 202–03
foreign banking institutions,
    supervision of:
    discussion, 197
    effects on Federal banking policy, 198
    grandfather clauses, 199
    International Banking Act of 1978, 197,
        198, 199
frequency of inspections, 200
internal audit, nature, 200
national banks, 200–01
numbers of personnel, 201
preparation, 201
reasons for, 192–93
responsibility for, allocation of, 195–97
    agencies supervising, 915
    deposit insurance, 196
    enforcement powers, 197
    FRS advantages, 196
    state-supported banks, 196
results:
    if bad, 207
    parts, 208
supervision, 192
surprise, 201
Exchange controls:
    government, problems with, 162
    international laws, 162
    risks, 162
    tolls, 161–62
    trade agreements, 162–63
    usual types, 161
Exchange rate determinants, theories
    about, 149–50
Export-Import Bank:
    credits from, 262–63
    guarantees from, 263
    loans by, 262
    nature, 261–62

F

Federal Reserve Act, Section 13, 83
Foreign banks in U.S.:
  agencies, 26, 27
  branches, 26, 27
  characteristics, 25
  entry to U.S., 25–26
  Federal regulation, 27
  International Banking Act of 1978, 26, 27
  New York State, 25
  Office of Comptroller of the Currency, 27
  representative offices, 26
  state regulation, 27
Foreign Credit Insurance Association:
  functions, 263–64
  multi-buyer coverage, 264
  nature, 263
  service coverage, 264–65
  single-buyer coverage, 264
  underwriting in, 264
  U.S. products, 264
Foreign exchange:
  accounts for, 111
  hard currencies, 110
  nature, 110
  New York City offices, 111–12
  ownership transfer, 111
  rates, types, 111
  soft currencies, 110–11
  telegraphic transfer, 111
Foreign exchange controls:
  and foreign trade, 161
  government monopoly, 160, 161
  legal barriers, 160
  nature, 159
  reasons for, 160
  and SEC rules, 160
  and U.S., 159–60
Foreign currency futures:
  closing out of contracts, 139
  forward contracts, difficulties with, 138–39
  IMM contracts, 138
  nature, 138
  regulation, 138, 139
Foreign currency market, mechanisms of:
  departments, 141
  government controls, 141
  international operations, 142
  safety, 141
  trading limits, 141
  transaction, initial, 140

Foreign currency trading, economic factors:
  balance of payments, 147
  capital flight, 145
  forward rates, 146
  inflation, 146
  indexes, economic, 146
  interest rates, 145
  market psychology, 145–46
  short-term, 147
  world, 145
Forgery of checks, 101–03
  certified and cashiers', 102
  drawer's signature vs. time of certification, 101–02
  finality of payment rule, 101
  knowledge of, 101
  negligence, 102
  payee's endorsement, forgery of, 102
  recrediting of accounts, 102–03
  signature, 101
  verification, 101–02
Fraud in transaction, in letters of credit:
  active, 66
  intentional, 66–67
  and UCC, 66

G

Gold, 154, 155
Guarantor, creditworthiness of, 204

H

Hedging:
  bank stamps, 137
  checks in foreign currency, 137
  commodities without restrictions, 138
  denominations, 136–37
  example, 121–22
  payment in future, 122
  reasons for, 136
  soft currencies, 137
  traveler's checks, 137

I

Imposter rule, 103
Import/export trade:
  forward transaction, 123
  lag, 123
  leading, 123
  risks, exchange, 123

Insurance, 57–58
Inter-American Development Bank:
    benefits, 267–68
    funds, sources, 267
    nature, 267
Interbank trading, Eurodollar, 169
Interest rate parity theory, 148
International Banking Act:
    activities, 19
    limits, 19
International banks:
    assets und numbers of, 22
    deposits, 21
    establishing, 20
    extending of credit, 14
    foreign currency loans, 14
    foreign use, 22
    general discussion, 13–14
    limit, 21
    loans, 21
    nature, new law about, 19
    in New York State, 13
    nonbank vs. interbank deposits, 21
    offshore branches, 20
    reasons for, 20
    services, range of, 14
    taxation, 19
    third parties, 20–21
    transactions, 20–21
International Development Agency, 260
International Financial Corporation,
    260–61
    loans by, 261
    reasons for, 260, 261
International Monetary Fund:
    credit tranche, 256
    draws, 255–56
    exchange rate, monitoring of, 257
    functions, 254
    General Agreement to Borrow program,
        256
    general resources transactions, 256
    intervention by, 255–56
        debt bomb, 255
        and U.S. quota, 255
    other services, 258
    personnel, 254
    programs, 254–55
    reserve tranche, 256
    stand-by arrangements, 256
    SDRs, 257–58
International money market:
    brokers, 114–15

    coverage, 115
    currencies on, 112
    functions, 112
    market growth, 113–14
        amounts, world, 114
        transfers, 113–14
        U.K. pounds, 113, 114
    nature, 112
    order procedure, 112
Investments, international money markets,
    123–25
Invoices, 57

J

Jargon, international money market,
    118–21

L

Letters of credit:
    agents for buyers, 46
    applications, 37–40
        assurance of performance, 38
        domestic, 38
        for export, 38
        financial, 38
        for import, 38
        independent nature of, 39
        vs. other instruments, 39–40
        and UCC, 40
    assignable/transferable credits, 44–46
        assignment principle, 45
        credit transfer vs. right to payment, 45
        and dividing of letter, 44–45
    authority to pay, 51
    authority to purchase, 51
    back-to-back, 47–48
        documents out of order, 48
        limits, case about, 47–48
        and UCC, 47
    clean, 41–42
    defined, 35–37
        collection, near buyer, 36
        remittance, 36
    discounting of, 42–43
        and bank's commitment, 43
    documentary, 41, 42
    establishment of, 40–41
    export vs. import, 42
    foreign currencies, 49–50
        conversion problems, 50
        customer, purchases by, 50

green clause, 44
history, 37
legal disputes:
  beneficiary, improper performance by,
    65–66
  beneficiary, payment to, 65
  customer, statements by against issuer,
    64–65
  draft, dishonor of, 65
  fraud, 66
  improper performance, 65
  issuer, dishonor by, 64
  issuing bank, stopping by, 66
  stop-payment order, 65–66
  and UCC, 65
interpretation problem, 46
irrevocable vs. irrevocable, 41
merchandise sale, 42
negotiation credit, 46
nonoperative, 51
with previous notice, 51
reasons for, 35
red-line clause, 44
revolving, 47
slight type, 42
skeleton, 43
specially advised, 43
standby, 48–49
  action, 48, 49
  default of, 49
  no-guaranty defense, 49
  reasons for, 48
  risk, 49
time type, 42
transferable, 45
world rules, 37
Liechtenstein:
  dummy corporations in, 232
  "entities" in, 232
  taxation in, 232
Limited branches, foreign banks:
  deposit sizes, 29
  nature, 27–28
  recent trends, 29
  regulatory bodies, 28
  restrictions, 28
  state lines, 29

M

Market development, for Eurodollars:
  OPEC, 167–68
  U.S. laws, 167

Marketplace, composition of in foreign
  currencies:
  rapid expansion, 140
  specialization, 139
  and time of day, 139
Money, concept of:
  dates, exchange, 153
  domestic vs. foreign currencies, 152
  extrinsic, 153
  as feature of state, 151–52
  government, 153
  intrinsic, 153
  legal tender, 151, 152
  metallism, 152
  metals, 151
  nominalism, 152
  obligations in foreign currencies,
    problems with, 152
  paper, 151
  reasons for, 150–51
  valorism, 152
Monetary approach theory, 148–49
Monetary exchange rate theories, 149
Monetary standard, international,
  evolution of:
  Bretton Woods system, 155–56
  and EEC, 156
  England, 154
  and fixed gold value, 155
  gold conversion, 154, 155
  gold pool, 155
  gold, U.S. ownership, 155
  hard currencies, 154
  reasons for, 154
Money supply, effects, 150
Money system, evolution of current:
  central banks, 158–59
  clean float, 157
  dirty float, 157
  discussion, 157
  fixed parity arrangement, 158
  government intervention, 157–58
  pegged currencies, 158

N

Notes, defined, 95

O

Offshore branches:
  application process, 23
  deposit size limit, 23, 24

and FRB, 23
foreign branching, 22–23
and foreign subsidiaries, 22
insured banks, 24
Regulation D, 24
Regulation K, 23–24
uninsured banks, 23
Options:
buyers, 130
reasons for, 127
sellers, 127
Swiss franc, vs. dollar, 128
U.K. pound, vs. dollar, 129
Overseas Private Investment Corporation:
nature, 265
project financing, 265–66
risk, 266–67
small business, 266
war, revolution, and insurrection,
insurance for, 266, 267

P

Payment, by letters of credit: See also
Letters of credit
banker's acceptance, 70
exchange fluctuations, 69
foreign currencies, 69
issuing bank, action of, 69–70
seller, 70
sight drafts, 69
time draft, 70
Portfolio balance theories, 149
Purchase power parity theory, 147–48

R

Rational expectations theory, 148
Reimbursement, 71–73
bank, documents held by, 71
bills of lading, 71–72
nature, 71
renewal of letters of credit, 72
Statement of Trust Receipt financing, 71,
72
titles, 72
trust receipt, 71
warehouse receipt, 72
Risk, assessment of:
country, instability of:
Bankhaus Herstatt failure, 174
discussion, 173
Eurocurrency, 174
remedies, 173

credit decisions, 174–76
factors, 175
FRS, 175–76
problems with, 175
currency, 171–73
alternate currency, repayment in, 173
asset theft, 173
availability of currency, 171–73
conversion, 171–72
Eurocurrency, 172
lender currency, 172
discussion, 171
Rollovers:
business people, 135
nature, 134
outdated paper currency, 136
outflow control, 135
physical foreign currency, 134
shipments, 135
sources, 134–35
verification of banknotes, 136

S

SDRs, 156–57, 257, 258
Sovereign immunity, waiver, 186–87
doctrine, 186
waiver, 187
Speculation, 122–23
Spot transaction:
currencies, 126
forward contract prices, 125–26
vs. forward rates, 127
long-term, 126
nature, 125
Swiss franc, ratio scale, 126
Stop-payment orders:
bank check, 107
domestic, 106
effect, 105
and estate, 106
factors, 105
failure to comply with, consequences,
105
foreign, 106
liability, 107
limits, 107
reasons for, 106–07
right to make, 106
timing, 108
Subsidiary banks, of foreign banks, 29–30
Swaps:
bookkeeping entries, 131
calculations in, 130

and Federal Reserve, 131
foreign banks, 132
limits, 132
nature, 130
network for, 131
preference for, 131
principles, 131
as purchase and sale, 130
Switzerland, banking in:
account blocking, 234
agreements with U.S., 233
attitudes to tax "evasion," 232–33
Bank for International Settlements,
229–30
cantonal, 225
components, 224
concession by, 233
courts of, trend away from secrecy,
235–36
credit cooperatives of (*Raiffeisen*),
225–26
and criminal matters, 233
denial of information by, 233
discussion, 223
double taxation, 233
Federal Banking Commission of, 229
Federal Council of, 229
foreign-owned, 227
fraud, 233
giro system, 227
General Aniline and Film Corporation,
sale of, 236–37
I.G. Farben, 236–37
and IRS, 233
laws about, 227–28
liquidity, 228
mortgage bond, 226–27
names, case about discovery of, 235
national, 224–25
National Bank giros, 227
postal giros, 227
private, 226
reasons for success, 237–38
and SEC, 234
secrecy, 223, 228, 230–31
knowledge in, 231
laws about, 228, 230
limits on, 230
neutralism in, 231
numbered accounts, 231
stability, 231
taxation, 231

securities trading, 233–34
self-regulation in, 230
supervision, 229
Swiss National Bank, 228–29
Syndication, of international loans: *See
also* Letters of credit
best-efforts, 177–78
borrowing needs, 176–77
direct, 178
discussion, 176
documents, 178
firm-commitment, 177, 178
indirect, 178
pooled funds, 176
preadvanced, 178
problems with, 178–79
startup, 177

T

Trade terms, use:
amount, 61
establishing letter of credit, 62
FAS, 60
FOB, 60
irrevocable letter of credit, 62
modification, 62
and other bank, 61
quotation of prices, 61
taxes, 61
timing, 61
weights, 61
Traders, international money market,
116–17

U

Uniform Commercial Code:
legal disputes, 65
letters of credit, 40, 47, 66
rejection of documents, 68–69
Uniform Rules for Collection, 88–89
U.S. foreign trade of, table, 124

W

World Bank:
governments, 259
lending by, 259
nature, 258–59